FOCUS ON LEADERSHIP

BOOKS EDITED BY LARRY C. SPEARS

Focus on Leadership: Servant-Leadership for the Twenty-First Century (with Michele Lawrence), 2002

The Power of Servant-Leadership, 1998

Insights on Leadership: Service, Stewardship, Spirit and Servant-Leadership, 1998

On Becoming a Servant-Leader (with Don M. Frick), 1996

Seeker and Servant (with Anne T. Fraker), 1996

Reflections on Leadership: How Robert K. Greenleaf's Theory of Servant-Leadership Influenced Today's Top Management Thinkers, 1995

As Contributing Author

Cutting Edge: Leadership 2000, edited by Barbara Kellerman and Larraine Matusak, 2000

Stone Soup for the World, edited by Marianne Larned, 1998

Leadership in a New Era, edited by John Renesch, 1994

FOCUS ON LEADERSHIP

Servant-Leadership for the Twenty-First Century

Edited by

Larry C. Spears and Michele Lawrence

JOHN WILEY & SONS, INC.

Published by John Wiley & Sons, Inc., New York.
Published simultaneously in Canada.

This publication is designed to provide accurate and authoritative information in regard to the subject matter covered. It is sold with the understanding that the publisher is not engaged in rendering professional services. If professional advice or other expert assistance is required, the services of a competent professional person should be sought.

Library of Congress Cataloging-in-Publication Data:

Focus on leadership : servant leadership for the twenty-first century / edited by Larry C. Spears and Michele Lawrence.
    p. cm.
Includes bibliographical references and index.
ISBN 978-0-471-41162-8
    1. Leadership.   2. Employee empowerment.   I. Spears, Larry C., 1955–
II. Lawrence, Michele.
HD57.7 .F63 2001
658.4′ 092—dc21

                                             2001026640

10 9 8 7 6 5 4 3 2 1

CONTENTS

Part One
Servant-Leadership and the Individual

Part Four

Servant-Leadership for the World

FOREWORD

THE HEART OF SERVANT-LEADERSHIP

Ken Blanchard

I AM EXCITED ABOUT this book! Why? Because I am a fan of Robert Greenleaf and think that servant-leadership is the foundation for effective leadership.

I had the pleasure of meeting Robert Greenleaf in the late 1960s, when I was at Ohio University in Athens, Ohio. I was attracted to the school because Vernon Alden had come, as president of the university, with the vision of creating the "Harvard of the Midwest." He had recruited all kinds of exciting people and resources to make this vision a reality.

I went to Ohio University in 1966 as an administrative assistant to the dean of the School of Business Administration, to help develop a graduate program in administration. In this role, I participated in the activities of the Ohio Fellows Group—a special undergraduate leadership program designed by Les Rollins, a longtime friend of Robert Greenleaf. Alden and Rollins were two of the first board members for The Greenleaf Center for Servant-Leadership (then called The Center for Applied Ethics).

When Greenleaf spent a weekend with the students, I was enthralled with his thinking. In fact, when I got a chance to teach, I tried to put his servant-leadership concepts into practice. At that time, I began my practice of always giving the students the final exam during the first day of class. When I started doing that, other faculty members would ask, "What are you doing?"

I would say, "I'm confused."

They'd say, "You act it."

Troubled, I would respond, "I thought we were supposed to teach these young people."

"You are," they would be quick to reply. "But don't give them the final exam ahead of time."

My servant-leadership response was: "Not only am I going to give them the final exam during the first day of class, but what do you think I'm going to do all semester? I'm going to teach them the answers! You better believe it, so when they get to the final exam, they'll get A's!" To me, life is all about getting A's, not about following the normal grade distribution curve.

During this period, Paul Hersey had come to Ohio University as chairman of the Management Department. In 1967, we started to write our textbook, *Management of Organizational Behavior* (now in its eighth edition), and to work on the development of Situational Leadership®. I knew Situational Leadership was a servant-leadership model, but the concepts I had learned from Greenleaf did not return to center stage in my work until the mid-1990s, when I began studying Jesus of Nazareth as a clear example of enlightened leadership. During this period, I was writing *Leadership by the Book,* with Bill Hybels, Senior Pastor of Willow Creek Community Church, and Phil Hodges, a longtime colleague.

I was first motivated to study Jesus as a leader when I was interviewed by Robert Schuller on *The Hour of Power* in 1983, as part of the publicity for *The One Minute Manager®*. In my interview, Reverend Schuller suggested that Jesus was a classic One Minute Manager: Once he had made his goals clear, he visited village after village, identifying people who were doing things right, and then praising or healing those gathered around him. If people were off base, he would reprimand them or redirect them.

My response was, "Interesting!" Those behaviors certainly exemplified the three secrets of the One Minute Manager: One Minute Goal Setting, One Minute Praisings, and One Minute Reprimands.

After that exchange on *The Hour of Power,* my spiritual journey began to intensify. When I started to read the Bible, I began to realize that everything I'd ever taught about leadership over the years, Jesus had already modeled. Jesus is not the only spiritual model, but his leadership style is often regarded as one of the most influential and effective the world has ever known. And he did it with twelve inexperienced people! The only person who had much education was Judas, who turned out to be his only turnover problem. Yet, with this ragtag group, Jesus was able to create a lasting impact. And central to Jesus' philosophy was servant-leadership. I believe Jesus exemplified the fully committed and effective servant-leader. He sent a clear message on the primary importance of servant-leadership when James and John seemed to be vying for a special leadership role among the disciples:

> You know that the rulers of the Gentiles lorded over them, and their high officials exercise authority over them. Not so with you. Instead, whoever wants to be great among you must be your servant. *(Matthew 20:25–27)*

The key phrase here is "Not so with you." Jesus was talking about a form of leadership very different from the model familiar to the disciples: a leader who is primarily a servant. He did not offer them a Plan B. Servant-leadership was to be their mode of operation. And so it should be for all leaders.

With that new insight, servant-leadership and what I had learned from Robert Greenleaf came center stage in my work again. I truly believe that servant-leadership has never been more applicable to the world of leadership than it is today. Not only are people looking for a deeper purpose and meaning when they must meet the challenges of today's changing world; they are also looking for principles and philosophies that actually work. *Servant-leadership works.* Servant-leadership is about getting people to a higher level by leading people at a higher level.

Absorb the teachings from this book's wonderful authors. Unless we begin to lead at a higher level, our future is in danger. Servant-leadership can make a difference in our life and in the lives of those we touch. But it takes heart. My hat is off to Robert Greenleaf, and to the efforts of Larry Spears, Michele Lawrence, and all the good

folks at The Greenleaf Center, for keeping Greenleaf's work alive
and for leading the servant-leadership charge.

KEN BLANCHARD

Dr. Ken Blanchard, cofounder and chief spiritual officer of The Ken
Blanchard Companies, a full-service human resource development group,
is characterized by friends, colleagues, and clients as one of the most
insightful and compassionate men in business today. Few people have
impacted the day-to-day management of people and companies more
than Ken Blanchard. He is a prominent and sought-after author, speaker,
and business consultant. His impact as a writer is far-reaching. His best-
selling book, *The One Minute Manager,* coauthored with Spencer
Johnson, has sold more than 10 million copies worldwide, has been
translated into more than 25 languages, and is still on best-seller lists. He
has established The Center for FaithWalk Leadership to help leaders of
faith walk their faith in the marketplace and follow the servant-leadership
model of Jesus of Nazareth.

PREFACE

FOCUS ON LEADERSHIP: *Servant-Leadership for the Twenty-First Century* owes much to the favorable public response to two earlier books in this series: *Reflections on Leadership: How Robert K. Greenleaf's Theory of Servant-Leadership Influenced Today's Top Management Thinkers* (John Wiley & Sons, 1995), and *Insights on Leadership: Service, Stewardship, Spirit and Servant-Leadership* (John Wiley & Sons, 1998). Both books have gone into multiple printings and have piqued the interest of tens of thousands of readers who are now exploring and implementing servant-leadership. *The Power of Servant-Leadership,* also published in 1998, offered readers a complementary sourcebook for how servant-leadership can be applied to personal and business endeavors.

Since the publication of the two servant-leadership anthologies, many new articles and essays have been written about servant-leadership. This volume brings together some of the most current and significant pieces on servant-leadership and on the growing influence of Robert K. Greenleaf's writings. Among them are several essays, written especially for this comprehensive collection, by some of today's leading thinkers, writers, and practitioners.

If you are intrigued, inspired, or moved by what you discover herein and wish to have more information concerning the wide array of servant-leadership programs and resources, contact us at:

The Greenleaf Center for Servant-Leadership
921 East 86th Street, Suite 200
Indianapolis, IN 46240
(317) 259-1241 (phone)
(317) 259-0560 (fax)
www.greenleaf.org (Web site)

LARRY C. SPEARS
MICHELE LAWRENCE

FOCUS ON LEADERSHIP

INTRODUCTION

TRACING THE PAST, PRESENT, AND FUTURE OF SERVANT-LEADERSHIP

Larry C. Spears

*The servant-leader is servant first. It begins with the natural feeling that
one wants to serve. Then conscious choice brings one to aspire to lead.
The best test is: Do those served grow as persons; do they, while being
served, become healthier, wiser, freer, more autonomous, more likely
themselves to become servants?*

Robert K. Greenleaf

THE MIGHTIEST OF RIVERS are first fed by many small trickles of
water. This observation is also an apt way of conveying my belief
that the growing number of practitioners of servant-leadership has
increased from a trickle to a river. On a global scale, it is not yet
a mighty river. However, it is an expanding river that has a deep
current.

The servant-leader concept continues to grow in its influence
and impact. In fact, we have witnessed an unparalleled explosion
of interest in and practice of servant-leadership during the past
decade. In many ways, it can truly be said that the times are only
now beginning to catch up with Robert Greenleaf's visionary call
to servant-leadership.

Servant-leadership, now in its fourth decade as a specific leadership and service concept, continues to create a quiet revolution in
workplaces around the world. This book and this introduction are

1

intended to provide a broad overview of the growing influence this unique concept of servant-leadership is having on people and their workplaces.

In these early years of the twenty-first century, we are beginning to see that traditional, autocratic, and hierarchical modes of leadership are yielding to a newer model—one based on teamwork and community, one that seeks to involve others in decision making, one strongly based in ethical and caring behavior, and one that is attempting to enhance the personal growth of workers while improving the caring and quality of our many institutions. This emerging approach to leadership and service is called *servant-leadership*.

The words *servant* and *leader* are usually thought of as being opposites. When two opposites are brought together in a creative and meaningful way, a paradox emerges. And so the words *servant* and *leader* have been brought together to create the paradoxical idea of servant-leadership. The basic idea of servant-leadership is both logical and intuitive. Since the time of the industrial revolution, managers have tended to view people as objects; institutions have considered workers as cogs within a machine. In the past few decades, we have witnessed a shift in that long-held view. Standard practices are rapidly shifting toward the ideas put forward by Robert Greenleaf, Stephen Covey, Peter Senge, Max DePree, Margaret Wheatley, Ken Blanchard, and many others who suggest that there is a better way to manage our organizations in the twenty-first century.

Today, there is a growing recognition of the need for a more team-oriented approach to leadership and management. Robert Greenleaf's writings on the subject of servant-leadership helped to get this movement started, and his views have had a profound and growing effect.

ROBERT K. GREENLEAF

Despite all the buzz about modern leadership techniques, no one knows better than Greenleaf what really matters.

—*Working Woman* magazine

The term *servant-leadership* was first coined in a 1970 essay entitled *The Servant as Leader,* by Robert K. Greenleaf (1904–1990). Greenleaf, born in Terre Haute, Indiana, spent most of his organizational life in the field of management research, development, and education at AT&T. Following a 40-year career at AT&T, Greenleaf enjoyed a second career that lasted 25 years: he served as an influential consultant to a number of major institutions, including Ohio University, MIT, Ford Foundation, R. K. Mellon Foundation, the Mead Corporation, the American Foundation for Management Research, and Lilly Endowment Inc. In 1964, Greenleaf founded the Center for Applied Ethics, which was renamed the Robert K. Greenleaf Center in 1985 and is now headquartered in Indianapolis.

As a lifelong student of how things get done in organizations, Greenleaf distilled his observations in a series of essays and books on the theme of "The Servant as Leader"—the objective of which was to stimulate thought and action for building a better, more caring society.

The Servant-as-Leader Idea

The idea of the servant as leader came partly out of Greenleaf's half-century of experience in working to shape large institutions. However, the event that crystallized Greenleaf's thinking came in the 1960s, when he read Hermann Hesse's short novel *Journey to the East*—an account of a mythical journey by a group of people on a spiritual quest.

After reading this book, Greenleaf concluded that its central meaning was that a great leader is first experienced as a servant to others, and this simple fact is central to his or her greatness. True leadership emerges from those whose primary motivation is a deep desire to help others.

In 1970, at the age of 66, Greenleaf published *The Servant as Leader,* the first of a dozen publications on servant-leadership. Since then, more than 500,000 copies of his books and essays have been sold worldwide. Slowly but surely, Greenleaf's servant-leadership writings have made a deep and lasting impression on leaders, educators, and many others who are concerned with issues of leadership, management, service, and personal growth.

What Is Servant-Leadership?

In all of his published works, Greenleaf discusses the need for a new kind of leadership model, a model that identifies serving others—including employees, customers, and community—as the number-one priority. Servant-leadership emphasizes increased service to others, a holistic approach to work, building a sense of community, and the sharing of power in decision making.

Who *is* a servant-leader? Greenleaf said that the servant-leader is one who is a servant first. In *The Servant as Leader* he wrote, "It begins with the natural feeling that one wants to serve, to serve first. Then conscious choice brings one to aspire to lead. The difference manifests itself in the care taken by the servant—first to make sure that other people's highest-priority needs are being served. The best test is: Do those served grow as persons; do they, while being served, become healthier, wiser, freer, more autonomous, more likely themselves to become servants?"

It is important to stress that servant-leadership is *not* a "quick-fix" approach. Nor is it something that can be quickly instilled within an institution. At its core, servant-leadership is a long-term, transformational approach to life and work—in essence, a way of being—that has the potential for creating positive change throughout our society.

Ten Characteristics of the Servant-Leader

> Servant leadership deals with the reality of power in everyday life—its legitimacy, the ethical restraints upon it and the beneficial results that can be attained through the appropriate use of power.
>
> —*The New York Times*

After some years of carefully considering Greenleaf's original writings, I have identified a set of 10 characteristics of the servant-leader

that I view as being of critical importance. These characteristics
are central to the development of servant-leaders:

1. *Listening.* Leaders have traditionally been valued for their
   communication and decision-making skills. These are also
   important skills for the servant-leader, but they need to be
   reinforced by a deep commitment to listening intently to
   others. The servant-leader seeks to identify the will of a
   group and to help clarify that will. He or she seeks to
   listen receptively to what is being said (and not said!).
   Listening also encompasses getting in touch with one's
   own inner voice and seeking to understand what one's
   body, spirit, and mind are communicating. Listening,
   coupled with regular periods of reflection, is essential to
   the growth of the servant-leader.

2. *Empathy.* The servant-leader strives to understand and
   empathize with others. People need to be accepted and
   recognized for their special and unique spirits. One
   assumes the good intentions of coworkers and does not
   reject them as people, even while refusing to accept their
   behavior or performance. The most successful servant-
   leaders are those who have become skilled empathetic
   listeners.

3. *Healing.* Learning to heal is a powerful force for
   transformation and integration. One of the great strengths
   of servant-leadership is its potential for healing oneself
   and others. Many people have broken spirits and have
   suffered from a variety of emotional hurts. Although this
   is a part of being human, servant-leaders recognize that
   they have an opportunity to "help make whole" those
   with whom they come in contact. In *The Servant as
   Leader,* Greenleaf writes: "There is something subtle
   communicated to one who is being served and led if,
   implicit in the compact between servant-leader and led, is
   the understanding that the search for wholeness is
   something they share."

4. *Awareness.* General awareness, especially self-awareness, strengthens the servant-leader. Making a commitment to foster awareness can be scary—you never know what you may discover! Awareness also aids one in understanding issues that involve ethics and values. It lends itself to being able to view most situations from a more integrated, holistic position. As Greenleaf observed: "Awareness is not a giver of solace—it is just the opposite. It is a disturber and an awakener. Able leaders are usually sharply awake and reasonably disturbed. They are not seekers after solace. They have their own inner serenity."

5. *Persuasion.* Another characteristic of servant-leaders is a reliance on persuasion, rather than on one's positional authority, in making decisions within an organization. The servant-leader seeks to convince others, rather than to coerce compliance. This element offers one of the clearest distinctions between the traditional authoritarian model and that of servant-leadership. The servant-leader is effective at building consensus within groups. This emphasis on persuasion over coercion probably has its roots within the beliefs of The Religious Society of Friends (Quakers), the denomination with which Robert Greenleaf himself was most closely allied.

6. *Conceptualization.* Servant-leaders seek to nurture their abilities to "dream great dreams." The ability to look at a problem (or an organization) from a conceptualizing perspective means that one must think beyond day-to-day realities. For many managers, this is a characteristic that requires discipline and practice. The traditional manager is focused on the need to achieve short-term operational goals. The manager who wishes to also be a servant-leader must stretch his or her thinking to encompass broader-based conceptual thinking. Within organizations, conceptualization is also the proper role of boards of trustees or directors. Unfortunately, boards can sometimes

become involved in the day-to-day operations (something that should always be discouraged) and fail to provide the visionary concept for an institution. Trustees need to be mostly conceptual in their orientation, staffs need to be mostly operational in their perspective, and the most effective CEOs and leaders probably need to develop both perspectives. Servant-leaders are called to seek a healthy balance between conceptual thinking and a day-to-day focused approach.

7. *Foresight.* Closely related to conceptualization, the ability to foresee the likely outcome of a situation is hard to define but easy to identify. One knows it when one sees it. Foresight is a characteristic that enables the servant-leader to understand the lessons from the past, the realities of the present, and the likely consequence of a decision for the future. It is also deeply rooted within the intuitive mind. As such, one can conjecture that foresight is the one servant-leader characteristic with which one may be born. All other characteristics can be consciously developed. There hasn't been a great deal written about foresight. It remains a largely unexplored area in leadership studies, but one most deserving of careful attention.

8. *Stewardship.* Peter Block (author of *Stewardship* and *The Empowered Manager*) has defined stewardship as "holding something in trust for another." Robert Greenleaf's view of all institutions was one in which CEOs, staffs, and trustees all played significant roles in holding their institutions in trust for the greater good of society. Servant-leadership, like stewardship, assumes first and foremost a commitment to serving the needs of others. It also emphasizes the use of openness and persuasion rather than control.

9. *Commitment to the growth of people.* Servant-leaders believe that people have an intrinsic value beyond their

tangible contributions as workers. As such, the servant-leader is deeply committed to the growth of each and every individual within his or her institution. The servant-leader recognizes the tremendous responsibility to do everything within his or her power to nurture the personal, professional, and spiritual growth of employees. In practice, this can include (but is not limited to) concrete actions such as making available funds for personal and professional development; taking a personal interest in the ideas of and the suggestions from everyone; encouraging workers' involvement in decision making; and actively assisting laid-off workers to find other employment.

10. *Building community.* The servant-leader senses that much has been lost in recent human history as a result of a shift in which large institutions, rather than local communities, have become the primary shapers of human lives. This awareness causes the servant-leader to seek to identify some means for building community among those who work within a given institution. Servant-leadership suggests that true community can be created among those who work in businesses and other institutions. Greenleaf said: "All that is needed to rebuild community as a viable life form for large numbers of people is for enough servant-leaders to show the way, not by mass movements, but by each servant-leader demonstrating his own unlimited liability for a quite specific community-related group."

These 10 characteristics of servant-leadership are by no means exhaustive. However, I believe that the list serves to communicate the power and promise that this concept offers to those who are open to its invitation and challenge.

Tracing the Growing Impact of Servant-Leadership

> Servant-leadership has emerged as one of the dominant philosophies being discussed in the world today.
>
> —*Indianapolis Business Journal*

Servant-Leadership as an Institutional Model

Servant-leadership principles are being applied in significant ways in a half-dozen major areas. The first area has to do with servant-leadership as an institutional philosophy and model. Servant-leadership crosses all boundaries and is being applied by a wide variety of people working with for-profit businesses; not-for-profit corporations; and churches, universities, health care, and foundations.

In recent years, a number of institutions have jettisoned their hierarchical decision making and replaced it with a servant-leader approach. Servant-leadership advocates a group-oriented approach to analysis and decision making as a means of strengthening institutions and improving society. It also emphasizes that the power of persuasion and of seeking consensus is superior to the old top-down form of leadership. Some people have likened this to turning the hierarchical pyramid upside down. Servant-leadership holds that the primary purpose of a business should be to create a positive impact on its employees and community. Profit should not be the sole motive.

Many individuals within institutions have adopted servant-leadership as a guiding philosophy. An increasing number of companies have adopted servant-leadership as part of their corporate philosophy or as a foundation for their mission statement. Among these are The Toro Company (Minneapolis, Minnesota), Synovus Financial Corporation (Columbus, Georgia), ServiceMaster Company (Downers Grove, Illinois), The Men's Wearhouse (Fremont, California), Southwest Airlines (Dallas, Texas), and TDIndustries (Dallas, Texas).

TDIndustries (TD), one of the earliest practitioners of servant-leadership in the corporate setting, is a Dallas-based heating and plumbing contracting firm that has consistently ranked in the top 10 of *Fortune* magazine's *100 Best Companies to Work For in America*. TD's founder, Jack Lowe Sr., came upon *The Servant as Leader* essay in the early 1970s and began to distribute copies of it to his employees. They were invited to read through the essay and then to gather in small groups to discuss its meaning. The belief that managers should serve their employees became an important value for TDIndustries.

Thirty years later, Jack Lowe Jr. and his colleagues, continue to use servant-leadership as the guiding philosophy for TD. Even today, any TDPartner who supervises at least one person must go through training in servant-leadership. All new employees receive a copy of *The Servant as Leader* essay; and TD has developed elaborate training modules designed to encourage the understanding and practice of servant-leadership.

Some businesses have begun to view servant-leadership as an important framework that is helpful (and necessary) for ensuring the long-term effects of related management and leadership approaches, such as continuous quality improvement and systems thinking. It is suggested that institutions interested in creating meaningful change may be best served by starting with servant-leadership as the foundational understanding and then building on it through any number of related approaches.

Servant-leadership has influenced many noted writers, thinkers, and leaders. Max DePree, former chairman of the Herman Miller Company and author of *Leadership Is an Art* and *Leadership Jazz* has said: "The servanthood of leadership needs to be felt, understood, believed, and practiced." And Peter Senge, author of *The Fifth Discipline,* has said that he tells people "not to bother reading any other book about leadership until you first read Robert Greenleaf's book, *Servant-Leadership.* I believe it is the most singular and useful statement on leadership I've come across." In recent years, a growing number of leaders and readers have "rediscovered" Robert Greenleaf's own writings through books by DePree, Senge, Covey, Wheatley, Autry, and many other popular writers.

Education and Training of Not-for-Profit Trustees

A second major application of servant-leadership is its pivotal role as the theoretical and ethical basis for "trustee education." Greenleaf wrote extensively on servant-leadership as it applies to the roles of boards of directors and trustees within institutions. His essays on these applications are widely distributed among directors of for-profit and nonprofit organizations. In his essay *Trustees as Servants,* Greenleaf urged trustees to ask themselves two central questions:

1. Whom do you serve?
2. For what purpose?

Servant-leadership suggests that boards of trustees need to undergo a radical shift in how they approach their roles. Trustees who seek to act as servant-leaders can help to create institutions of great depth and quality. Over the past decade, two of America's largest grant-making foundations (Lilly Endowment Inc. and the W. K. Kellogg Foundation) have encouraged the development of programs designed to educate and train not-for-profit boards of trustees to function as servant-leaders. John Carver, the noted author on board governance, addresses this particular application in Chapter 14 of this book.

Community Leadership Programs

The third application of servant-leadership concerns its deepening role in community leadership organizations across the country. A growing number of community leadership groups are using Greenleaf Center resources as part of their own education and training efforts. Some have been doing so for more than 20 years.

M. Scott Peck, who has written about the importance of building true community, says the following in *A World Waiting to Be Born:* "In his work on servant-leadership, Greenleaf posited that the world will be saved if it can develop just three truly well-managed, large institutions—one in the private sector, one in the public sector, and one in the nonprofit sector. He believed—and I know—that such excellence in management will be achieved through an organizational culture of civility routinely utilizing the mode of community."

Service-Learning Programs

The fourth application involves servant-leadership and experiential education. During the past 25 years, experiential education programs of all sorts have sprung up in virtually every college and university—and, increasingly, in secondary schools, too. Experiential education, or "learning by doing," is now a part of most students' educational experience.

Around 1980, a number of educators began to write about the linkage between the servant-leader concept and experiential learning under a new term called "service-learning." Service-learning has become a major focus for experiential education programs in the past few years.

The National Society for Experiential Education (NSEE) has adopted service-learning as one of its major program areas. NSEE has published a massive three-volume work called *Combining Service and Learning,* which brings together many articles and papers about service-learning—several dozen of which discuss servant-leadership as the philosophical basis for experiential learning programs.

Leadership Education

The fifth application of servant-leadership concerns its use in both formal and informal education and training programs. This is taking place through leadership and management courses in colleges and universities, as well as through corporate training programs. A number of undergraduate and graduate courses on management and leadership incorporate servant-leadership within their course curricula. Several colleges and universities now offer specific courses on servant-leadership. Also, a number of noted leadership authors, including Peter Block, Ken Blanchard, Max DePree, and Peter Senge, have acclaimed the servant-leader concept as an overarching framework that is compatible with, and enhancing of, other leadership and management models such as total quality management, systems thinking, and community-building.

In the area of corporate education and training programs, many management and leadership consultants now utilize servant-leadership materials as part of their ongoing work with corporations. Among these companies are Synovus Financial, The Toro Company, and Arthur Andersen. A number of consultants and educators are now touting the benefits to be gained in building a total quality management approach upon a servant-leadership foundation. Through internal training and education, institutions are discovering that servant-leadership can truly improve how business is developed and conducted, while still successfully turning a profit.

Personal Transformation

The sixth application of servant-leadership involves its use in programs relating to personal growth and transformation. Servant-leadership operates at both the institutional and personal levels. For individuals, it offers a means to personal growth—spiritually, professionally, emotionally, and intellectually. It has ties to the ideas of M. Scott Peck *(The Road Less Traveled)*, Parker Palmer *(The Active Life)*, Ann McGee-Cooper *(You Don't Have to Go Home from Work Exhausted!)*, and others who have written on expanding human potential. A particular strength of servant-leadership is that it encourages everyone to actively seek opportunities to both serve and lead others, thereby setting up the potential for raising the quality of life throughout society.

Servant-Leadership and Multiculturalism

For some people, the word *servant* prompts an immediate negative connotation because of the oppression that many workers—particularly women and people of color—have historically endured. For some it may take a while to accept the positive usage of the word *servant*. However, those who are willing to dig a little deeper come to understand the inherent spiritual nature of what is intended by the pairing of *servant* and *leader*. The startling paradox of the term *servant-leadership* serves to prompt new insights.

In a Greenleaf Center newsletter article titled "Pluralistic Reflections on Servant-Leadership," Juana Bordas has written: "Many women, minorities and people of color have long traditions of servant-leadership in their cultures. Servant-leadership has very old roots in many of the indigenous cultures. Cultures that were holistic, cooperative, communal, intuitive and spiritual. These cultures centered on being guardians of the future and respecting the ancestors who walked before."

Women leaders and authors are now writing and speaking about servant-leadership as a twenty-first-century leadership philosophy that is most appropriate for both women and men to embrace. Patsy Sampson, former president of Stephens College in Columbia, Missouri, is one such person. In an essay on women and servant-leadership, *The Leader as Servant*, she wrote: "So-called (service-oriented) feminine characteristics are exactly those which are consonant with the very best qualities of servant-leadership."

A Growing Movement

> Servant-leadership works like the consensus building that the Japanese are famous for. Yes, it takes a while on the front end; everyone's view is solicited, though everyone also understands that his view may not ultimately prevail. But once the consensus is forged, watch out: With everybody on board, your so-called implementation proceeds wham-bam.
>
> —*Fortune* Magazine

Interest in the philosophy and practice of servant-leadership is now at an all-time high. Hundreds of articles on servant-leadership have appeared in various magazines, journals, and newspapers during the past few years. Many books on the general subject of leadership have referenced servant-leadership as the preeminent leadership model for the twenty-first century. And, a growing body of literature is available on the understanding and practice of servant-leadership.

The Greenleaf Center for Servant-Leadership is an international, not-for-profit educational organization that seeks to encourage the understanding and practice of servant-leadership. The Center's mission is to fundamentally improve the caring and quality of all institutions through a servant-leader approach to leadership, structure, and decision making.

In recent years, the Greenleaf Center has experienced tremendous growth and expansion. Its programs now include the following: the worldwide sales of more than 120 books, essays, and videotapes on servant-leadership; a membership program; workshops, retreats, institutes, and seminars; and an annual International Conference on Servant-Leadership. A number of notable Greenleaf Center members have spoken at the annual conferences, including: James Autry, Peter Block, Max DePree, Stephen Covey, Meg Wheatley, M. Scott Peck, and Peter Senge, to name but a few. These and other conference speakers have described the tremendous impact that the servant-leader concept has had on the development of their own understanding of what it means to be a leader.

Paradox and Pathway

The Greenleaf Center's logo is a variation on the geometrical figure called a "mobius strip." A mobius strip, pictured here, is a one-sided surface constructed from a rectangle by holding one end fixed, rotating the opposite end through 180 degrees, and applying it to the first end—thereby giving the appearance of a two-sided figure. It thus appears to have a front side that merges into a back side, and then back again into the front.

The mobius strip symbolizes, in visual terms, the servant-leader concept—a merging of servanthood into leadership and back into servanthood again, in a fluid and continuous pattern. It also reflects the Greenleaf Center's own role as an institution seeking to both serve and lead others who are interested in leadership and service issues.

Life is full of curious and meaningful paradoxes. Servant-leadership is one such paradox. Slowly but surely, it has gained hundreds of thousands of adherents over the past quarter-century. The seeds that have been planted have begun to sprout in many institutions, as well as in the hearts of many who long to improve the human condition. Servant-leadership is providing a framework within which many thousands of known and unknown individuals are helping to improve how we treat those who do the work within our many institutions. Servant-leadership truly offers hope and guidance for a new era in human development and for the creation of better and more caring institutions.

PART ONE

SERVANT-LEADERSHIP AND THE INDIVIDUAL

Robert K. Greenleaf coined the term *servant-leadership* in his seminal 1970 essay, "The Servant as Leader." Since then, the servant-leader concept has had a deep and lasting influence on many modern leadership theories and practices. Greenleaf spent his first career—40 years—at AT&T. He retired as director of management research in 1964. That same year, Greenleaf founded The Center for Applied Ethics (later renamed The Greenleaf Center for Servant-Leadership). For another 25 years, he had an illustrious second career as an author, teacher, and consultant. Greenleaf, who died in 1990, was the author of numerous books and essays on the theme of the servant as leader. His books include three posthumous collections: *The Power of Servant-Leadership* (1998), *On Becoming a Servant-Leader* (1996), and *Seeker and Servant* (1996). During his lifetime, he published two other books: *Teacher as Servant* (1979) and *Servant-Leadership* (1977). Many other separately published essays are available through The Greenleaf Center.

This short excerpt from Greenleaf's essay "The Servant as Leader" contains an essential understanding of the origin and definition of servant-leadership. Greenleaf relates how his reading of Hermann Hesse's *Journey to the East* led to his developing the servant-as-leader terminology.

1

ESSENTIALS OF SERVANT-LEADERSHIP

Robert K. Greenleaf

SERVANT AND LEADER—can these two roles be fused in one real person, in all levels of status or calling? If so, can that person live and be productive in the real world of the present? My sense of the present leads me to say yes to both questions. This chapter is an attempt to explain why and to suggest how.

The idea of the servant as leader came out of reading Hermann Hesse's *Journey to the East*. In this story, we see a band of men on a mythical journey, probably also Hesse's own journey. The central figure of the story is Leo, who accompanies the party as the servant who does their menial chores, but who also sustains them with his spirit and his song. He is a person of extraordinary presence. All goes well until Leo disappears. Then the group falls into disarray and the journey is abandoned. They cannot make it without the servant Leo. The narrator, one of the party, after some years of wandering, finds Leo and is taken into the Order that had sponsored the journey. There he discovers that Leo, whom he had known first as servant, was in fact the titular head of the Order, its guiding spirit, a great and noble leader.

One can muse on what Hesse was trying to say when he wrote this story. We know that most of his fiction was autobiographical, that he led a tortured life, and that *Journey to the East* suggests a turn toward the serenity he achieved in his old age. There has been much speculation by critics on Hesse's life and work, some of it centering on this story, which they find the most puzzling. But to me, this story clearly says that the great leader is seen as servant first, and that simple fact is the key to his greatness. Leo was actually the leader all of the time, but he was servant first because that was what he was, deep down inside. Leadership was bestowed on a man who was by nature a servant. It was something given, or assumed, that could be taken away. His servant nature was the real man, not bestowed, not assumed, and not to be taken away. He was servant first.

I mention Hesse and *Journey to the East* for two reasons. First, I want to acknowledge the source of the idea of *the servant as leader.* Then I want to use this reference as an introduction to a brief discussion of prophecy.

In 1958, when I first read about Leo, if I had been listening to contemporary prophecy as intently as I do now, the first draft of this piece might have been written then. As it was, the idea lay dormant for 11 years during which I came to believe that we in this country were in a leadership crisis and that I should do what I could about it. I became painfully aware of how dull my sense of contemporary prophecy had been. And I have reflected much on why we do not hear and heed the prophetic voices in our midst (not a new question in our times, nor more critical than heretofore).

I now embrace the theory of prophecy which holds that prophetic voices of great clarity, and with a quality of insight equal to that of any age, are speaking cogently all of the time. Men and women of a stature equal to the greatest prophets of the past are with us now, addressing the problems of the day and pointing to a better way to live fully and serenely in these times.

The variable that marks some periods as barren and some as rich in prophetic vision is in the interest, the level of seeking, the responsiveness of the hearers. The variable is not in the presence or absence or the relative quality and force of the prophetic voices. Prophets grow in stature as people respond to their message. If their early attempts are ignored or spurned, their talent may wither away.

It is seekers, then, who make prophets, and the initiative of any one of us in searching for and responding to the voice of contemporary prophets may mark the turning point in their growth and service. But since we are the product of our own history, we see current prophecy within the context of past wisdom. We listen to as wide a range of contemporary thought as we can attend to. Then we choose those we elect to heed as prophets—both old and new—and meld their advice with our own leadings. This we test in real-life experiences to establish our own position.

One does not, of course, ignore the great voices of the past. One does not awaken each morning with the compulsion to reinvent the wheel. But if one is servant, either leader or follower, one is always searching, listening, expecting that a better wheel for these times is in the making. It may emerge any day. Any one of us may discover it from personal experience. I am hopeful.

I am hopeful for these times, despite the tension and conflict, because more natural servants are trying to see clearly the world as it is and are listening carefully to prophetic voices that are speaking now. They are challenging the pervasive injustice with greater force, and they are taking sharper issue with the wide disparity between the quality of society they know is reasonable and possible with available resources and the actual performance of the institutions that exist to serve society.

A fresh, critical look is being taken at the issues of power and authority, and people are beginning to learn, however haltingly, to relate to one another in less coercive and more creatively supporting ways. A new moral principle is emerging, which holds that the only authority deserving one's allegiance is that which is freely and knowingly granted by the led to the leader in response to, and in proportion to, the clearly evident servant stature of the leader. Those who choose to follow this principle will not casually accept the authority of existing institutions. Rather, they will freely respond only to individuals who are chosen as leaders because they are proven and trusted as servants. To the extent that this principle prevails in the future, the only truly viable institutions will be those that are predominantly servant-led.

I am mindful of the long road ahead before these trends, which I see so clearly, become a major society-shaping force. We are not there yet. But I see encouraging movement on the horizon.

What direction will the movement take? Much depends on whether those who stir the ferment will come to grips with the age-old problem of how to live in a human society. I say this because so many, having made their awesome decision for autonomy and independence from tradition, and having taken their firm stand against injustice and hypocrisy, find it hard to convert themselves into affirmative builders of a better society. How many of them will seek their personal fulfillment by making the hard choices, and by undertaking the rigorous preparation that building a better society requires? It all depends on what kind of leaders emerge and how they—we—respond to them.

My thesis, that more servants should emerge as leaders, or should follow only servant-leaders, is not a popular one. It is much more comfortable to go with a less demanding point of view about what is expected of one now. There are several undemanding, plausibly argued alternatives from which to choose. One, since society seems corrupt, is to seek to avoid the center of it by retreating to an idyllic existence that minimizes involvement with the "system" (with the system that makes such withdrawal possible). Then there is the assumption that since the effort to reform existing institutions has not brought instant perfection, the remedy is to destroy them completely so that fresh, new, perfect ones can grow. Not much thought seems to be given to the problem of where the new seed will come from or who the gardener to tend them will be. The concept of the servant-leader stands in sharp contrast to this kind of thinking.

Yet it is understandable that the easier alternatives would be chosen, especially by young people. By extending education for so many so far into the adult years, normal participation in society is effectively denied when young people are ready for it. With education that is preponderantly abstract and analytical, it is no wonder that a preoccupation with criticism exists and that not much thought is given to "What can I do about it?"

Criticism has its place, but as a total preoccupation it is sterile. In a time of crisis, like the leadership crisis we are now in, if too many potential builders are completely absorbed with dissecting the wrong and striving for instant perfection, then the movement so many of us want to see will be set back. The danger, perhaps, is to hear the analyst too much and the artist too little.

Albert Camus stands apart from other great artists of his time, in my view, and deserves the title of prophet, because of his unrelenting demand that each of us confront the exacting terms of our own existence, and, like Sisyphus, accept our rock and find our happiness by dealing with it. Camus sums up the relevance of his position to our concern for the servant as leader in the last paragraph of his last published lecture, entitled *Create Dangerously:*

> One may long, as I do, for a gentler flame, a respite, a pause for musing. But perhaps there is no other peace for the artist than what he finds in the heat of combat. "Every wall is a door," Emerson correctly said. Let us not look for the door, and the way out, anywhere but in the wall against which we are living. Instead, let us seek the respite where it is—in the very thick of battle. For in my opinion, and this is where I shall close, it is there. Great ideas, it has been said, come into the world as gently as doves. Perhaps, then, if we listen attentively, we shall hear, amid the uproar of empires and nations, a faint flutter of wings, the gentle stirring of life and hope. Some will say that this hope lies in a nation; others, in a man. I believe rather that it is awakened, revived, nourished by millions of solitary individuals whose deeds and works every day negate frontiers and the crudest implications of history. As a result, there shines forth fleetingly the ever-threatened truth that each and every man, on the foundations of his own sufferings and joys, builds for them all.

Who Is the Servant-Leader?

The servant-leader is servant first—as Leo was portrayed. Becoming a servant-leader begins with the natural feeling that one wants to serve, to serve first. Then conscious choice brings one to aspire to lead. That person is sharply different from one who is leader first, perhaps because of the need to assuage an unusual power drive or to acquire material possessions. For such people, it will be a later choice to serve—after leadership is established. The leader-first and

the servant-first are two extreme types. Between them are the shad-
ings and blends that are part of the infinite variety of human nature.

The difference manifests itself in the care taken by the servant
first to make sure that other people's highest priority needs are being
served. The best test, and most difficult to administer, is this: Do
those served grow as persons? Do they, while being served, become
healthier, wiser, freer, more autonomous, more likely themselves to
become servants? And what is the effect on the least privileged in society; will they benefit, or, at least, not be further deprived?

All of this rests on the assumption that the only way to change
a society (or just make it go) is to produce people, enough people,
who will change it (or make it go). The urgent problems of our
day—the disposition to venture into immoral and senseless wars,
destruction of the environment, poverty, alienation, discrimination,
overpopulation—exist because of human failures, individual failures, one-person-at-a-time, one-action-at-a-time failures.

If we make it out of all of this (and this is written in the belief
that we will), the system will be whatever works best. The builders
will find the useful pieces wherever they are, and invent new ones
when needed, all without reference to ideological coloration. "How
do we get the right things done?" will be the watchword of the day,
every day. And the context of those who bring it on will be: All men
and women who are touched by the effort grow taller, and become
healthier, stronger, more autonomous, and more disposed to serve.

Leo the servant, and the exemplar of the servant-leader, has one
further portent for us. If we assume that Hermann Hesse is the narrator in *Journey to the East* (not a difficult assumption to make),
at the end of the story he establishes his identity. His final confrontation at the close of his initiation into the Order is with a small
transparent sculpture: two figures joined together. One is Leo, the
other is the narrator. The narrator notes that a movement of substance is taking place within the transparent sculpture.

> I perceived that my image was in the process of adding to and
> flowing into Leo's, nourishing and strengthening it. It seemed
> that, in time . . . only one would remain: Leo. He must grow,
> I must disappear. As I stood there and looked and tried to

understand what I saw, I recalled a short conversation that I had once had with Leo during the festive days at Bremgarten. We had talked about the creations of poetry being more vivid and real than the poets themselves.

What Hesse may be telling us here is that Leo is the symbolic personification of Hesse's aspiration to serve through his literary creations—creations that are greater than Hesse himself—and that his work, for which he was but the channel, will carry on and serve and lead in a way that he, a twisted and tormented man, could not—as he created.

Does not Hesse dramatize, in extreme form, the dilemma of us all? Except as we venture to create, we cannot project ourselves beyond ourselves to serve and lead.

To which Camus would add: *create dangerously!*

Dr. Stephen R. Covey is vice chairman of Franklin Covey Company, the largest management and leadership development organization in the world. He is perhaps best known as the author of *The 7 Habits of Highly Effective People,* a book with a compelling message that has kept it on numerous best-seller lists for more than ten years. Those familiar with his work will not be surprised to learn that Dr. Covey has been recognized as one of *Time* magazine's 25 most influential Americans.

In this essay, drawn from his keynote speech at the Greenleaf Center's 1999 conference, Dr. Covey describes what he calls the four roles of leadership—modeling, pathfinding, alignment, and empowerment—using examples and a nautical metaphor. Covey says the true test of leadership is the one that Robert K. Greenleaf described, and true servant-leadership produces servant-leadership in others. Stephen Covey was a keynote speaker at the Greenleaf Center's 1996 and 1999 annual international conferences.

2

SERVANT-LEADERSHIP AND COMMUNITY LEADERSHIP IN THE TWENTY-FIRST CENTURY

Stephen R. Covey

I WANT TO SAY a word about this conference: it's a beautiful illustration of win–win situations, because servant-leadership is the enabling art to accomplishing any worthy objective. It's glorious to see these two organizations—The Greenleaf Center for Servant-Leadership and the National Association for Community Leadership—come together, and to see others join together, and to let go of the ego investment in words, semantics, and agendas, to realize the transcendent agenda that unifies us and the transcendent values of respect and service, servant-leadership, and the enabling values.

My purpose now is to describe what I call "the four roles of leadership." The first role is simply to be an example, a model: one whose life has credibility with others, has integrity, diligence, humility, the spirit of servant-leadership, of contribution. This is the most fundamental of our roles. Someone asked Albert

Schweitzer how kids learn. He said, "Three ways. First, example. Second, example. Third, example." Nothing is as powerful as example. I don't care how much or how little you know. When you teach what you yourself are still learning, you also enroll people as a support for you, to help you live it. You give your knowledge to others by trying to live it; yes, it's hard. You show humility: This modeling is the foundation of true leadership. People who genuinely care and who have this personal integrity merit the confidence of others.

The second role of leadership is pathfinding. That's the vision role—the role of deciding what your mission is and what your values are; what you're trying to accomplish. The big mistake most organizations tend to fall into—and, in many firms, leaders tend to fall into—is to announce to other people what their mission is. Because if there's no involvement of the people in forming the mission, there's no commitment from the people. The mission won't be the operative, powerful, empowering focus it's intended to be. For true pathfinding, you must always study what the needs of people are. You must try to discern what the value systems are and how you can come up with a strategic plan within those values to meet those needs. That's essentially what pathfinding involves.

The third role of leadership is alignment. Once you have chosen the words that define what your vision, your mission, your values are, then you have to make sure that all of the structures and systems inside the organization reflect that. This is the toughest part of the pathfinding role. Because once you realize you have to align structures and systems, once you realize you're not just in some kind of vision workshop for the mental exercise, but that your organizational structures and systems will be governed by your visions and values—I'm telling you, you will start to take seriously the concept of coming up with a proper goal or vision or mission. Unless you institutionalize your values, they won't happen. All you'll do is talk about them—about the value of servant-leadership, about the value of community leadership, about cooperation, innovation, diversity—but unless they're institutionalized, built into the very criteria of structures and systems to support the strategy, the vision, the mission that you're after, they will not happen. That's why that alignment role is so vital. You can't come up with competitive compensation systems and still say you value cooperation. You can't say you value the long term when you're totally governed by short-term data. You can't say you value creativity when march-step conformity is the thing that's continually enforced. You can't say you value diversity when really deep in the bowels of recognition systems are prejudices about different kinds of groups or people. But you can get commitment and involvement by many people if your value system is truly exemplified by your organization's structure and policies. And if your values are based on natural laws or principles that are universal and self-evident, then you institutionalize that moral authority. You're no longer dependent on the moral authority of a particular individual.

The fourth role of leadership is empowerment—empowering people. The fourth role is essentially the fruit of the first three. When you have a common vision and value system, and you have put into place structures and systems reinforcing that vision, when you have institutionalized that kind of moral authority—it is like lifeblood feeding the culture, the feelings of people, the norms, the mores—feeding it constantly. Now, you're really out of people's way. You don't have to be focused on morals. You don't have to be focused on procedures; you have a few, but relatively few. You can focus instead on vision and values and release the enormous human creativity, the human ingenuity, the resourcefulness, the intelligence of people to the accomplishment of those purposes. Everything connects together: the quality of the relationships, the common purpose and values. You find that people will organize themselves. They'll manage themselves. People are drawn to doing their own best thing and accomplishing that worthy purpose, that vision. That's empowerment!

Let me give you a visual image for each of those roles from a nautical source. The first role, *modeling,* is an anchor. That means you personally are anchored to the principles of integrity, of service, of contribution, of kindness, of respect—all these most basic principles and values. The second image is the image of a map, with the ship going toward its destination. *Pathfinding* means that the ship knows where it's going. It has a destination. The third image, for *alignment*, is the steering wheel. When the steering wheel of this big ship is turned, all of the structures and systems, the huge rudder, the trimtab of the rudder, everything else is geared to responding to the direction that has been given from this wheel. All the parts of the ship are coordinated, everything is focused, aligned. The fourth image, the one of *empowerment*, is the fully masted sailing ship. With the sails set up fully, responding to the wind, you have the release of that human potential: everyone cooperates together to take that ship to its destination.

Now I want to introduce one other image: the image of a trimtab. The trimtab is the small rudder on the big rudder of a ship—a small surface but when you turn it, it turns the larger surface. Sometimes the resistance of the ocean is so strong that you can't turn the rudder directly so you turn a small trimtab, which is easier to turn. It gets leverage against the water, and that can enable the rudder to turn; and when the rudder turns, you can direct the ship to its destination. I love this image of a trimtab because every one of us can become a trimtab figure—inside our families, inside our communities, inside our organizations. It doesn't make any difference what your position is. Any person can become a trimtab figure.

People often ask if modeling always comes first. My experience is that there *is* an element of modeling that comes first, otherwise there's no credibility. But the highest form of modeling is when you're carrying out the other three roles. You model when you help people get involved in the process of deciding the destination, the pathfinding role. You are modeling tremendous respect for others when you are willing to align structures and systems that affect you as well as everyone else, and you make yourself accountable. You have essentially modeled integrity. The greatest gift you can give to other people is themselves. You do this when you affirm in people their basic gifts and talents and capacities, their ability to become trimtabs themselves, to become change catalysts. When you do that, you show tremendous reverence for people, you show humility, you show respect, you show caring—that's modeling.

The true test of leadership is the one that Bob Greenleaf described: you model these four roles of leadership so that others around you are empowered to find their own paths, and they in turn are inspired to help even more people find their paths. Greenleaf said your servant-leadership produces servant-leadership in others. You don't just serve, you do it in a way that makes them independent of you, and capable and desirous of serving other people. Anyone can be a servant-leader. Any one of us can take initiative ourself; it doesn't require that we be appointed a leader, but it does require that we operate from moral authority. That's the great need. The spirit of servant-leadership is the spirit of moral authority. It says, "I'm not into me. I'm into serving you and other people. And I know for me to be a servant, I have to be a model or I'll lose the spirit of servant. I'll just want to have 'the appearance' of serving so that people will think more of me." Then they lose the kind of humility Robert Greenleaf spoke about.

You can release tremendous synergy when you empower people, and you can do it most effectively when you come to any situation not with a competitive, win–lose attitude, but with a win–win attitude. It only takes one person to think win–win. Not two. So when you join together with other groups, you have different vocabularies, different kinds of agendas, a different focus, and so forth. The natural thing with people is to want to be understood. No: Instead, seek to understand the other first. That's the spirit of the servant-leader: "I want to understand you. What are your concerns? What are your interests? Why don't we both win?" Now *that* empowers us *both;* it releases our potential. The key to empowerment is to listen to other people and to value their differences.

Let me tell you about a colleague I sometimes team-teach with when I'm in South Africa. He's well known in that country for his successes, and his businesses are prospering. And with the new South African economic reality—with the global economy, the releasing of the sanctions, the dismantling of apartheid—a lot of businesses are really languishing. And businessmen press him. They say, "Colin, how did you do this? What are you doing?" He basically starts with a story of playing Monopoly with his son, beating his son in a very competitive game, and then really emotionally piling on, kind of gloating. And his son says to him, "Father, does it matter that much to you? It's only a game." And the father at the time was going through Seven Habits training, writing his personal mission statement, and he said, "What has happened to me? What has my life been based upon?" It was based upon technique, power, training, education, but not principles. So he went deep inside all the rationalizations in his mind and his heart, including apartheid. And he really let it out. He tells businessmen this story. That's not the story they want to hear. They want to hear techniques. They want to know what program he recommends. He says, "It starts with oneself." And it does. Starting with himself was the key. He went from power leadership to servant-leadership. He became interested in others, empowering others.

There's one last point I'd like to make. There are four needs in all people. We must survive in our body: we must live. We must relate to others: we must love. We must grow and develop, use our talents: we must learn. And we must also have value, make a difference: we must leave a legacy. To live, to love, to learn, to leave a legacy. Where these needs overlap, you find that internal motivation, the fire within. If you do not have an outward focus to leave a legacy, the fire will go out in other areas. Did you know that? People will be wanting more for themselves. The culture will divide, and people will learn toward their own ends. But when you are making a living, building a family, having good relationships, constantly growing and learning, all with intent to contribute, to serve, the fire goes on. It ignites. If a lit match gets close to another match, it will ignite the other match. It's the warmth of caring that does it. Then the fire goes on. If I were to take that match and put it to a candle, it would burn for a long period of time. What if I were to translate that candle into an electrical system or something even bigger?

Starting with your own fire, you can create something that will burn bright for many people and last a lifetime—through alignment of structures and systems, through the institutionalization of the principles we have talked about—you can empower others to live, to love, to learn, to leave a legacy. You can be a servant-leader.

Michael Jones is a gifted pianist, author, speaker, and educator. He has 11 recordings on the Narada Record label, and has sold more than two million units of his "pianoscapes." Jones has written numerous articles on creativity as well as *Creating an Imaginative Life,* an award-winning collection of stories and insights on the creative process. He has been a member of the core faculty of the MIT Dialogue Project and now speaks and leads seminars on the relationship between creative practice and leadership. His Web site is www.pianoscapes.com.

Too often, we think work is what we are. Michael Jones professes that our lives are what we are and our challenge is to let our life be our art. In this essay, he takes us on the journey of his own unfolding as an artist and leads us to the conclusion that the imaginative life starts with a sense of the aesthetic, where we often sense reality before we understand it. He echoes Greenleaf's stated qualification for leadership: the ability to tolerate a sustained awareness so that the leader sees the world (and self) as it truly is. Michael Jones was a keynote speaker at the Greenleaf Center's annual international conference in 2000.

3

SERVANT-LEADERSHIP AND
THE IMAGINATIVE LIFE

Michael Jones

I HAVE BEEN INTERESTED in the nature of the gift community and how our gifts are seen by others, often not by ourselves. In the honoring of other persons through the way we see the gift living in them, we can be the moon that reflects back to them the light of their own sun.

I think we're very familiar with the market economy, since that has been a dominant part of our culture. Many of us have been inducted into that from the time we first walked into school. But a more invisible part of the economy has been the economy of gift exchange, the sense that we bear gifts and that those gifts are an important part of how we touch the heart of another. Those gifts reach others because we were made for this purpose by nature beyond anything else we might do. So, while we may see our skills and abilities as part of what we bring to the marketplace, they are not always our primary strengths. There are also these more transcendent qualities, qualities which are often invisible to us because they're so close to who we naturally are. And yet when we live our lives from these gifts, magic happens, perhaps because, as the Italian Renaissance philosopher Marsilio Ficino says, "Heaven favours those things it has itself begun."

I can remember how this sense of reaching others happened for me several years ago. I was at the Esalen Institute in California for part of a winter. My wife and I were traveling, on the road for about six months, and we kept trying to anticipate where were we going to be each week so we could figure out with whom we might stay. We would make phone calls, but nobody would call back, so we were getting a clue that maybe this wasn't working. A friend of ours had said before we started this trip, "Travel with a candle rather than a flashlight. See if you can live your journey in the same way that you live your music." So we traveled through the country with a candle, only looking ahead about twenty-four hours at a time. In fact, whenever we tried to plan further, things simply didn't work out. And we did this—following the leadings of the candle—down through Florida, across the South, into California, and then to the Esalen Institute.

Because I was also traveling to Japan to do some concerts, we stopped for a time in California so I could rehearse and get ready for the trip. One evening, a young man came up to me while I was sitting at the piano. As I was getting up to leave, he stopped me and said, "I really enjoy your music." I thanked him. Then he said, "There's just one thing." "What's that?" I asked. "Well," he said, "you sound too much like Michael Jones." Knowing he had my attention now, he started to lecture me saying, "You have to develop your own style. You can't sound like somebody else the rest of your life. You have to find your own musical voice." By this time he had developed quite a head of steam. I was getting progressively more uncomfortable, however, and not quite sure how to respond. I finally stopped him and said, "Look, really. My name *is* Michael Jones." He looked at me for the longest time. "No, you're not," he said emphatically. And I knew he was serious. So we sat on the piano bench arguing about who I was.

It was an important moment for me, because I realized that I had spent almost all of my life, more or less, in a place of exchange with other people. Others knew me. I knew them. In my work as a consultant, that's largely how my life had worked. But a couple of years before, I had started to record my work, and it had captured the interest of many people. Now people were meeting me on the road who had already met me in my music. In a sense, they felt they knew me better than I knew myself, through the time they had spent with my music.

I also realized that this kind of interchange with someone who knew me through my music would not happen in Canada, at least not in my experience. I have a cousin who became a very famous playwright in Canada and says, "What happens when you become a famous playwright in Canada? Nothing." I was not used to the kind of meeting where somebody would engage with me the way this young gentleman had. His comments provoked me to reflect upon the events that had led me to be in this place at this particular time, to have taken a different road that created the circumstances for this meeting to have taken place.

I had been an organizational consultant for many years. Although I had studied music for about 15 years and loved it, I felt— as many of us do—it was time to move on, to assume a more responsible, adult life. I couldn't figure out how music might fit into that. I also had a background in psychology, which led to professional work in leadership development and organizational consulting. I spent a lot of my time doing that kind of work, often in off-site retreat settings. Once I was in a hotel outside of Toronto with a group of financial managers for a week. At midweek, we decided to take some time off. We were in a wonderful little town with good restaurants, so a group of us went off to eat. I came back to the hotel early so I could prepare for the next day. There was a little spinet piano near the registration desk; the hotel looked relatively empty, so I thought I might sit down and play for a while. If you're a pianist, you might recognize the impulse—you can't walk by a piano without touching it. So I sat down and started to play. At that time, I felt that my own music was a little too personal to share in public settings, so I had worked up cover arrangements of popular tunes, and I relied on those to draw from, whenever I played in a setting like this. I did that for a while, but then, because nobody was around, I shifted into my own music, then back into some cover tunes, and back and forth. After about 20 minutes, I had a sense of somebody moving toward me from the lounge down the hall. I looked up and saw an older gentleman weaving toward me with a glass of red wine precariously perched between his thumb and his forefinger.

As he got closer, I became uneasy. I thought, "Oh, he's going to ask for a request, and it will probably be a song I haven't learned, and this is going to be uncomfortable." I was really looking forward to some quiet time to relax and reflect. He grabbed at the piano to steady himself, plopped down in an easy chair just beside the instrument, and listened as I continued to play. When I stopped, he asked me, "What was that music?" I said, "Well, I think that was probably a little bit of 'Moon River.'" And he said, "No. No, there was something before that. What was that music?" I thought for a moment and I said, "I think that was probably a little of my own music." He said, "Well, I really enjoyed that. But you are wasting your time with . . . ." I said, "I think what I was playing was 'Moon River.'" "Well, you're really wasting your time with 'Moon River,'" he said. I was taken aback by his directness, and we talked for a bit. He said, "Do you work here at the hotel?" I said, "Oh, no, no, no. I'm a consultant. I'm busy trying to change the world." To my disappointment, he didn't seem at all impressed by that. Then he asked, "How many other people do this kind of consulting work that you do?" I said, "Well, probably 20 or 30, I would guess, in the Toronto area." And then he looked at me, and at that moment what I most recall about that meeting was how clear and sober his eyes appeared, from how he seemed a few minutes before. He said, "Who's going to play that music if you don't play it yourself?"

I felt that question drop in a way that I had not heard a question drop inside of me before. I realized it was a question for which I had no answer. We just sat and looked at each other. It was one of those silences that are immense, filled with meaning. Then he stood up, a little uneasy, and steadied himself by putting his hand on my shoulder, and said, "This is your gift—don't waste it." Then he picked up his wine glass and pointed himself back toward the lounge and—weaving unsteadily across the lobby floor—disappeared from sight. Meanwhile, I sat there on the piano bench, stunned by the question and the sense that it had just changed my life.

Who *will* play my music? I asked myself. I realized that, for many years, I had been reluctant to ask myself that very question. I remember, in fact, reflecting to friends, "I'd like to do something creative so that there's some memory of me when I'm gone . . . like taking up poetry or sculpture or something." And people would ask, "What about your music?" And I'd say, "No, I mean something really special." I realized how much I discounted that very thing I had been made for, which had been so much a source of love and pleasure when I was a child.

It's as the American painter Georgia O'Keeffe once said, "That which is most precious to us is often so close to us that we don't know that it's there." It seems so ordinary that we can't imagine why anybody would want to pay that much attention to it. And maybe this *ordinariness* is the source of our salvation. It keeps our gift within human dimensions and protects us from the hidden dangers of some overblown inflation.

But within the ordinariness of the gift, there is something else that *is* extraordinary—something that is not in the territory of ego inflation but rather in the domain of the imagination. If we follow our gift—in the way that I had followed the candle—it will take us on an adventure into a dimension of life that is perhaps larger and more profound than we could possibly envision when we began. And I realized: that was what was behind the resistance I had to bringing the music more into the center of my life: I had a sense that it was going to take me into parts of myself and parts of the world where I didn't think I wanted to go. For example, it might take me into a more public life of stages and audiences and media attention that would be very uncomfortable because the music was very personal for me. I was also very shy and introverted, very inward. I wanted to make a difference but do it from behind the scenes. I don't think there was ever a stage I saw in my life that I did not want to avoid! The idea that I might go back to music, and the prospects of where it might lead me, were the reasons I'd not asked myself that question. Yet Pablo Neruda, the Chilean poet, writes in his *Memoirs* that sometimes we are warned. When we get too far off track in terms of where our real life purpose is, somebody or something calls us back.

I felt in that moment I was being called back to the centrality of my own life. As the gentleman from the hotel lounge disappeared, I found some new thoughts turning over, and some other familiar ones started to surface as well. I had thoughts such as: "Well, if I do what he's suggesting, I'm probably going to go broke. Secondly, I'm not that good. Thirdly, I don't think . . . ," and so on. I went off in search of him to tell him, "Look—let's have a discussion about this!" Of course, he was nowhere to be found. (When I shared this story some years later, a friend said, "I hear that angels come to us in the forms of drunks and children." So perhaps I'd had a visitation that night.)

But several other things also unfolded from that evening. First, I never played "Moon River" ever again. In fact, I didn't play anybody else's music after that night. I know there are wonderful ways to bring our creative interpretations to other people's work, but he reminded me that something was coming through in my own work that didn't seem to be evident in playing anyone else's. I started to see that it was a matter of devoting myself to the articulation of a voice that was uniquely my own to bring forth. The second thing was: I realized I could not bring any believability to my work if I wasn't living it in my own life. I was meeting with a group the following morning—I was still a consultant leading retreats, after all—and the topic we were exploring was "Vision and Purpose." But my work had become abstract. I was talking the words but somehow I wasn't living the spirit of the work, because I had been avoiding it in my own life. As a result, I began to think differently about my consulting practice. As contracts wrapped up, I didn't try to renew them. Instead, I took advantage of this "found time" to play the piano instead. The third thing I found was that I had to learn to wait, because the answer to that question was not going to be coming in any immediate sense. I didn't have any idea what the form of the music might be, what it might look like, what it might lead me to. The best I could do was simply wait and see what might come to me. In that waiting, I found some guidance by turning to poetry, because I discovered that poets understand something about waiting upon the imagination and entering into this other dimension of life that was just opening up consciously for the first time for me. My psychology background was not much help to me here. It seems true that at times the skills that bring us to a certain part of our life are not the same ones we need when it comes to changing our life. We need to open up to new metaphors, new ways of seeing possibilities. I think it was Sigmund Freud who said once that no matter where his research led, a poet had already been there before him. Poets are articulators of the life of the imagination. And that's what this waiting was teaching me. By not trying to make something happen based on what I thought ought to happen, but instead learning how to sense into and follow what was already happening naturally, I was learning to do the work of the imagination.

The thread of continuity for me since that evening was always the question: Who will play *my* music? I believed that as long as I held on to that question, the question would do the work, leading me into what, in a sense, was the life I was here to live. With such questions, we find that we fail not because the questions are too large, but because they are too small. Henry Moore, the sculptor, said, "You need to hold questions that cannot be fully completed or lived out within the span of your own lifetime." Beethoven is an example of a composer whose questions were larger than his own life. You hear it in the greatness of his music. The greatness is in the question. If he had composed his music with the answer already set in his mind, he would not have been as great a composer, and his music would not have pulled us in as deeply as it does. From my experience as a composer, it is the question—this ongoing inquiry into life's eternal mystery—that is the imagination's instrument for attracting us deeply into life. I have noticed that when I am no longer in the question, I am not as sensitized to the nuances of movement and touch, and soon the music stops as well.

How often we find there's some significant, precious part of ourselves that somehow doesn't go with us in the morning when we travel to work. It can't seem to find its place in what we're doing. In many ways, it may be the most precious and—what might we say?—most gifted parts of ourselves that are left out. There is no answer to this dilemma for most of us. There is only the question. And, if we can hold it as a question, playing with it, inquiring into what the answer might feel or look like, and being curious about its possibilities, it will lead us to things we could not have planned with the strategic part of our mind. Being here, speaking and performing with you this afternoon, is not part of a long-term strategy. I could never have put all these elements together. But through holding the question of what it might mean and feel like to bring this deeper integration into my life, I have discovered that I am now able to bring *all* of myself—the piano, the music, the stories, the ideas, everything that makes up my own voice—into the room at the same time!

Another thing about "living in the question" is that it heightens the sense that we live in an ever-present terror, that we're on the precipice of the unknown—of a void or an abyss—in which we are not sure of our footing or of what stands in front of us. In the life of the imagination, this doesn't change! As a friend said to me once, "Remember, music is *not* your career, teaching is. Through being improvisational and heartfelt—and true to the feeling of your music—you are discovering how to bring that same quality into your words. So you can expect that by allowing the words to come from the same place you play, you're going to have those moments when you feel lost and don't know what to say next." The question is: How do you handle that moment? Will you keep going, even though those moments seem to come up more and more frequently as you hold your conversations—and your life—at this frontier where the familiar and the unfamiliar world meet? Perhaps this explains why one of St. Augustine's favorite words for *heart* was *abyss*. It is through this experience of being *lost* that the imaginative, sensing, feeling heart comes most alive. We are familiar with the courage of the lion heart and the endurance of the heart committed to long days and hard work. We know the sentimental—and sometimes compassionate—heart that expresses itself through pop songs' expressions of care and loss and love. We are less familiar with the imaginative heart, the heart that sees deeply and arises from having an aesthetic attitude toward our life and our work.

It is in this moment of being lost, when we have no choice but to "stand still," that we discover the true dimensions of the aesthetic heart. It leads us instinctively to finding our way back to that "sense of place" we knew as a child. It was a way of being in the world in which we had no plans, no agendas; we simply met the world as it presented itself to us. This is the way of being present to the world that the poets speak of, the sense that wherever we are is the place of the heart and therefore can be called home. We hear this sense of being present to the moment beautifully expressed in the words of Spanish poet Antonio Machado when he says, "You walking, your footprints are the road and nothing else;

there is no road, walker: You make the road by walking." That was the challenge the old man presented to me that night in the hotel. In asking the question, he was also saying: It's time to find your own path through life, a path that cannot be imitated or lived out by anyone but yourself. And that path offers itself only one step at a time. If we can see the road winding far ahead, it is very likely that we have stumbled upon someone else's road and need to find our way back to our own. In other words, in the life of the imagination, there is no goal. The road is always just beneath our feet. If we follow it, we will recognize that we are in the right place, but we will do so only *after* we have arrived.

Through the music, I was finding the key to that sense of place that was home to the imagination for me. About that time, I came across a commentary by the Canadian poet Dennis Lee, who was inspired by something similar. Lee was describing one of the greatest gifts he was given by a mentor of his, a philosopher in Canada by the name of George Grant. Grant helped him to see the rightness of "loving our own"—in Lee's case, this affection was found in the few acres of land on a lake north of Toronto where he spent summers as a boy. By loving our own, he says, we come to find that place of the heart, that feeling of belonging, which we can grow out from; the place where the life of the aesthetic begins. That place of the heart for me was similar to Dennis Lee's: It was the unforgettable craggy shorelines, the inviting feeling of diving into cold, deep lakes, the chorus of loons at night, the sparkle of sunlight on water, the wind whispering through the great white pines. What gave me the most delight as a pianist was discovering ways to find a musical expression for that. I wanted to not only represent this sense of place in a conceptual way, but also in a way that would evoke what it might be like to *be* rain, to *be* wind. I wanted to merge with the very thing I was trying to recreate an impression of, so I could *be* the thing I was playing and speaking. An aesthetic sensibility involves this willingness to breathe in or take in the world, to receive life in all of its many ways.

As I think of the life of imagination and its relevance for leadership, I believe we are called to reclaim the aesthetic as our central vocation or calling. If the world is to have a future, it will have an aesthetic future. I believe that aesthetics—the capacity for imaginative sensing, for feeling and seeing deeply—is the primary new work for leaders. When I speak of aesthetics, I am thinking of it not as a conceptual framework, but as a lived experience. Robert Greenleaf, who is the founding spirit and inspiration for bringing us here today, said: "One qualification for leadership is the ability to tolerate a sustained wide span of awareness so that the leader sees it [and I believe by 'it' he was referring to the world] as it really is." This *experience* of the aesthetic precedes its *understanding*. And to know it truly, we need to begin with our own life, in our own unique way of "knowing" things; in the qualities of movement, smell, and touch; and through those activities and relationships that most bring alive for us that sense of what the love of place means for us. Marsilio Ficino, the Renaissance philosopher I spoke of earlier, says: "It is useful for us to search for that region which best suits us, a place where our spirit is advanced and refreshed, where our senses remain thriving and where things nourish us." This is a physical place, but it is also a disposition of the imaginative heart. And we come to this disposition when we let go of what we believe *ought* to be happening, and in so doing we will discover a deepening awareness of what is already trying to happen naturally in our life. This animal sense, or developing a nose for the innate intelligence of things—one which our rational mind often fails to detect—expresses itself most commonly through a life dedicated to practices that bring us into closer proximity with an expressive language, with beauty, and place, by living without a script, and sharing with others those gifts that are unique to them and to ourselves. The root of vocation is *vocare,* which means voice. Every life is, I believe, a journey into discovering our own voice. We do this through recognizing the restorative power of an expressive or living speech. A living speech *is* music, it is a way of speaking in which the words are no longer simply an instrument for getting things done. Rather, *we* become instruments for the expression of the Word, of our own truth, of the atmosphere of our own mind, our own authority and unique viewpoint that reflect our way of seeing the world. We find this atmosphere by placing ourselves in the presence of beauty, so that the words themselves become the heartfelt expression of praise for the many ways life is acting upon us.

Artists often begin their work from this inner place of knowing. As Dennis Lee says, "It is by allowing ourselves to be claimed by this childhood place of the heart that we find the ground to move ahead from. It equips us to love lesser things later on." To move toward the world with an imaginative heart helps "bring the country up." It instills the leader with an elevated perception for seeing not only the far hill but also what lies behind. By training the hand, the eye, and the nose to sense truly what is real, they are able to intuitively make the right moves that keep the larger interests of the world in view.

To conclude, I believe that servant-leaders are also called to be leaders of the aesthetic and, as such, leaders of the imaginative and sensing heart. They can do this through embracing such practices as: listening for the restorative power of language and story; keeping faith with the living word; making a home for others through the appreciation of beauty and place; developing the sense of seeing gifts in others through first being committed to calling up and living out the gifts that are in themselves. By learning to "live in the question" and lead without a script, through being open and responsive to the emergent as it is revealed through what the world is already trying to be, leaders can learn to let life live them rather than feeling they must always be trying to make things happen through attempting to grasp the future or reaching out. By serving the imagination in this way, we are also being served by it. As Marsilio Ficino said; "Heaven favors things that it has itself begun." And what heaven begins are found in those inexplicable sparks of inspiration that fire the imaginative heart and cause us to act. It is appropriate that we should draw upon a Renaissance philosopher to begin and conclude this talk because the sensibility I am speaking of has, at its root, a Renaissance sensibility. As we embrace the aesthetic in our life and work, we join the company of many others, known and unknown to us, who have accepted a similar challenge in embracing their own giftedness and furthering the work of the imagination. Through this imaginative labor, we may experience what it means to truly belong and feel at home in the world again. Who will play your music if you don't play it yourself?

Russ S. Moxley is a senior fellow at the Center for Creative Leadership in Greensboro, North Carolina. Over the past thirty years, he has been an executive coach, a trainer/facilitator in a variety of management and leadership development programs, an organizational development practitioner, a writer and editor, and a senior-level manager in two different organizations. Russ Moxley is the author of *Leadership & Spirit: Breathing New Vitality and Energy into Individuals and Organizations*. He received his master's degree in theology from the Perkins School of Theology at Southern Methodist University in Dallas.

Russ Moxley says that to be successful over the long haul, organizations need systems, structures, and practices of leadership that call forth the energies of all. He proposes that rather than look to one person as the leader, we start looking at leadership as being a partnership between two or more persons. In this essay, he elaborates on the benefits and challenges of such a model: rethinking power structures; supporting shared goals and responsibilities; respecting each person's contributions; and structuring leadership relationships that allow our organizations to honor diversity.

4

LEADERSHIP AS PARTNERSHIP

Russ S. Moxley

LEADERSHIP IS TYPICALLY UNDERSTOOD as something an individual provides. Leaders lead. They provide a compelling vision. They set direction and determine strategy. They motivate and inspire.

This understanding has worked reasonably well, particularly in industrial settings, but it has its limitations because there is only so much that any individual can do. First, with the increasing diversity of the workforce, it is very difficult for any one person to create and articulate a common goal. Today, a shared goal is possible only when the diverse interests and different agendas of many stakeholders are combined. Second, the resources—the gifts, skills, and energies—of a single person will invariably run out. To be successful over the long haul, organizations need systems, structures, and practices of leadership that call forth the energies of all employees.

I would like to suggest an alternative to individual leadership: leadership as partnership. Practicing this kind of leadership requires that two or more people share power and join forces to move toward the accomplishment of a shared goal. It is a relationship in which people are equals. Leadership is cocreated as individuals relate as partners and develop a shared vision, set a direction, solve problems, and make meaning of their work. Leadership as partnership is a distributed process shared by many ordinary people rather than the expression of a single individual.

Five Requirements for Leadership as Partnership

1. *There must be a balance of power.* A partnership will not work when one person has power and others don't, or when some people have power and some don't. When one person or one group uses positional or coercive power, the partnership stops. Rather, each individual must claim his or her personal power and use it to cocreate win–win situations and reach a shared goal.

2. *There must be a shared goal.* Even though there may be differing opinions of how to reach a goal, everyone in a partnership must share an understanding of what the goal is. Individuals will experience differences and conflict, but, as partners, they must learn to accept and honor them.

3. *There must be a shared sense of responsibility and accountability.* Whether in a one-to-one relationship, a group, or a larger community, partnership requires that everyone be responsible and accountable for the work. Work can't be done by *us* or *them*. It can only be done by all of us. In a partnership, the buck is on everyone's desk, not just the CEO's.

4. *Partnership requires respect for the person.* Each person in a partnership must believe in the inherent worth and value of every other person. People must recognize that each person has gifts, skills, and energies to offer. Partnership thus honors diversity, in word and deed. It requires that everyone be treated with dignity and respect.

5. *Partnership must be applied in all areas of organizational life.* Partnership will not work if it is applied only to unimportant issues. It must take on the tough challenges. Try to use it only in some situations and it will not work in any.

Perhaps the best way to understand how a partnership is different from individual leadership is to look at how it works in three different settings: a one-to-one relationship, a team, and an organization. The following examples are taken from my personal experience with individuals and organizations.

Partnership in a One-to-One Relationship

Robbie is a brand manager in a large manufacturing organization. He is knowledgeable, hardworking, focused, optimistic, considerate, and a quick study. Recently, he has had a series of conversations with his boss about problems with the final development and launch of an important new product. The boss not only expressed appropriate concern about the delay but also told Robbie exactly what needed to be done to get the product back on a fast track. Robbie knew from experience that what the boss told him to do would not work, but he did it anyway.

Robbie wanted the boss to do things differently, not just in this one instance but in all their work together. First, he wanted the boss, before he gave an order, to ask what Robbie thought needed to be done. Robbie also wanted the boss to ask whether there was anything that he, the boss, could do to help. Instead, by being high-handed, the boss made Robbie feel not only that he was responsible for the delay but also that he had no power to correct it.

In this case, Robbie and the boss had a shared goal, so one of the requirements of partnership was in place. But the boss sidelined Robbie—he assumed he alone knew what needed to be done, decided he didn't have time to discuss it, and saw his role as being directive. Robbie, however, wanted dialogue, not direction. He wanted to be a partner, not be overpowered. He wanted to be treated as a person, not a puppet. The boss needed to engage Robbie as a full participant in getting the task accomplished. And Robbie needed to have sufficient courage to speak his truth to the boss.

Partnership in a Team

Business was good for a major consumer product company, but the young president knew that the executive team could be stronger. Relationships among the six members of the team were cordial on the surface, but unresolved conflicts and tensions were evident just beneath it. Individuals had built fiefdoms and now worked hard to protect them. They avoided interdependence. Conflicts were pushed up to the president to resolve. Responsibility and accountability were not shared. The finger-pointing exceeded the working toward shared goals. Differences in style and personality were not honored; indeed, there was no appreciation that diversity might be a strength on which team members could build.

When the executives finally admitted this gap between the appearance of harmony and the reality, they took steps to create a team that represented true partnership. They worked on different ways of being and acting together, acknowledging conflict, spelling out assumptions, engaging in real dialogue, solving problems rather than passing them on, and sharing problems faced by the organization.

Changes came slowly but perceptibly. Over time, the executive team members became more open and less guarded, more collaborative and less competitive, more willing to put issues on the table and less likely to engage in sabotage after a meeting. They developed new understandings of their roles, of how they could practice partnership as leadership, and over time they developed the capacities to act on this new understanding.

In this case, once the partnership approach was adopted by the executive team, it improved both the company's performance and the work climate for the executives. Backbiting became a thing of the past. Individual goals were abandoned, and shared commitment to company goals was held up as the highest value.

Partnership in an Organization

Managers of a major airline, still operating under the authoritarian style of the company's first president, realized that this style would not allow them to develop the *esprit de corps* that seemed critical to long-term success. The president's attitude fostered compliance, not commitment. The top-down, command-and-control style did not elicit the inspired performance that this growing company needed.

A new president developed and implemented a different approach to leadership: partnership. Employees were encouraged to be accountable, even in areas for which they didn't have authority. Pilots learned to work with ramp agents, and customer-service agents learned to assist skycaps. The culture focused on the organization as a family—a group of individuals who were in this venture together, not out for themselves.

Yet individuality was honored, especially through creative enterprises such as storytelling and making humorous videos about working at the airline. The employees also focused on fundamentals—on-time arrivals, quick turnarounds, and low-cost fares. They took their work seriously.

Today, this airline has become a highly prized employer and its profitability has remained consistently excellent.

Individuals and Partnerships

The preceding examples make it seem as though the individual as leader is an endangered species. The opposite is true. The role of the individual is enhanced in this new partnership approach because it centers on the importance of *all* individuals.

Even though leadership is not the province of a single individual in the partnership approach, the personhood of each employee becomes important. The gifts, skills, and energies of each person within the relationship are honored and used. There is no "more than" or "less than"; no "one up" or "one down"; no person who has power over others and makes them feel powerless. In partnership, power is cocreated as people share it.

Often, an individual is the catalyst for starting the leadership process, for suggesting new ways of working and being together. The refreshing perspective of one person often finds new meaning and purpose in work.

The role of the individual is also enhanced because it is interdependently defined—one person becomes the spokesperson, another is the organizer, another is responsible for the processes that keep the partnership strong and growing.

This new approach to leadership suggests a change in perspective. We need to move toward more interdependent ways of thinking and acting. If the rugged individuals we once held up as heroic leaders cannot acknowledge a need for connectedness, they may fail to adapt to an environment where individuals *and* communities are honored.

Hamilton Beazley is an associate professor of Administrative Sciences at George Washington University. His major fields of expertise are organizational behavior, organizational culture, leadership, and spirituality in organizations. Before launching an academic career, he served in the for-profit and not-for-profit sectors. His wide range of talents led Dr. Beazley to cocreate a BBC television series titled *Secrets Out;* to found a successful consulting firm; and to serve as president of the National Council on Alcoholism and Drug Dependence, Inc.

Julie Yancich Beggs is currently chief learning officer for the Greenleaf Center. At the start of her professional career, she was the Assistant Director of Campus Activities for Butler University in Indianapolis, Indiana. While at Butler, she developed "The Hampton House," a special-interest housing facility where student servant-leaders can live and learn together. The Hampton House is one of three housing models, within the United States, that are based on Robert K. Greenleaf's book *Teacher as Servant.*

In *Teacher as Servant,* Robert K. Greenleaf described the type of environment that he believed would be conducive to the development of servant-leaders and servant-led organizations. Hamilton Beazley and Julie Beggs draw on direct experience and ongoing research of three university living units that are patterned on Greenleaf's fictional "Jefferson House." *Teacher as Servant* presents the theory and practice of this unique pedagogical model within academic living units, but the authors believe that this pedagogy can also be the basis for the development of servant-leaders in for-profit and not-for-profit organizations of all types.

5

TEACHING SERVANT-LEADERSHIP

Hamilton Beazley and Julie Beggs

NUMEROUS INSTITUTIONS AND HUNDREDS of individuals around the world have answered the call to servant-leadership that Robert Greenleaf issued more than three decades ago. Greenleaf's dream of a "good society" created by servant-leaders working through their institutions has inspired an accelerating commitment to the study and practice of servant-leadership and to servant-led organizations. Servant-leadership is now being taught in America's colleges and universities and is itself being practiced in institutions of higher learning. This trend is all the more significant because the paradox of the servant as leader (and the leader as servant) is often confounding upon cursory examination, is not easily captured, and is not amenable to quick application.

How servant-leaders and servant-led institutions can be developed is a significant question to which increasing research has been devoted. Of particular interest are very recent developments on American college and university campuses, from which some answers are emerging regarding how servant-leadership can be taught and the opportunities that foster its development and practice. The focus of this chapter is on the development of servant-leaders in higher education. The conclusions drawn are the result of continuing research in this area by the authors.

What Has Been Done to Date

Several different types of programs have been developed in higher education to cultivate servant-leaders. Broadly speaking, such programs can be divided into:

- ○ *Curricular* programs (e.g., a master's degree in organizational leadership that is based on servant-leadership, courses devoted exclusively to servant-leadership theory and practice, or sections on servant-leadership within a leadership or organizational behavior course);

- ○ *Cocurricular* programs (e.g., a living-learning unit dedicated to the study and practice of servant-leadership; servant-leadership programs offered outside the classroom by staff members who gather students in informal groups to discuss the concept; or a one-credit, one-hour seminar in servant-leadership offered over four years with institutional scholarships awarded each year);

- ○ *Institutional* (e.g., new mission statements grounded in servant-leadership; the establishment of centers for servant-leadership to develop servant-leaders throughout the campus; revised policy statements, or faculty and staff development seminars that focus on servant-leadership).

A Living Laboratory

When Robert Greenleaf first wrote of servant-leadership in the 1970s, his intended audience was college students. Because of the turbulence of the period, he was concerned about the future of the nation and, in particular, its potential for greatness because of the disaffection of the young and their disinclination to work within established institutions. Greenleaf's consulting work in leadership focused on different types of organizations and on various age groups, but he was "betting his chips" on what could be done with the young. He feared that their spirit, their willingness to serve, and their ability to lead might be wasted or conditioned out of them. Therefore, in his early writings and particularly in his parable entitled *Teacher as Servant,* he delved into how servant-leadership might be cultivated among the young and how it could be used to change society in dramatic and lasting ways.

In *Teacher as Servant,* Robert Greenleaf describes an imaginary university living unit, Jefferson House, in which servant-leadership is taught to, and practiced by, the students who live there, under the guidance of a wise physics professor: Dr. Billings. The narrator of the story, a young business executive employed by a servant-led institution, recounts his four-year experience at Jefferson House. What is unique about *Teacher as Servant* is that it describes the type of environment that Greenleaf believed would be conducive to the development of servant-leaders and servant-led organizations. Through the narrator's story of his experiences at Jefferson House, Greenleaf describes a design for developing servant-leaders on campus and explores how institutions might be changed through the presence of servant-leaders.

Over the past few years, the fictional Jefferson House has served as a model for the creation of three servant-leadership houses on university campuses in the United States. These houses, which accommodate undergraduate students in a residence hall setting, are Leadership House at the University of South Florida, Tampa; Hampton House at Butler University, Indianapolis; and Leadership House at East Tennessee State University, Johnson City. A study of these three houses makes it possible to identify some of the elements required to teach servant-leadership and to create a structured environment that fosters its practice. These houses, as well as other university servant-leadership programs, provide a living laboratory and convincing evidence that servant-leadership can be intentionally taught, constructively practiced, and effectively learned. This essay focuses on students in college and university settings, but its principles are also applicable to businesses and to other institutions.

The pedagogical model that Greenleaf offers in *Teacher as Servant* is conceptually an *apprenticeship.* The term is appropriate because it implies both instruction in theory and supervision in practice by someone committed to both the concept and the individual attempting to master it. Apprenticeship is necessary in servant-leadership because the real power of servant-leadership is only grasped through the continual practice that characterizes any art or discipline. Although the concept is simple, its execution is not. No precise formula guides its implementation. Its expression is always an individualized experience based on the person's unique set of talents and skills. Each individual and every organization, therefore, will be different in the way it teaches and practices servant-leadership.

Instruction in Servant-Leadership

The primary resources for instruction in Greenleaf's vision of servant-leadership are his original writings. Each piece provides a slightly different perspective on his thinking regarding the theory and practice of servant-leadership as it specifically relates to students and, in a broader way, to others in a community. A study of servant-leadership begins with Greenleaf's seminal essay *The Servant as Leader.* A more complete articulation of Greenleaf's ideas is available in his book, *Servant-Leadership: A Journey into the Nature of Legitimate Power and Greatness.* Two other essays are helpful when working with students: *Have You a Dream Deferred* and *Education and Maturity.* Hermann Hesse's *Journey to the East* triggered the concept in Greenleaf's mind and is also a good read. The Greenleaf Center for Servant-Leadership offers a variety of other books, readings, and videos on servant-leadership that expand the concept and provide numerous examples of practical application. Greenleaf did not originate the concept; he coined the term. Numerous other sources relating to the practice of servant-leadership as a governing philosophy—whether religious or secular—are also available for instructional purposes.

Within a living-learning environment, a discussion of Greenleaf's parable, *Teacher as Servant,* can be a powerful way to understand servant-leadership and how it is fostered. The timing of the reading varies according to preference. Some houses read it during their first semester, as an introduction to the program; others read it during their last semester, as a conclusion and an opportunity for retrospection. For house advisers, Greenleaf's essay, *The Leadership Crisis,* is highly recommended.

In addition to readings and videos, invited speakers provide students with useful insights, practical applications, and different perspectives, as well as an opportunity to have their questions answered.

Instruction in servant-leadership in any organization includes both formal and informal elements. Formal instruction is sponsored by the organization itself (the university, the servant-leadership house, or a business organization); informal instruction occurs through one-on-one mentoring and in informal discussions. The elements of the apprenticeship model that business organizations and institutions of higher education have used to teach and foster servant-leadership are important. Because the concept of servant-leadership seems contradictory, it has to be explained. The idea of serving first rather than leading first—of developing the servant perspective rather than the leadership perspective—is not easy to grasp in the beginning. Nor is the duality of the servant-leader—one who is fully servant and fully leader, so that even while serving, he or she is nonetheless leading. A solid course of instruction should be the first step when an individual or an institution begins its journey into servant-leadership. Here are the seven central concepts that provide the framework for teaching servant-leadership:

1. *Serving first.* Servant-leadership begins with the concept of serving first and, out of a desire to serve, seeking to lead through the judicious and appropriate use of power. The goal or idea is to improve the lot of those who are led by increasing their autonomy, health, wisdom, and freedom, thereby ensuring that the least privileged in society will either benefit or will not be further deprived.

2. *Greenleaf's credo and "best test."* An explanation of Robert Greenleaf's credo (the goal of servant-leadership is to create a more caring and just society where "the less able and the more able serve each other with unlimited liability") in conjunction with his "best test" of a servant-leader ("Do those served grow as persons; do they, while being served, become healthier, wiser, freer, more autonomous, more likely themselves to become servants? And will the least privileged in society benefit or not be further deprived?").

These two concepts provide a grounding in Greenleaf's work by clarifying his objectives, and provide a marker for students while on their learning journey.

3. *Being served by.* Greenleaf spoke of the goal of servant-leadership as being "to serve and be served by." The second half of the phrase is sometimes missed in discussions on servant-leadership, yet it is as important as the first. If everyone were serving others, but no one was being served, it would be an odd world. More people than might be imagined have to learn how to be served with gratitude and joy rather than with embarrassment or resentment. Those who cannot accept cannot truly give; those who cannot be served by others cannot truly serve others.

4. *Maintaining oneself.* The idea of being of service to another while still maintaining one's own integrity, boundaries, and responsibility to self is a central theme in Greenleaf's writings. Servant-leaders are not martyrs; they are careful practitioners of the appropriate use of power and of the word "No."

5. *Servanthood as a positive.* Servant-leadership is empowering rather than demeaning. It is far from servitude or slavery because it is offered out of love rather than out of coercion. It comes from judicious power appropriately applied, not from an abdication of power or from illusions of power. Exploration of this idea can overcome negative stereotypes regarding servants and serving.

6. *The rewards of servant-leadership.* The rewards of servant-leadership, which often stem from its paradoxes, may not be clear until they are explained. Such paradoxes as "in giving, one receives" are not necessarily clear either in principle or in application.

7. *Relation to other leadership theories.* Some review of other leadership theories in relation to servant-leadership is important. Greenleaf's theory is a form of transformational leadership that is consonant with such other leadership

concepts as stewardship, systems thinking, and the learning organization.

The practice of servant-leadership involves the development or enhancement of multiple capacities for which students often need instruction and to which their attention should be regularly focused. Among the more important of these capacities are:

○ *Listening.* A servant listens well because, through listening, understanding grows and problems can be framed, understood, and solved.

○ *Empathy.* An empathetic orientation enables an individual to identify with another, to emphasize commonalities rather than differences, and to appreciate other perspectives as valid and legitimate.

○ *Willingness to change.* A servant-leader is open to the process of personal growth, to new ideas, and to change that is not merely responsive, but anticipatory. For servant-leaders, change is a lifelong commitment.

○ *Reflection and contemplation.* Servant-leadership requires reflection and contemplation. These actions are not often associated with students or busy executives, yet they are essential for self-exploration and personal awareness, which are at the heart of servant-leadership.

○ *Collaboration and consensus.* It is important for students to understand and to experience collaboration and consensus and the ways in which they differ from competition and majority vote.

Instruction in servant-leadership includes experiential exercises as well as discussions about concepts. Among the forms of experiential learning that can be effectively employed are the following:

○ *Team-building exercises.* Servant-leadership is inclusive rather than exclusive, devoted to community-building rather than to isolation. Exercises designed specifically to build community are desirable, particularly at the beginning of a semester. All-day participation in a rope course, experiential learning initiatives, and collaborative games are examples.

○ *Retreats.* A retreat at the beginning of the semester builds community, sets a precedent for individual contemplation, and establishes ground rules for group learning. A retreat at the end of the semester provides an opportunity for retrospection.

○ *Readings and dialogue groups.* Readings and discussion groups make it possible for students to explore the meaning of servant-leadership and its many manifestations in their lives. If possible, the discussion session should be led by someone other than the formal group instructor or adviser.

○ *Group projects.* As described in *Teacher as Servant,* students should be encouraged to propose, design, and implement various projects that provide service to their university or community.

The role of the adviser or instructor is critical to the learning process. That role should be one of facilitator rather than director. In other words, an adviser models servant-leadership and instructs in its principles, allowing students the freedom to be wrong and to make mistakes as they feel their way into understanding. By refusing to make the difficult decisions or to intervene when easy answers are to no avail, the adviser makes it possible for students to experience the difficulties and the rewards of practicing servant-leadership.

The Practice of Servant-Leadership

The advantage of a servant-leadership house or a servant-leadership program is that it provides a structured environment in which to implement the principles of servant-leadership that were first explored through instruction. Servant-leadership reveals its power and takes on meaning in the crucible of daily life, whether in business, an educational institution, or a college residence hall. Students in Hampton House, for example, discover that while they may debate the principles and merits and ramifications of servant-leadership, someone must still wash the community dishes that fill the sink and take out the trash that blocks the door. The mundane aspects of living and the difficulties of relating to other individuals who have differing needs, perspectives, and desires do not disappear because they are addressed within the context of servant-leadership. Rather, they are approached in a different way and gradually become opportunities for personal growth, community development, and grateful service rather then ego struggles for power and status.

Practice is essential to the development of mature servant-leadership. But because the point of servant-leadership is to live more richly, productively, and effectively, such practice is merely a discipline, not an imposition. This practice aspect of apprenticeship is what makes an institution (educational or business) the ideal setting in which to learn servant-leadership and to discover its tangible and intangible rewards. When servant-leadership becomes a goal of the organization—or part of its vision—those who adopt it become mentors to each other. Learners are thus apprenticed to mentors but also to one another. They learn in community and thus strengthen their community and their ability to form partnerships among themselves. Groups become teams, and organizations become finely-honed instruments for the service of their multiple stakeholders.

In the practice of servant-leadership, people confront their weaknesses, their egos, and their limitations, and so are empowered to deal with them. In the practice of servant-leadership, they come to see the missed opportunities to serve and be served, and to appreciate how difficult it may be to accept the serving of others. It is easier to make a "leader" than a "servant," to indulge hierarchies and control than to embrace service and collaboration. Practice begins with serving, not because it is more important than leading (it can't be more important because it is part of leadership), but because it is more difficult.

Changes

Students in servant-leadership houses—and employees in servant-led organizations—develop certain distinguishing attributes as they go through the change process that occurs within the development of servant-leadership. These markers may also develop with other forms of leadership and so should be considered correlative rather than definitive, but they will always be present with servant-leadership. One of the pleasures of being associated with a servant-leadership house is being able to watch the development of servant-leadership in the students as they confront the realities of its implementation and grow from its practice. By observing the students at the beginning of the school year, then at its end, and then after another year and another, it is possible to identify categories of change that seem to take place. Some of these changes are:

○ Students develop a genuine sense of community; that is, they identify with each other as members of a group that is committed to certain ideals and actions, and they exhibit a real compassion for each other.

○ They develop, first, a tolerance for diversity; then they embrace it as a means of discovering new perspectives and greater understanding. They become less judgmental and more accepting, less likely to be sure they are right and more likely to invite the opinions and ideas of others.

○ They learn that, despite their egos and ambition, there are times when it is better to follow than to lead.

○ They learn the rewards of service and become inclined to do more of it and to encourage others to do likewise.

○ They come to appreciate the power of collaboration and consensus, and how both can be achieved in the context of diversity and disagreement.

○ They take what they have learned in the house and apply it to their world outside, first within the university and, later, within the larger community.

○ They learn to engage in reflective practice, i.e., to observe their own behavior and to make changes in that behavior on the basis of experience as they continue their exploration of servant-leadership and its applicability to their lives.

○ They find more meaning in the lives they lead, more satisfaction in what they do, and more opportunities in the trials and tribulations of the world. They are more sensitive to the plight of others and more grateful for their own good fortune.

The development of such attributes is surely among the most prized of all objectives of higher education in a free society. That they should be achieved through residence halls devoted to servant-leadership is only slightly less remarkable than the concept itself. Counterintuitive, paradoxical, beset by negative stereotypes associated with the word *servant* and extravagant connotations associated with the word *leadership,* servant-leadership nonetheless continues its steady growth in application and acclaim. Those who have studied at or worked with servant-leadership houses, been employed by servant-led organizations, or experienced the rich rewards of adopting servant-leadership as a personal philosophy are not surprised by the spreading interest in servant-leadership. For them, the paradoxes and promises are part of the rich tapestry of leadership and personal growth that converges in servant-leadership, challenging them to higher achievement, bolder experimentation, and more meaningful lives.

Lea E. Williams describes herself as "an educator by training and experience, a teacher by temperament, and a writer by passion." She currently lives in Greensboro, North Carolina, where she is executive director of the Women's Leadership Institute at Bennett College. *Servants of the People: The 1960s Legacy of African American Leadership* is her first book. Dr. Williams was formerly vice president of Educational Services at the United Negro College Fund.

In this essay, an excerpt from her book *Servants of the People,* Lea Williams tells the story of Fannie Lou Hamer, a sharecropper's daughter from Mississippi, who fought for equal rights for blacks, pricking the conscience of the nation with the strength of her convictions and determination. Fannie Lou Hamer was truly a servant-leader, serving selflessly and fearlessly the causes she believed in. This examination of Hamer's life can teach us much about courage and servant-leadership. Lea Williams was a keynote speaker at the Greenleaf Center's 1998 and 1999 annual international conferences.

6

FANNIE LOU HAMER, SERVANT OF THE PEOPLE

Lea E. Williams

*I said, "Now, you cain't have me fired 'cause I'm
already fired, and I won't have to move now, because
I'm not livin' in no white man's house."*

*I said, "I'll be here every thirty days until
I become a registered voter."*

—Fannie Lou Hamer, Interview quoted in
My Soul Is Rested (Howell Raines)

BRAVING INTENSE RACIAL HATRED and entrenched white supremacy, Fannie Lou Hamer began a personal and political odyssey during the Freedom Summer of 1962. The young civil rights volunteers who streamed into Sunflower County, Mississippi, that summer tapped a wellspring of discontent that had long been denied expression by the yoke of racism. Fannie Lou Hamer, who had been, along with others, brutally controlled by fear and intimidation, became one of the most outspoken voices in the fight for equality in Mississippi. Freedom had a high price tag. In attempting to register to vote, Hamer was evicted from her home on a sharecropping plantation, jailed, and viciously beaten, the last of which left her health permanently impaired; yet, she refused to be deterred.

65

Denial of the right to vote notwithstanding, Hamer believed firmly in the power of the ballot box to balance gross economic disparities between blacks and whites and dismantle legally sanctioned abuses of civil rights. She challenged President Johnson to live up to the nation's professed democratic ideals. Speaking before the credentials committee at the 1964 national convention on behalf of the Mississippi Freedom Democratic Party's bid to be seated, Fannie Lou Hamer said: "[W]e want to register, to become first-class citizens, and if the Freedom Democratic Party is not seated now, I question America."

Fannie Lou Hamer, credited with helping to open the southern political process to black participation, crusaded throughout the state, conducting citizenship classes and urging black Mississippians to register to vote. She used the courts to argue the unconstitutionality of the poll tax, discriminatory state election laws, and fraudulent election results. She pricked the conscience of the nation with the fervor of her convictions and her uncompromising determination.

While political enfranchisement was her longest running battle and undergirded all that she did, it was not the only crusade she waged. Wherever she went, Hamer talked about the conditions of black Mississippians—the grinding poverty, economic deprivation, inadequate education, and poor health care. She created entrepreneurial ventures to stimulate economic self-sufficiency and improve education. She advocated equal rights for blacks, but also invited poor whites to join the struggle to secure a better future for themselves and their children. Few answered the call, but those who did received fair treatment. Fannie Lou Hamer was truly a servant-leader, serving the causes in which she believed selflessly, tirelessly, and fearlessly.

A few weeks after her death in 1977 from cancer, the Mississippi legislature, whose members had excoriated her on previous occasions, unanimously passed a resolution praising her service to the state. Her funeral was attended by civil rights leaders representing the broadest possible spectrum of the movement—moderates to militants, integrationists to separatists. In his eulogy, United Nations Ambassador Andrew Young, a civil rights activist and longtime admirer, said: "None of us would be where we are now had she not been there then." What can the life of Fannie Lou Hamer teach us about leadership?

Servant-Leadership

Of the many styles of leadership that researchers have documented—bureaucratic, charismatic, democratic, intellectual, executive, patrimonial, and representative—Fannie Lou Hamer exemplifies a rarer type, characterized by Robert K. Greenleaf as servant-leadership. The servant-leader is committed to serving others through a cause, a crusade, a movement, a campaign with humanitarian, not materialistic, goals.

The test of this type of leadership is twofold: Those being served must grow and evolve as persons, and those least privileged in society should benefit. The servant-leader, when initially taking on the leadership task, never knows for sure what the results will be because it is difficult to predict whether others will benefit. However, the servant-leader, eschewing opportunistic motives of personal gain and self-aggrandizement, is willing to take great risks to achieve a higher good.

The servant-leader is one who is guided by an overarching, prophetic, transforming vision—carefully conceived and simply articulated. By precept and example, the leader guides others toward that vision, converting followers one-by-one through singular acts of bravery, courage, and determination. Generally, the servant-leader avoids the limelight and works behind the scenes, where the needs are greatest and the rewards, when they come, are most gratifying.

Because the terrain that the leader and followers traverse is usually fraught with obstacles and resistance, the servant-leader must be willing to lead in the face of danger and adversity. Shared trials and tribulations nurture the bonds of trust between the leader and the followers, and this is critically important, given the risks to personal safety that are often involved in trying to achieve the goals they are moving toward. Because honesty and integrity validate the leader's credibility, followers are willing to assume a high degree of risk. Typically, the servant-leader possesses a charismatic, persuasive personality that inspires confidence and helps the follower weather the times of doubt and despair that inevitably arise in emotion-laden causes in which ideological lines are sharply drawn and opponents attempt to derail efforts and question leaders' motives. Hamer had this quality of persuasiveness, derived from a spiritual fervor that drew people to her.

The servant-leader works in the trenches with people from varied backgrounds who have had diverse ranges of experience. Servant-leadership should facilitate cooperative interaction among those diverse groups. John Brown Childs expresses this as the concept of mutuality. Under this concept, oppressed groups can communicate with one another as fellow sufferers. All can work toward a common goal, but without an omniscient leader who is advancing an immutable agenda derived from a single vantage point. Accepting followers for who they are, and channeling their energies and talents in the right direction is a sensitive, time-consuming task requiring patience and diplomacy. Coming from the same socioeconomic group that she was trying to empower, Fannie Lou Hamer understood the unarticulated yearnings of poor Mississippians and knew their unspoken fears. Yet, she sought their full participation in the march toward freedom. While modeling the highest standards of excellence for a diverse constituency, the servant-leader never rejects people because of their inherent shortcomings. Instead, the leader demonstrates empathy, understanding, and tolerance, realizing that imperfections are part of the human condition.

Initially, without having a vested interest in an established organizational image to conserve and project, Hamer worked from the perspective of mutually shared responsibility with other black Mississippians in deciding the methods and means of enfranchisement. This perspective differed from that of organizational leaders such as Whitney M. Young of the National Urban League and Roy Wilkins at the NAACP. They disseminated a vision of civil rights based on long-established institutional history and traditions. This vanguard perspective reflected a more cautious, elitist view. It also imposed hierarchical thinking about how to overcome legal injustices and gain economic power. Hamer, on the other hand, wanted the people to take responsibility for their own liberation, although a lack of basic literacy and a low level of self-esteem sometimes prevented the masses from assuming the power they had—another reason why citizenship education was so important in the southern sphere of the movement.

Finally, the servant-leader is attuned to inner qualities—intuition, foresight, awareness, and perception—that aid decision making. Knowingly or unknowingly, these leaders use their intuitive sense to make judgments when a leap of faith is required. Having the foresight to project ahead, to interpret events and shrewdly chart the appropriate course of action, gives leaders the edge that followers recognize and respect. Lastly, heightened awareness and openness to sensual perceptions keep the leader tuned in to the environment and to followers, in order to discern the impact, or likely impact, of decisions. These qualities are an aspect of intelligence that transcends the knowledge acquired through academic training and formal schooling. The confident leader trusts these intuitive qualities and is guided by them.

When leading a cause, such as civil rights, the ultimate goal can seem elusive; its attainment may often be in doubt. Yet, the servant-leader is sustained by, and draws strength from, an abiding faith—faith in God, faith in self and in others, faith in the vision and in the integrity of the cause. Fannie Lou Hamer alluded often to her trust in God and how that belief was a sustaining power in her life. Like Martin Luther King Jr. and many of the southern activists, she came from a religious background and had a deep spirituality. Faith plays a defining role because it assures the servant-leader that even in the midst of fear and confusion, amid turmoil and uncertainty, appropriate actions and responses will somehow be revealed. The servant-leader walks by faith and not by sight. This helps the leader remain centered in troubled times. Intuitive attributes are desirable in any leader, but the servant-leader, in particular, listens to and believes in these inner qualities.

A Call to Conscience

Fannie Lou Hamer was the youngest of 20 children born to Jim and Ella Townsend; she was born in or near Montgomery County, in north-central Mississippi, on October 6, 1917. Two months after her birth, the family moved west to Sunflower County in the

Mississippi Delta, where they sharecropped on the plantation of E. W. Brandon. Fannie Lou Hamer started picking cotton at the age of six and continued until well into middle age. Sharecropping kept families tied to the land through an unfair system of overpriced goods and services, which the plantation owner controlled. The system entrapped families in debt and quashed any chance of economic independence.

During the planting and harvesting season, from April to November, the work in the fields was grueling and unrelenting. Generation after generation stayed on the land with little hope of a better life for themselves or their children. Schools were inadequate and, when available, convened only for a few months during the off-season. After sixth grade, Fannie Lou Hamer ended her formal schooling and worked full time to help support her family. James D. Anderson explained the pattern of school leaving that was typical of that time and place:

> Despite the structure and work rhythms of the southern agricultural economy, black children did not voluntarily sacrifice formal schooling for gainful employment. Rather, there were no public or private schools available to the great majority of black children, and in the absence of school facilities, employment seemed the next best opportunity. Both heavy use of black children in the agricultural labor force and the limited availability of black public schools reflected the planters' domination of the rural South. Where public schools were available, black parents in general accepted the loss of child labor and additional household income so that their children would attend school.

According to Anderson, the migration of black laborers from the rural farm areas to the cities was an attempt to emancipate their children from the drudgery of daily labor so they could attend school.

Fannie Lou Hamer was one of the victims of poor schooling and indifferent health care. Along with near illiteracy, perhaps the cruelest injustice, in a life filled with hardship and travail, was her involuntary sterilization in 1961. She entered the hospital to have a small, benign uterine tumor removed; without her knowledge or consent, the doctors performed a hysterectomy. It later came to public attention that this was an all-too-common occurrence among poor black women in the South. A few years later, another tragedy struck when Mrs. Hamer's daughter Dorothy, an only child, hemorrhaged to death after giving birth. She died as the Hamers sped toward Memphis, over 100 miles away, seeking medical care because nearby hospitals, like many in the South, refused to treat blacks.

Controlling blacks' reproduction and fear of black male sexuality have been continuing themes throughout African American history, with devastating consequences. Black males were often assaulted and mutilated sexually before, or after, a lynching. During slavery, women, married or not, were made to produce children to maintain a free labor force. And, of course, female slaves were routinely seduced and raped by slave masters and overseers. One hundred years after emancipation, poor health care, uninformed consent, and nonconsent still entrapped many black women, preventing them from controlling their own reproductive systems.

A history of unrelenting brutality and tragedy prepared southern blacks for the massive resistance of the civil rights movement. It began when young civil rights workers from the Southern Christian Leadership Conference (SCLC) and the Student Nonviolent Coordinating Committee (SNCC) descended on Mississippi in 1962, urging blacks to register to vote. This was the beginning of the voter registration drive. Fannie Lou Hamer and her husband Perry were sharecroppers on the Marlow cotton plantation in Ruleville, a small Delta town in Sunflower County. Although the Hamers worked in the fields from dawn to dusk during the planting and harvesting season, they barely eked out a living. SCLC and SNCC volunteers found in Fannie Lou Hamer an inspired leader in the Mississippi freedom movement. In Howell Raines's oral history of the civil rights movement, Hamer describes the arrival of the volunteers:

> Well, we were living on a plantation about four and a half miles east of here. . . . Pap had been out there thirty years, and I had been out there eighteen years, 'cause we had been

married at that time eighteen years. And you know, things were just rough. . . . I don't think that I ever remember working for as much as four dollars a day. Yes, one year I remember working for four dollars a day, and I was gettin' as much as the men. So then that was in 1962 when the civil rights workers came into this county.

She embraced the voter registration drive because political enfranchisement offered the means by which to claim long-denied rights and gain a measure of economic and educational equality. Registering herself and others to vote became the all-consuming passion of Fannie Lou Hamer's life, aptly defined by David Loye as the passionate embrace of an ideal. In middle age, this woman of humble beginnings, with little formal education, found her voice and became a leader in the voter registration drive. The history of unchecked violence against blacks in Mississippi prepared Fannie Lou Hamer for the high personal cost of her decision.

Mississippi had an infamous history of barbarous cruelty to blacks. In addition to the weight of legal sanctions, southern segregation and conventions were enforced through death threats, destruction of property, night rider attacks, fire bombings, and, of course, lynching—all routine forms of intimidation. Lynching was used to punish everything from minor infractions to the most serious crimes—the homicide of whites, even in self-defense, and accusations of rape. The 539 black Mississippians lynched from 1882 to 1968 was the largest number nationwide.

In the mid-1930s, when Adam Clayton Powell Jr. was openly picketing against job discrimination by local Harlem stores and the hiring practices of the New York City bus lines, southern blacks chafed under the brutal yoke of legal racism, and risked life, limb, and property if they dared speak out or protest. Twenty years after Powell's mass action in Harlem, blacks finally boycotted the Montgomery city bus line, the first major postbellum civil disobedience in the South. Whereas Adam Clayton Powell Jr. could return safely home after picketing, Fannie Lou Hamer found herself immediately evicted from her sharecropper's shack after she attempted to register to vote in 1962. She recalled the words of the plantation owner:

"I mean that. You'll have to go back to Indianola [in Sunflower County] and withdraw, or you have to leave this place." So I said, "Mr. Dee, I didn't go down there to register for you. I went down there to register for myself."

So I knowed I wasn't goin' back to withdraw, so wasn't nothin' for me to do but leave the plantation.

Alone and isolated in rural towns and hamlets, southern blacks were effectively controlled by fear, which squelched the unity that would have encouraged rebellion. Civil rights volunteers reached those rural areas with the message that blacks had voting rights guaranteed by the U.S. Constitution, and they could exercise them. Local leaders like Fannie Lou Hamer sought to register potential voters. They conducted citizenship classes modeled on the Highlander Folk School workshops and civil disobedience techniques, which Septima Poinsette Clark—a stalwart civil rights crusader and educator—had started throughout the South.

Fannie Lou Hamer, Septima Clark, and countless others worked without expectation of reward or honors. Most indigenous southern leaders had few material possessions when they took up the cause of civil rights. But what they did have—a menial job, a plantation shack, usurious credit at a local or plantation store, even family and friends—was imperiled by the stand they took. The prospect of material gain was certainly not a motivation, because it was rarely ever available. The parable told in the gospel according to Saint Luke, recounting how Christ responded to the almsgiving of the rich man and the poor widow, is apropos:

> He looked up and saw the rich people dropping their gifts into the chest of the temple treasury; and he noticed a poor widow putting in two tiny coins. "I tell you this," he said: "this poor widow has given more than any of them; for those others who have given had more than enough, but she, with less than enough, has given all she had to live on."

Even southern blacks of better means than Hamer, despite their education and profession, had relatively little security at the hands of retaliatory politicians and employers. The experience of Septima

Clark confirms the possible fate that awaited those who engaged in civil rights activities. In 1956, at the age of 58, Clark was dismissed from her teaching job in the public school system of Charleston, South Carolina, for refusing to quit the NAACP. The state legislature, in an attempt to minimize the effectiveness of the NAACP, had stipulated that no city employee could affiliate with any civil rights organization. Although Clark had taught since 1947, she was also denied her pension. She waged, and won, a 20-year battle to have the retirement funds restored. Fortunately, Myles Horton, director of the famous Highlander Folk School, hired Clark immediately after her dismissal to teach citizenship classes in voting rights and adult literacy.

In attempting to understand Fannie Lou Hamer's call to leadership, Kay Mills, her biographer, says that "some alchemy of inborn intelligence, deep spirituality, strong parents, love of country, and a sharecropper's gutty instincts for survival made her different." Additionally, the ruthless cruelty of whites became so overbearing that it loosened the bonds of fear that had gripped blacks, creating a receptive climate for the civil rights movement. In Mrs. Hamer, the northern volunteers and the advocacy of the NAACP touched and released deep wellsprings of discontent that had been bred by the viciousness of southern racism and were struggling within her for expression. Their message of freedom and equality—and, moreover, how to seize it—fell on fertile soil. Finally, the civil disobedience training of the Highlander Folk School disciples, who fanned out throughout the South, provided a conceptual and philosophical framework for thinking about liberation and equality. This tempered and disciplined the smoldering outrage, turning it into constructive action. Motivated by the indomitability of the human spirit that yearns to be free and, at last, emancipated from the shackles of fear, grassroots leaders like Mrs. Hamer emerged, willing to endure the strife, deprivation, and terror that awaited. They became, by their example, a towering moral and political force throughout the South.

Prophetic Visionary

Leadership is predicated on a guiding vision. Believing that she, as an individual, could make a difference, Fannie Lou Hamer envisioned what might be for black Mississippians. According to Greenleaf, individual actions are responsible for the good and evil in the world, and Mrs. Hamer's personal vision, truly prophetic given the racist climate in which it was born and sustained, was to remove the obstacles to black voter registration, first in Sunflower County and then in Mississippi, her corner of the world. As her horizons broadened with exposure to the wider world, her vision also expanded and encompassed economic development, day care, and health and nutrition education. Fannie Lou Hamer absorbed, acknowledged, and communicated lessons from her own experiences—those that were difficult, and meant to demean, as well as those that were uplifting—and used them to connect with, educate, and guide others. She was proof that leadership can be learned on the job, through experience and through systematic acquisition of knowledge and skills.

In addition to her involvement in the Mississippi Freedom Democratic Party (MFDP), Mrs. Hamer also ran for Congress—challenging Representative Jamie Whitten, the powerful chairman of the House Appropriations Subcommittee on Agriculture—and contested a seat in the Mississippi state senate. She filed lawsuits against illegal state election practices (*Hamer v. Campbell,* 1965) and school desegregation (*Hamer v. Sunflower County,* 1970), and started the Freedom Farm Cooperative. The achievements and successes were not hers alone—others also worked diligently in support of the same causes—but she was, without a doubt, the most visible and often the sustaining force behind many reform efforts.

In articulating the enormous political and economic needs of the Ruleville community, Mrs. Hamer brought to light the horrendous exploitation of black people. The fact that these inequities could no longer be ignored augured well for the "least privileged in society," one of the tests Greenleaf proposes for the servant-leader. She knew from a lifetime of living and working on Delta plantations the perils of black life in Mississippi. Her advocacy derived from this knowledge, and she used it to improve the lives of Mississippians. For example, in creating the Pig Bank, an extension of the Freedom Farm Cooperative, she sought to supplement the nutritionally deficient diets of the rural poor and, at the same time, offer a measure of economic self-sufficiency. The Pig Bank—financially supported by the National Council of Negro Women with the strong advocacy of Dorothy I. Height, the organization's president—was a simple, but inspired, idea. The bank would loan a gilt and a boar to a family and allow them to keep the piglets. In return, families were to share pregnant gilts with their neighbors, thus producing a multiplier effect. By the end of the third year, it was reported that approximately 300 families had participated in the program.

Although visionary in concept, the Pig Bank and Freedom Farm, unfortunately, were plagued by a host of shortcomings; failure to implement professional management techniques and specialized knowledge of modern farming methods were among the most serious. In addition, an overly ambitious agenda soon clouded the co-op's main mission. It expanded beyond food production to purchasing food stamps, buying clothing, and even awarding student scholarships. The diverted funds subsidized bona fide needs, but funders nevertheless voiced concern about what they considered extraneous expenditures. As in most cases where outside funding is involved, supporters tacitly dictated the parameters of power and controlled the tactics of leaders. Perhaps a more legitimate concern was the failure to plan long term and the lack of overall fiscal accountability due to lax, almost nonexistent, financial controls, which raised questions and eroded confidence in the project.

A plethora of related problems also surfaced. Most disappointing was the resistance of the community to the cooperative concept. Various observers at the time speculated that blacks resented the arduous work associated with farming because it kept them shackled to the land and served as a painful reminder of the lifetime of drudgery they had endured on Delta plantations since slavery. The failures were omissions rather than commissions, and misfeasance rather than malfeasance; nevertheless, they handicapped the farm project and hastened its demise.

According to Fred E. Fiedler, matching the leader's skills to the task at hand is a precondition of effective leadership. Freedom Farm certainly demonstrated Fannie Lou Hamer's visionary approach to problem solving. She aimed to improve the nutritional health of her community and create a solid economic base. Often, when Freedom Farm was in dire straits and the danger of foreclosure was imminent,

Mrs. Hamer secured an infusion of funds to sustain its operation. Yet, sustaining the farm called for more than vision, hard work, and sheer determination. It entailed mastering the intricacies of standard accounting procedures, properly maintaining expensive farm equipment, and ensuring efficient planting and harvesting of crops. Unfortunately, Mrs. Hamer and those around her never perfected these skills. Without the financial and managerial expertise and formal networks available to a major organization, Fannie Lou Hamer had few resources, other than indigenous talent, readily at hand to assess and assist in remedying the shortcomings in the Pig Bank and Freedom Farm.

When Whitney M. Young ran into managerial problems at the National Urban League, a powerful, resourceful board of trustees engaged a consulting firm to assess the problems and propose solutions. Once Young accepted the report and decided on a course of action, he could hire a staff that would implement the plan. Like Young, Hamer had to answer to supporters, but the resources at her disposal were fewer. An ongoing, internal support structure and needed technical expertise were largely missing. As a result, managerial difficulties persisted. After five years, the farm foundered, having realized only a fraction of its full potential.

Struggling to assert leadership and control over their own destiny 100 years after emancipation, black Mississippians still faced problems similar to those of the manumitted slaves. Although leaders worked arduously to attain a modicum of economic independence by creating jobs and enhancing educational opportunities, blacks were nevertheless constrained in pursuit of those modest goals by the oppressive environment in which they lived. In the early 1970s, after enfranchisement, blacks in Mississippi were still having difficulty grasping a foothold on the next rung of the economic ladder. Even strong leadership, as demonstrated by Fannie Lou Hamer and buttressed by civil rights and social legislation, failed at times to attenuate the stubbornly resistant barriers impeding black progress.

In defiance of federal legislation, staunch segregationists continued to avoid the law by resisting integration and practicing overt discrimination to keep blacks inadequately housed, fed, clothed, and educated. Locked into second-class citizenship along with the

masses, black leaders suffered the same handicaps as their followers. Without adequate education, training, and exposure, they were
initially very naïve politically and unsophisticated about business
matters. Having no secure economic base, they were also vulnerable to the enormous pressure and intimidation relentlessly exerted
by the white power structure. Amazingly, even in this stultifying, repressive environment, black leaders managed to accomplish quite
remarkable feats: they educated blacks about citizenship and registered them to vote.

Inspirational Leader

Fannie Lou Hamer's inspiration was firmly grounded in a spiritual
context and sustained by her Christian faith. Her religious beliefs
were the source of her strength. Personal faith, which has historically and traditionally sustained African Americans under brutal
conditions in their sojourn through slavery and even now, was a
strong palliative against the pervasive poverty and racism that sur-
rounded Hamer and, in a less determined person, could have weak-
ened resolve. Greenleaf suggests that individuals who are unusually
open to inspiration are the visionaries whose insights guide others.
They personify the essence of leadership; they are the individuals in
the forefront who show others the way.

Personal inspiration derives from many sources: exposure to
learned individuals and seminal thinkers; debate of complex ideas
and critical issues; opportunities for philosophical, reflective
thinking; divine intervention resulting from spiritual meditation.
As Fannie Lou Hamer worked in the movement, and began to represent the grassroots element, she encountered the eclectic, diverse
circle of libertarians, political strategists, entertainers, and scholars whom the civil rights campaign attracted. Her thinking was
profoundly influenced by what seemed to her to be radically new
concepts about freedom and self-empowerment espoused by these
individuals. They were no less moved by her poignant, eloquent
articulation of the sufferings and sacrifices of rural Mississippians. A synergistic, interdependent relationship resulted, releasing
Mrs. Hamer's natural rebelliousness and piquing an intellectual

awakening that was radical in scope. This empowered Fannie Lou Hamer to transcend the limitations of her own circumstances. Her example of endurance emboldened, strengthened, and lifted an entire community's aspirations and determination to tackle and overcome the repression and terror associated with racism.

The sociologist Daniel Thompson concludes that despite the inequalities they experienced, black leaders retained an abiding faith in America's democratic principles. Fannie Lou Hamer certainly never lost sight of those ideals. On the contrary, she continued to be inspired by them and had faith in their eventual attainment. Although she had the opportunity to migrate North as many of her brothers and sisters had, she remained in Mississippi. Refusing to relinquish her claim on the state or on America, she passionately and defiantly proclaimed her patriotism:

> People who tell me to go back to Africa, I got an answer for them. I say when all the Italians go back to Italy, and all the Germans go back to Germany, and all the Frenchmen go back to France, and all the Chinese go back to China, and when they give the Indians their land back and they get on the *Mayflower* and go back to where they came from, then I'll go home too.

Fannie Lou Hamer was committed to making America a better place for all its citizens. Her self-appointed crusade was to communicate to the outside world the debilitating consequences of the rural poverty that was systematically imposed on black people—the poor health care, high mortality and morbidity rates, inadequate schools, malnutrition, and disease. She was a powerfully persuasive advocate. From the time she volunteered to register to vote until her death 15 years later, she was often in the limelight. Her voice was heard at mass rallies in small towns throughout Mississippi, urging blacks to vote, enlightening congressional committees, demanding legal intervention to speed school desegregation. Her example of outspoken courage in the midst of a constant barrage of threats and without legal or police protection helped overcome the paralyzing fear that for years had silenced the voices of the black masses.

With a gift for cutting to the essence of issues, she seized whatever forum was at hand to promote the causes in which she fervently believed. Eleanor Holmes Norton, a young civil rights lawyer at the time, described Fannie Lou Hamer as being extraordinarily brilliant in her ability to articulate ideas not fully formed by others. Norton said she had ". . . the capacity to put together a mosaic of coherent thought about freedom and justice, so that when it was all through, you knew what you had heard because it held together with wonderful cohesion. . . . She [had] put her finger on something truly important that all of us had felt but she had said."

Many young civil rights volunteers working in Mississippi, such as Norton and Marian Wright Edelman, continued their activism in later careers. Norton, a Yale University Law School graduate, was active with SNCC and MFDP. Her activism included a stint at the American Civil Liberties Union and as head of the New York City Commission on Human Rights. She was appointed by President Carter to chair the Equal Employment Opportunity Commission (EEOC). In an ironic twist, during her tenure at the ACLU, she defended the right of former Alabama Governor George Wallace to hold an outdoor political rally at Shea Stadium when he was running for President. In 1990, Norton became the congressional representative for the District of Columbia. Marian Wright Edelman, also a Yale Law School graduate, defended blacks throughout the state of Mississippi and was the first black woman to pass the Mississippi bar. Like so many of the legal stars of her generation, she interned with the NAACP Legal Defense and Educational Fund. Edelman is best known for founding the Children's Defense Fund and for her tireless advocacy on behalf of poor children. Fannie Lou Hamer's courage, determination, and spirituality inspired these women.

Refusing to Compromise

One aspect of servant-leadership that Greenleaf cautions against is a tendency toward overzealousness that may cause a leader to adhere singlemindedly to a position based on principle when compromising is the wiser course of action.

There must be some order because we know for certain that the great majority of people will choose some kind of order over chaos even if it is delivered by a brutal non-servant and even if, in the process, they lose much of their freedom. Therefore the servant-leader will beware of pursuing an idealistic path regardless of its impact on order.

At times, compromising was difficult for Fannie Lou Hamer. For her, as with A. Philip Randolph, certain principles were simply inviolable, and she dogmatically defended them even when such adherence narrowed her circle of influence, rather than expanding it as effective leaders advise. James M. Kouzes and Barry Z. Posner posit six disciplines of credibility, including the leader's ability to come to *consensus* on common values within a group process. Fannie Lou Hamer sometimes lacked this ability to achieve consensus, as shown in the case of a power struggle that divided the Mississippi Freedom Democratic Party and allowed a compromise group, known as the Loyalists Democratic Party, to usurp the MFDP's agenda. The conflict also exposed Fannie Lou Hamer's political vulnerability and naïveté.

Since Reconstruction, blacks had been effectively disenfranchised in southern politics, first by the Republican Party, for whom blacks overwhelmingly voted until Franklin D. Roosevelt's election, and then by the Democratic Party. By the 1964 election, the voter registration drive had kindled black resolve. Determined to participate in Democratic state politics, blacks organized the Mississippi Freedom Democratic Party as an opposition movement. In Atlantic City, at the Democratic National Convention in 1964, the Freedom Party attempted to unseat the regular state delegation, whose loyalty to the national party was tenuous at best, partly because of conflicts over the cherished southern tradition of racial segregation. Fannie Lou Hamer was a founding member of the MFDP and at the center of the confrontation.

Preceding the convention, the Freedom Democrats held mock elections throughout the state, often the first in which blacks had participated, and selected an alternative slate of 68 delegates and alternates to attend the convention. The MFDP forced a hearing before the credentials committee; it petitioned the committee, in vain, to unseat the regular delegation. The riveting testimony of Mrs. Hamer and others, broadcast on television, became part of the lore of the civil rights movement and focused national attention on the bitter consequences of the black struggle for enfranchisement in Mississippi. It shamed a nation and embarrassed President Lyndon Johnson, who was seeking election as president in his own right after having succeeded the slain President John F. Kennedy.

When the credentials committee rendered its decision, after considering several iterations of a compromise proposal, Fannie Lou Hamer was outraged by what she viewed as a sellout of the principles championed by MFDP. The compromise designated two members of the Freedom Democrats—Aaron Henry and Ed King—to be seated as at-large delegates. Further, guest passes would be issued to the other MFDP delegates, and each member of the all-white delegation would be required to take a loyalty oath in order to be seated. Finally, the agreement promised that future delegations would have black representation. Because of her outspoken rebuke of Senator Hubert H. Humphrey Jr., President Johnson's emissary, during the initial meeting called to hammer out a compromise, Mrs. Hamer was excluded from subsequent meetings. Although she found ample platforms from which to express her views on the negotiations, she was persona non grata in the inner sanctum where the agreement was made. Mrs. Hamer usually insisted on her own uncompromising terms when negotiating with power brokers, both whites and blacks. These were the individuals whose promises too often foundered on the shoals of political expediency, and blacks were seldom a powerful factor in influencing the outcome.

To forge a compromise, Humphrey turned to more predictable members of the delegation such as Robert ("Bob") Moses, a Harvard-educated volunteer. Starting in 1960, Moses, a teacher at Horace Mann, a private school in New York City, had spent summers in Mississippi working with SNCC in the voting rights campaign. When he arrived in Atlantic City for the 1964 convention, he soon found himself embroiled in working out a compromise to seat the MFDP. Most blacks rallied behind the compromise, particularly moderate civil rights leaders like Roy Wilkins and Whitney Young, who urged Fannie Lou Hamer to concede. She refused. The Mississippi Freedom Democratic Party left the convention still divided over the imposed resolution of their petition. Mrs. Hamer and Bob Moses both felt betrayed when the compromise was announced publicly while the negotiations were still in progress.

Four years later, when the Democrats convened in Chicago, new party rules, provoked by the MFDP's challenge, had radically altered the southern political process: delegations would henceforth more accurately reflect the racial composition of the counties and states they represented. Interestingly, the Loyal Democrats of Mississippi, a biracial coalition of moderate Democrats, was formed following the 1964 convention. They controlled the compromise platform, which was aimed at appealing to a broader base of constituents. A. Philip Randolph endorsed the coalition. Since the mid-1960s, Randolph and the Brotherhood of Sleeping Car Porters had developed and benefited from cooperative relations with whites, especially Jewish labor leaders in the AFL–CIO. Randolph was genuinely convinced of the necessity and effectiveness of interracial coalitions.

Not surprisingly, the Loyalists soon overshadowed the Mississippi Freedom Democratic Party's predominantly black, working-class delegation, and came to represent the voting rights agenda. The Mississippi Freedom Democratic Party was thought to be too radical and too aggressive in advocating economic and political change. The ascendancy of the Loyalists to prominence resulted from "[a] tug-of-war for the soul of the reform movement." It was probably inevitable that the more temperate, middle-class faction, represented by the politically savvy and well-connected Loyalists, would win this struggle, which was as much a class battle as it was a racial conflict.

Greenleaf poses a rhetorical question appropriate to this situation when he asks: "How do we get the right things done?" Sometimes that may require compromising and accepting an imperfect victory rather than risking certain defeat. However, Fannie Lou Hamer was not a compromiser when it came to empowering working-class and poor Mississippians. Those who portrayed Hamer as immoderate, undisciplined, and unpredictable were the very disciplined, predictable moderates—blacks and whites—who had a vested interest in the status quo. Black moderates, negotiators, and compromisers—the Whitney M. Youngs of the civil rights movement—were more comfortable asking for an equitable share within the existing socioeconomic system rather than demanding a radical overthrow of the established order. After all, middle-class black moderates were first in line to reap the fruits of integration; the working class and poor needed revolutionary economic and social change before they could gather their harvest.

Although the MFDP failed to attain all of its goals at the 1964 convention, it could point to some solid accomplishments. The Atlantic City challenge ultimately revolutionized Democratic Party politics. Over time, record numbers of black politicians were permitted to win election to state and local offices, where issues that directly affect people's daily lives are most often decided. Ominous on the horizon was the 1995 Supreme Court ruling in *Miller v. Johnson,* which denied race as a legitimate factor in drawing congressional districts' lines and has provided African Americans with more equitable representation in Congress, but threatens to unravel many of the gains that resulted from the civil rights movement.

In addition to voting rights, the MFDP was ahead of the times in voicing concern about the exclusion of women from leadership positions in the Democratic Party and in opposing the Vietnam War, even before Martin Luther King Jr., an early objector, asserted his concern. But detractors complained that Hamer's adherence to principles, to the exclusion of "reasonable" compromise, undermined MFDP's voice in political reform in Mississippi. Instead, the moderate Loyalists, reaching across the political divides to collaborate with regular Mississippi Democrats and other factions objectionable to MFDP, effectively usurped the promise of the Freedom Democrats in 1964. But, driven by the fear that the poor would remain disenfranchised even if the political structure of Mississippi was changed, Fannie Lou Hamer refused to yield control of the party to factions whose loyalties were untested. Given the poverty still plaguing poor Mississippians, Hamer's concerns were legitimate. Experience teaches how control of black organizations has been adversely affected when dominant groups assume leadership positions. True to experience, MFDP's revolutionary aims were adversely affected when the Loyalist group and its compromise agenda set the negotiating points.

Drawing Conclusions

Servant-leader aptly describes Fannie Lou Hamer. She was selflessly devoted to securing voting rights for blacks in her native Mississippi despite the unpunished violence, punctuated by murderous rampages and destruction of property, intended to keep black rebellion in check. Her rewards were, at best, meager and late in coming. There was a Fannie Lou Hamer Day at Ruleville's Central High School in 1970, and the town of Ruleville declared a Fannie Lou Hamer Day the year before she died.

At times, Mrs. Hamer embraced a losing cause because she believed in it, as when, in ill health, she attended the 1972 Democratic convention in Miami and was persuaded, by feminists, to support the vice presidential nomination of Frances "Sissy" Farenthold, a state legislator from Texas. There was never a chance that Farenthold would secure the vice presidential slot; her nomination was purely a symbolic gesture. Fannie Lou Hamer, among others, seconded the nomination. Farenthold was defeated when the convention overwhelmingly approved Senator Tom Eagleton, George McGovern's choice for a running mate. Mills concluded that perhaps Mrs. Hamer yearned once again to be in the spotlight that was less frequently available in her later years. However, Mrs. Hamer was not usually a pawn in other people's games; she was too inspired by her own vision.

Mrs. Hamer lived her entire life in the state of Mississippi. In answering those who asked why she did not abandon the state that had so ill-treated her, she said, "You don't run away from problems—you just face them." She squarely faced problems despite the tremendous, ever-present risks. In so doing, she helped create a movement in Mississippi that enfranchised blacks and helped free whites of some of their prejudices. For example, Fannie Lou Hamer recounts boarding a plane in Memphis, in 1975, with Champ Terney, a Mississippi attorney who had earlier argued against school integration in a court case brought by Mrs. Hamer. He was also the son-in-law of Senator James O. Eastland, the most famous resident of Sunflower County and a staunch segregationist. He invited Mrs. Hamer to sit in the seat next to him and even offered her a ride home from the airport. She said: "[We've] come a long way because I've known the time that he'd have gotten off the plane rather than ride with me."

She was not materially enriched by her involvement in the movement. In this regard, Fannie Lou Hamer was a spiritual soul mate of A. Philip Randolph. However, Randolph lived a comfortable, though modest, middle-class existence for most of his adult life and had less reason to be tempted by the offers of material gain he received. Mrs. Hamer lived most of her life in poverty; only in late middle age did she attain a modest house and relative economic security, which made her commitment all the more exemplary. Sadly, in the final years of her life, debilitated by illness, Fannie Lou Hamer felt deserted by her friends. The Hamer house was strangely quiet because people no longer came seeking her help or enlisting her support for their causes. Perry "Pap" Hamer complained that when his wife needed care in her last days, the only people who came were those he paid. When illness quieted her voice, Fannie Lou Hamer was neglected by former suitors.

Fame, potentially a usurper of servant-leadership, can be seductive, luring leaders to abandon their beliefs and commitments for the momentary spotlight of public adulation. Adam Clayton Powell Jr. was such a victim. Given to public posturing, he thought little of grabbing headlines with outrageous remarks. He frequently and remorselessly distorted conversations and betrayed private confidences of other civil rights leaders to gain a political advantage. Fannie Lou Hamer was much more selfless, for her fame was unsought. Her loyalty was to the lowliest as opposed to higher political or career aspirations. Regrettably, when she was seen less often in public forums, her star faded, but her impact would outlast transitory fame. Servant-leadership seeks not its own rewards; rather, it measures success by how much followers grow and evolve as persons, and whether the "least privileged in society" have benefited. By these standards, Fannie Lou Hamer was richly rewarded.

Over the years, Fannie Lou Hamer's sacrifices and tireless advocacy became the building blocks of democratic enfranchisement for blacks in Mississippi, a testament to her servant-leadership. Her favorite spiritual, "This Little Light of Mine," which came to be her theme song—all who heard her sing it were deeply moved—is an appropriate coda for her life. Fannie Lou Hamer believed her little light could make a difference in rural Mississippi. She explained: "I grew up believin' in God, but I knew things was bad wrong, and I used to think, 'Let me have a chance, and whatever this is that's wrong in Mississippi, I'm gonna do somethin' about it.'" When her chance came, she did something about it, leaving those she touched forever changed.

With forty years of corporate experience, Max DePree is chairman emeritus of Herman Miller, Inc., a member of *Fortune* magazine's National Business Hall of Fame, and a recipient of the Business Enterprise Trust's Lifetime Achievement Award. He serves on the board of Fuller Theological Seminary, and is a member of the advisory board of the Peter F. Drucker Foundation for Nonprofit Management. His leadership insights are expressed in his books: *Leadership Is an Art, Leadership Jazz, Leading Without Power,* and *Called to Serve.* The DePree Leadership Center was established in 1996 in response to the transforming influence of Max DePree.

Max DePree recognizes that leadership really is a quest, a search that never ends for most of us. In our quest to become better leaders and to recognize servant-leaders, DePree says, three things that are vital for the long term are needed now: (1) an understanding of the fiduciary nature of leadership; (2) a broadened definition of leadership competence; and (3) the enlightenment afforded leaders by a moral purpose.

Max DePree was a keynote speaker at the Greenleaf Center's 1993 annual international conference.

7

SERVANT-LEADERSHIP: THREE THINGS NECESSARY

Max DePree

IF THERE'S ONE THING I've come to believe about leadership, it's this: Leadership is a serious meddling in other people's lives. Because I believe that to be true, I have to take seriously what it means to be a leader. Maybe that's why I've committed so many words on leadership to paper.

It's difficult to stop talking about leadership because there are so many corners to explore. You can't reduce leadership to a formula. Leadership really is a quest, a search that never ends for most of us. It certainly hasn't ended for me. These thoughts are a way for me to search out another dimly lit corner of leadership in my own mind.

To say that an undercurrent in our society is pushing us to reflect on the role and expectations of leadership is an understatement. In public discussions everywhere—about institutions, the government, corporations, the family—people who are truly committed are coming to grips with what it really means to be a leader. I receive letters all the time from people who are searching, as I am, for a deeper understanding of leadership. To examine our expectations of leaders in the future seems to me to be a good idea. Everybody seems to know a good leader when we see one in action. But toward what should we work in trying to make *ourselves* better leaders?

One of the most important questions leaders ask themselves is: What shall we measure? In some areas, we are pretty good at deciding what to measure and how to measure it. When we think about organizational results, we can usually recognize at least the more obvious marks of vitality in a capitalist system. We know the financial and operational ratios that indicate to some extent whether an organization can survive.

On a broader scale—and perhaps with the most important things—we seem to be less sure. What should we measure about the character of our national leaders? How should we measure it? What constitutes lying in governmental processes or corporate behavior? Does practiced untruth carry consequences for society? Is a person's or a family's reputation a disposable part of our organizational lives? Are we content with the way results are distributed in the capitalist system?

Indeed, what are we to measure? For leaders *are* measured, whether they like it or not. There is no such thing as a closet leader, and measurement is part of being in the public eye. But when we think of measurement and leadership, it's easy to fall into the trap of oversimplifying things.

Success in capitalism—and thus, successful leaders in capitalism—have been all too often rated according to the so-called bottom line, a literal reality on an income statement that doesn't transfer well into the world of metaphor and true significance. This simple measurement is neither satisfying nor adequate.

How many simplistic things are satisfying or adequate? Matthew Arnold, an English writer and poet, warns us in his book *Culture and Anarchy* about simplistic thinking—the thinking that "one thing is necessary." I'm borrowing part of the title of this chapter from his book. When we think broadly about the obligations and potential of leadership, it's tempting to try for easy answers, to focus on "the one thing necessary." I would like to discuss *three* things I feel are necessary for leaders. (Of course, many things are necessary, but we've got to start somewhere.)

I strongly believe that three things should be placed at the top of any leaders' lists, whether those leaders guide institutions, governments, corporations, or families. These three things are needed now, and they are vital for the long term:

1. *An understanding of the fiduciary nature of leadership.*
2. *A broadened definition of leadership competence.*
3. *The enlightenment afforded leaders by a moral purpose.*

First, some thoughts on the fiduciary nature of leadership. *The Oxford English Dictionary* (given to me by Herman Miller when I retired as CEO) offers two helpful definitions of fiduciary: "of the nature of, proceeding from, or implying trust or reliance;" and "one who holds anything in trust; a trustee." It seems to me that the concept of fiduciary leadership is self-evident.

Long ago, Edmund Burke taught us that the governed consent to be governed. This great concept is the enabler of civil society and speaks directly to leaders. Leaders hold many things in trust for their followers, for leadership is a fiduciary job. The followers (of whom only some are employees) count. Leaders only hold temporarily, in trust, the opportunities and accountabilities that followers delegate to them. Leaders direct all that they hold in trust toward the common good, as defined by everyone's right to life, liberty, and hope. Fiduciary leaders see us not as the sum of separate issues, but as an interdependent family with complex needs and goals and opportunities. We all need to be included.

Our acceptance of the fiduciary nature of leadership as an assumption guides us down five essential paths:

Path 1. Leadership is not a position. To my knowledge, a promotion has never made anyone a leader. Leadership is a fiduciary calling. Inherent in this calling is the knowledge that hope plays a critical part in the lives of followers. Fiduciary leaders design, build, and then serve inclusive communities by liberating human spirit and potential, not by relying only on their own abilities or experience or judgment.

Path 2. We are learning every day how important it is for organizations to become centers of learning and collaboration. By making it possible for people to grow and to work together, fiduciary leaders try to invest and enlarge the knowledge and talent that they hold in trust for individuals. I strongly believe that learning and collaboration take place most easily in inclusive organizations.

Path 3. Fiduciary leaders balance two essential ideas: individual opportunity and a concept of community. In this balance, they insist on disciplined accountability to and for others.

Path 4. Fiduciary leaders, seeing the importance of trust, work to build it. I once received a note from an outstanding industrial designer who has worked for Herman Miller for many years. The note said, "Your trust is the grace that enables me to be creative." This is what leadership looks like through the eyes of a follower. When followers see conflict among leaders, they are rendered impotent. But when leaders give and expect trust, the organization reaps undreamed-of benefits. Trust may be the most motivating force in organizations. Trust is clearly the basis for covenantal relationships, which are far more productive than contractual ones.

Path 5. Trustees leave legacies; so do fiduciary leaders. The *Constitution on the Church in the Modern World,* from Vatican II, reminds us that "the future is in the hands of those who can give tomorrow's generations reasons to live and hope." A Native American saying tells us that the world does not belong to us; we merely borrow it from our grandchildren.

An acceptance of the fiduciary nature of leadership implies, for me, at least two actions: (1) broadening our definition of leadership competence; and (2) finding a clear moral purpose for our actions as leaders. We usually measure the competence of leaders in the more tangible areas of finance, operations, sales, and technology. I'd like to suggest that we need to bring a new balance to our measurements of competence. *We need to think more about how well leaders handle relationships.*

It's no mystery that organizations stand a better chance of reaching their potential when the gifts of everyone are brought to bear on reality than when an organization limits itself to the gifts of a few people at the top. From this perspective, I'd like to propose five areas in which leaders can build their competence.

Area 1. The leader perceives, defines, and expresses reality. Consider this story about reality for three men in a nursing home. Two of them, not perfectly clear of mind, made a habit of escaping together. The nurses and the manager were understandably worried about the dangers to these two. Something had to change. One day, the manager, at his wits' end, asked my father-in-law, also a resident, what he could do about these two old friends. My father-in-law replied with a shrewd grasp of reality. "These two men have lived a long time, and their habits are not going to change. All of their lives, they have put on their hats when they go outside. I'm sure if you hide their hats, they'll no longer try to escape." Sure enough, that solved the problem.

There are many realities: competitive realities having to do with technology and service and quality; realities of behavior (our mothers used to tell us that we may do anything we want as long as we're willing to live with the consequences; imagine what a corporation would be like if that were the only statement from the CEO!). Defining and expressing reality for an organization is important because it ends the numbing isolation that is so prevalent and so deadly today.

Area 2. A competent leader knows that the future lies in the selection, nurture, and assignment of key people. Vision and strategy are important, but they are not nearly as important as the provision for key leaders and future leaders. Some people from Herman Miller's research group had been conducting some experiments in a high school in Benton Harbor, Michigan. As part of their work, they interviewed the school superintendent and asked him his strategy. He responded succinctly, "My strategy is to be alive at four o'clock!" I think he had a good understanding of the proper role of strategy.

Area 3. A competent leader bears personal responsibility for knowing, understanding, and enabling the creative people in an organization. Creative work lies at the heart of organizations. We need to know who, through innovative thought and action, provides for our future. Creative people cannot be left to languish on the fringes of organizations. They must be intimate and accountable. Designer

Charles Eames taught me how important it is, in dealing with innovation, to understand the nuances of the word *appropriate*. Being
appropriate means having the right answer to the right question.
Appropriate innovation goes beyond the limits of *excellence,* a word
that today has become almost as banal as *bottom line.*

Area 4. Competent leaders are transforming leaders. Competent
leaders guide their organizations, and the people in them to new
levels of learning and performance, transforming the present into
a reaching toward potential. And, as Charles Handy says, "The
total pragmatist cannot be a transforming leader." Transforming
leadership is a process of learning and risking and changing lives.
(Now you can see one of the reasons I believe that leadership is a
serious meddling in other people's lives!)

Area 5. Competent leaders discover, unleash, and polish diverse
gifts. Every person comes to our organizations, our institutions,
and our families with unique gifts. The great majority of these people welcome the promise of transforming leaders. As we are helped
to new levels of achievement by competent leaders, our organizations mature and become more effective. If we as individuals remain stifled, our organizations will die.

The last of my three things necessary for leaders, and another
inescapable implication of fiduciary leadership, is a clear moral
purpose. Without moral purpose, competence has no measure, and
trust has no goal. A defining thought gives me a way to think about
leadership and moral purpose.

In every church and monastery in Celtic Britain and Ireland, a
fire was kept burning as a sign of God's presence. This is the way I
as a Christian see moral purpose—as a sign of God's presence in
our leadership. It's up to leaders to keep the signs of moral purpose
alive and visible in organizations. Let me propose some signs of
moral purpose. I'm sure you will add others to my list.

Sign 1. The first sign of what I call God's presence is a whole-
hearted acceptance of human authenticity. We are all authentic. We
are not authentic because we have been hired by a company, nor because we have been admitted as a student to a particular college,
nor because we have married a particular man or woman. We are
not authentic because of government programs spelling out the rules

for hiring minorities or people with disabilities. As parts of a great cross-cultural society, we form a cornucopia of gifts and talents. We are genuinely insiders in this world because we are God's mix—we are made in his image. Authenticity needs to dominate our relationships and our understanding of justice. The implications of this belief are enormous for leaders.

Sign 2. Because we are authentic, we are entitled to certain rights as insiders: the right to belong; the right to ownership; the right to opportunity; the right to a covenantal relationship; the right to inclusive organizations. Leaders with a clear moral purpose work to make these rights real.

Sign 3. Another sign of moral purpose in a leader is truth. The degree of truth in our lives and organizations critically affects our present and future relationships. Unfortunately, we see objective untruthfulness all around us—in Senate hearings, in corporate advertising, in unhappy families, in the daily media. From his own experience there, theologian Eberhard Jungel has thoughtfully reviewed the recent history and demise of communism in East Germany. For me, his crucial conclusion was "if . . . one begins to analyze why 'realized socialism' finally failed, one should seek the decisive cause in its objective untruthfulness." To assume blithely that untruthfulness has no consequence for our world is mighty risky.

But what is truth? Is it a concept? A person? Is truth communication? Quality? Predictability? A leader's promise? It seems to me that truth in its many facets is all of these things. It also seems to me that in our most private moments, every one of us knows truth in our hearts.

Sign 4. Leaders with clear moral purpose are vulnerable—a gift of all true leaders to their followers. Moral purpose enables leaders to be vulnerable because it changes the rules of measurement. A clear moral purpose removes the ego from the game. It means that leaders no longer need to succeed on the terms that make some leaders intolerant, inaccessible, and insufferable. Vulnerable leaders are open to diversity of gifts from followers. They seek contrary opinion. They take every person seriously. They are strong enough to abandon themselves to the strengths of others.

Sign 5. Leaders with a clear moral purpose to their actions take very seriously realistic and equitable distribution of results in the capitalist system. I'm not talking about redistributing wealth, but distributing the normal results of profit-making institutions, and, for that matter, many nonprofit organizations. What is fair and motivating to authentic insiders from whom leaders demand a meaningful contribution? As *I Corinthians* reminds us: "Who plants a vineyard without eating any of its fruit? Who tends a flock without getting some of its milk?" Who, indeed?

When I was CEO at Herman Miller, we capped the cash compensation of the CEO at 20 times the average compensation. For many years, we have had productivity gain sharing in cash bonuses, and, quarterly, we have paid out profit sharing in fully negotiable Herman Miller stock. These practices didn't happen accidentally. They are all attempts to distribute the results of our work equitably.

Of course, not all results are tangible. And not all compensation consists of money or stock. During a consulting session at Beth Israel Hospital in Boston, I was confronted by a small but militant group of physicians. They fired this question at me: "Why do you always think of a bonus as cash?" They suggested time, safety, and the chance to spend time with the president of the hospital. The equitable distribution of results may be the most convincing sign of a leader who is clearly guided in his or her job by moral purpose.

Sign 6. I'd like to suggest, as a sign of God's presence, personal restraint. Leaders work in public, under constant scrutiny. You may not like that—in fact, I often resented the intrusions that came with my job—but that's reality. Because leaders function in public, perceptions of leaders are crucial to their performance. What message does our lifestyle send to people about what we think is right, who matters, and what moves followers? What signal are we sending with our power, our status, and our perks?

What is the real purpose of talent and wealth? Surely they are gifts from God to us, but are those gifts only for our use? How can we share equitably, and how are we to employ, for the common good, the unearned gift of access? Access—to resources, education, or opportunity, for example—is a gift that, like talent or wealth, exacts accountability. How in the context of capitalism and in a world of limited resources are we to understand and practice simplicity? How are we to assess our individual liberty and license—essential to us—and modulate our liberty and license in light of the common good?

I certainly don't have the answers to all of these questions, but I do think that as each of us finds his or her own answers, we will come to understand how a moral purpose can guide our work as leaders.

I have tried to discuss three things that I think are necessary to leadership. Leadership is a quest for many things, but surely the three important ones are: (1) an understanding of the fiduciary nature of leadership; (2) a new meaning of competence; and (3) clear moral purpose.

I'd like to end with a story that illustrates for me just how much trust followers place in the hands of their leaders; how much competence followers expect in their leaders; and how necessary it is for leaders to have a clear moral purpose for their actions.

Carla drove a lift-truck on the second shift. She came into my office while I was CEO of Herman Miller, made herself comfortable, and told me about her family's vacation trip from Michigan to Florida when she was a little girl. "We were driving through a county in one of the deep south states," she said. "My father was wearing his white cowboy hat. It seemed like I never saw my father without his cowboy hat. A deputy sheriff stopped our car. In those days, we knew that black people should not roll down the windows or unlock the door at a time like this. The deputy rapped his nightstick hard on the window next to my dad's head and said loud enough for us all to hear, 'Boy, when you're in this county, you drive with your hat off.' My dad put his hat on the seat beside him until we passed the county line. I made up my mind then that I would always speak up against that kind of treatment."

We talked some more together, and Carla told me that the minority program at our main plant was not going as well as I had thought it was. Carla could not let some of the incidents go unprotested. She had taken the first and most difficult step; she had led the way. I asked Carla what she wanted me to do. She said, "You're the CEO. It's your job to tell us what you believe." I told her I would do that.

As in many cases, a follower had shown a leader what was necessary.

PART TWO

SERVANT-LEADERSHIP IN THE WORKPLACE

Dr. Warren Bennis is Distinguished Professor of Business Administration at the University of Southern California and a consultant to governments and multinational companies throughout the world. Author of more than a dozen books, including the bestsellers *Leaders* and *On Becoming a Leader,* Bennis's insights have fundamentally shaped the way we think about leaders today. Warren Bennis was also one of the earliest endorsers of Robert K. Greenleaf's seminal work, saying that *Servant Leadership: A Journey into the Nature of Legitimate Power and Greatness* was "A gem of a book on leadership."

In this essay, an excerpt from *Old Dogs, New Tricks,* Warren Bennis elucidates what he believes are crucial traits of the contemporary leader. The student of servant-leadership will find some of the traits discussed here—trust, vision, meaning, distributed leadership—reminiscent of servant-leadership, while other traits complement and enrich our understanding of what the twenty-first century requires of effective leaders. Bennis is a scheduled presenter at the Greenleaf Center's 2002 international conference on servant-leadership.

8

BECOME A TOMORROW LEADER

Warren Bennis

THE MORE AUTHENTIC WE become and the more attuned to the times, the better we can lead the transformation of our organizations.

Authentic people have a bias toward action. They keep saying, "You're never going to get anywhere if you keep sitting in the dugout." The only way you succeed, ultimately, in whatever you do, is to get up there and take your swings—and sometimes that means taking a swing at someone else who you think is doing something wrong or dangerous for the company. That's action, too.

Every good leader has had a willful determination to achieve a set of goals, a set of convictions, about what he or she wanted the organization to achieve. In the leader, character is having the vision to see things not just the way they are but the way they should be—and doing something to make them that way. Leaders have the capacity to convert purpose and vision into action. It just isn't enough to have the great vision people can trust. It has to be manifest in some external products and results. Most leaders are pragmatic dreamers or practical idealists.

Most of the leaders whom I have interviewed said they learn more from failure than from success. They possess the ability to learn from themselves and their mistakes, and they know how to get the best and worst out of people. There is nothing like power to reveal your own humanity and character—especially power in crisis situations, because that's when you hit rock bottom. As one CEO told me, "That's when the iron enters your soul and gives you resiliency to cope." There's nothing like being a person of responsibility if you need a lesson about who you are. Nothing.

Many companies are the direct reflection of their leaders. Effective leaders are all about creative collaboration, about creating a shared sense of purpose. A central task for the leader is the development of other leaders by creating conditions that enhance the ability of all employees to make decisions and create change. The leader actively helps his or her followers to reach their full potential. As Max DePree once put it: "The signs of outstanding leadership appear primarily among the followers."

How do you go about becoming a good leader? Figure out what you're good at. Hire only good people who care, and treat them the way you want to be treated. Identify your one or two key objectives or directions, and ask your coworkers how to get there. Listen hard and get out of their way. Cheer them. Switch from *macho* to *maestro*.

Ten Traits

Tomorrow's leaders must learn how to create an environment that embraces change, not as a threat but as an opportunity. Some leaders will be successful at this; others will fail.

1. *Successful leaders have self-awareness and self-esteem.* They sense when a different repertoire of competencies is needed, without being threatened by the need to change. They have the diagnostic ability to understand what new things are required, or what things should be unlearned, plus the behavioral flexibility to change. GE's Jack Welch had enough diagnostic ability to say, "The

way I was doing things is not going to work," and then he was also able to change his behavior.

2. *Leaders ensure that boundaries are porous and permeable.* You need the foresight to see things before the curve, before others do. And the only way you get that is by being in touch with your customers, with society, with the outside world, and by having the boundaries permeable and porous enough to get your information. That's why people at the periphery are usually the most creative and often the least consulted.

3. *Competitive advantage will be the leadership of women.* I suspect that by the year 2005, about 50 percent of the vice presidents for finance will be women, and women will appear much more often in top management positions. One of our competitive advantages will be the full deployment of the talent of women in our workforce. We must dispel the myth that the only way for a woman to succeed is to act like a man. One irony is that male leaders have been trying to shed the same macho character traits that women have been encouraged to imitate. Dr. Helen Tartakoff, a Harvard psychoanalyst, said that generally women have exactly the opposite character traits, and that these feminine traits contain the potential for improving the human condition.

What has got to change is not women's character traits but corporate cultures, because most of them have been playing male-chauvinist games for too long. The power structures and avenues of opportunity have excluded women for years. Successful leadership doesn't depend on masculinity or femininity. It's not about being tough or soft, assertive or sensitive. It's about having a particular set of attributes which all leaders, both male and female, seem to share.

4. *Leaders have a strongly defined sense of purpose and vision.* They also develop the capacity to articulate it clearly. Leading means doing the right things; managing means doing things right. Too many organizations are overmanaged and underled because the people at the top are better at making policies, practices, and procedures than they are at creating a compelling, overarching vision. They are managers, not leaders. They are looking at how to achieve

greater efficiency and how to control their systems and structures more effectively. They are looking at how to do things right.

We need more leaders—people who do the right things. Managers are people who do things right. There's a profound difference. When you think about doing the right things, your mind immediately goes toward thinking about the future, thinking about dreams, missions, visions, strategic intents, and purposes. When you think about doing things right, you think about systems and processes. You think about how-to. Leaders ask the *what* and *why* questions, not the *how* questions. Leaders think about empowerment, not control. And empowerment means not stealing responsibility from people. Grace Hopper, a management expert who was the first female admiral in the U.S. Navy, has said, "You manage things, but you lead people."

Tomorrow's leaders will spend much of their time nurturing and developing other leaders within the organization. Today's leaders need to prepare themselves and their people for the challenges of tomorrow. Over the years, I studied many terrific groups, many creative collaborators. And in every case where they really reached epiphanies, there was a leader who enrolled people in an exciting, insanely significant vision; a leader who was capable of reeling in advocates and supporters to work with him or her. They all believed that they would make a dent in the universe. What leaders need to realize is that people would much rather live a life dedicated to an idea or a cause that they believe in, than lead a life of aimless diversion. Effective leaders are all about cause and meaning—creating a shared sense of purpose because people need purpose. That's why we live. And the power of an organization will be in that shared sense of purpose. With a shared sense of purpose, you can achieve anything.

In the twenty-first century, we will need leaders who know what is important in the long term. Who have a vision, dream, mission, or a strategic intent. Who remind people continually of what's important and create an environment where people know why they are there.

To communicate a vision, you need more than words, speeches, memos, and laminated plaques. You need to live a vision, day in, day out, embodying it and empowering every other person to execute that vision in everything he or she does; anchoring it in realities, so that it becomes a template for decision making. Actions do speak louder than words.

5. *Leaders generate trust.* Leaders will have to be candid in their communications and show that they care. They've got to be seen to be trustworthy. Most communication has to be done eyeball-to-eyeball, rather than in newsletters, on videos, or via satellite. The leader must generate and sustain trust, and that also means demonstrating competence and constancy.

"Strike hard and try everything," wrote Henry James. You're never going to get anywhere unless you risk and try and then learn from each experience. Leaders have to play even when it means making mistakes. And they have to learn from those mistakes.

6. *Leaders have a bias toward action.* Not just reflection, but action. A combination of both of them, of course, is what we all want. And then you need to get feedback on how you are doing. You have to cultivate sources of reflective backtalk by getting people around you whose counsel you treasure, people who are capable of telling the truth, people you can depend on, people who have the future in their bones. You need these people. You can't do it alone. You need people who can take the vision and run with it.

7. *Leaders create not just a vision, but a vision with meaning—* one with significance, one that puts the players at the center of things rather than at the periphery. If companies have a vision that is meaningful to people, nothing will stop them from being successful. Not just any old vision will do: it must be a shared vision with meaning and significance.

The only way a vision can be shared is for it to have meaning for the people who are involved in it. Leaders have to specify the steps that behaviorally fit into that vision, and then reward people for following those steps. Then they need some feedback loops, to make sure that the vision is still relevant and salient, and has some resonance. Again, without meaning and resonance, vision statements are only stale truths.

8. *Leaders must become very comfortable with advanced technology* and the changes that it will bring. On my seventieth birthday, my children were all there; they're in their late twenties and early thirties. One of their birthday gifts to me was two hours of instruction on using the Internet and the World Wide Web. Two of them gave me gifts of software.

In this high-tech, high-touch world, we're going to see a totally new breed of people for whom advanced technology is just a natural part of life. Leaders will have to be not only comfortable with advanced technology but, at the same time, engage even more hands-on than ever before. They will also need more interpersonal competence.

9. *Leaders must act big if they are small, and small if they are big.* What we see in the global economy is that both small and big companies can be successful. It's just a matter of finding the right scale for a particular organization and industry, and then providing the right structure and leadership.

As Rosabeth Moss Kanter points out, companies worldwide are becoming PALs: they are "pooling, allying, and linking." This is particularly true of small companies, which are creating networks, joint ventures, R&D consortia, and strategic partnerships that cut across corporate and national boundaries. They are "buying the power of bigness," as Jay Galbraith says, to gain scale in marketing, purchasing, and manufacturing.

Small firms also have new technologies on their side—like computer-based manufacturing and distribution, sophisticated marketing databases, the latest telecommunication systems—all of which are formidable competitive weapons that allow them to build global markets quickly. But this in no way signals the end of the large corporation. Giant companies have some very formidable advantages: economies of scale, resources, skilled people, know-how, social clout, long-term planning, and stability. They just wish they could get all the benefits of size without all the problems of bureaucracy and the other diseconomies of scale that size brings with it. To compete, these giants have got to behave like small, fast-moving companies. They have to recreate themselves as collections of small, independent, manageable units. Hence the worldwide focus on reengineering, downsizing, subcontracting, decentralization, spin-offs, and intrapreneuring.

10. *Ultimately, leaders make federations of corporations.* Most successful organizations combine the best characteristics of both big and small companies. The most practical solution, particularly for the large corporation, is federalism. Federations work better than monolithic organizations because, along with strength, they offer flexibility. They are more nimble and adaptive. They have all the inherent advantages of being big but all the benefits of being small.

Everywhere we look in the world today, from ABB to Benetton and from General Electric to Coca-Cola, we see new corporate confederations made up of numerous semiautonomous units, all collaborating together and joined by a common vision. Essentially, what makes a federation work are the principles described by James Madison in the late eighteenth century. They are just as valid for corporations as they are for nations. First, you diffuse power to all the semiautonomous units to become noncentralized, not just decentralized. Second, decision making must be shared between the units and the central authority. Nobody dictates terms and conditions to anybody else. Everything is negotiated. Third, there is an overarching vision and purpose, and some form of written constitution that lays out the company's operating principles. The units may even have their own constitutions, but they must be in harmony with the vision and principles of the federation. Fourth, the units need to understand where their boundaries are, whether these are business or product line boundaries or, as is the case with Coca-Cola's bottlers and Benetton's retailers, geographic boundaries. Fifth, you need to balance power not only between the units and the central authority but between the units themselves, so that none of the units dominates the others. Sixth, the units must have autonomy. They have to be free to be self-governing, as long as they don't violate the federation's universal operating principles. And this is the most difficult characteristic of federalism. It's the source of the continuing tension: the power of the central authority versus the power of constituent units.

In many cases, this tension can be fatal because the tendency is to go to one of the extremes. Either the federation overgeneralizes, or it lacks a unifying vision and constitution to hold it all together, and it finally disintegrates. So this is where you need true leadership. Leaders provide the necessary balance. Leaders of federations don't think of their associates as troops. And associates don't think of their leaders as generals. The leader of the new federal corporation has to be a leader of leaders. You can't be the only one making decisions. Rather, you have to create an environment in which other leaders, who subscribe to your vision, can make effective decisions—an environment in which people at all levels are empowered to be leaders.

Coca-Cola is a global federation of fiercely independent franchised bottlers and distributors. The late CEO Roberto Goizueta once had a meeting with these folks and asked them three times in one speech to please "paint your trucks red." He didn't command them to do it. He pleaded with them.

Percy Barnevik, CEO of Asea Brown Boveri, describes his organization as "a federation of national companies with a global communications center." ABB has only 100 employees in its Zurich headquarters, but I've heard Barnevik say he has 5,000 leaders. So it's not the central staff that holds ABB together, it's the common vision of globalism and excellence that those 5,000 leaders subscribe to. And, again, this is what I mean by a leader of leaders. Percy Barnevik doesn't command and control the troops. He simply enunciates clearly the company's performance standards and then he gives his associates the freedom to find the best ways of achieving those standards. He doesn't try to manage their jobs for them.

One of my favorite metaphors for this is Schumacher's balloon man—now perhaps a woman—who holds a fistful of strings attached to balloons, each representing an entrepreneurial unit. She doesn't control the balloons—they all have their own individual buoyancy. She simply holds them together in her hand.

The leader of federations must have faith in the power of people to solve their problems locally. He or she is responsible for establishing the *why* and the *what*—the overarching vision and purpose—but the rest of the leaders are responsible for the *how*.

Danah Zohar was born and educated in the United States. She studied Physics and Philosophy at MIT, and then did her postgraduate work in Philosophy, Religion, and Psychology at Harvard University. She is the author of the best-sellers *The Quantum Self* and *The Quantum Society,* which extend the language and principles of quantum physics into a new understanding of human consciousness, psychology, and social organization. In 1997, she published *Who's Afraid of Schrödinger's Cat?,* a survey of twentieth-century scientific ideas, and her business book, *ReWiring the Corporate Brain.* Her latest book is *SQ—Spiritual Intelligence.* Zohar is a visiting fellow at Cranfield School of Management. She also teaches in The Leading Edge course at Oxford Brookes University and in the Oxford Strategic Leadership Program at Oxford University's Templeton College.

This essay is an excerpt from her book, *ReWiring the Corporate Brain: Using the New Science to Rethink How We Structure and Lead Organizations.* Zohar says that servant-leadership is the essence of quantum thinking and quantum leadership: It is compatible with the quantum model of self where "I see myself as a cocreator, as an active agent in this universe who makes things happen." Danah Zohar was a keynote speaker at the Greenleaf Center's 2001 annual international conference.

9

SERVANT-LEADERSHIP AND
REWIRING THE CORPORATE BRAIN

Danah Zohar

Oh, this is the animal that never was.
They did not know it and, for all of that,
they loved his neck and posture, and his gait,
clean to the great eyes with their tranquil gaze.
Really it was not. Of their love they made it,
this pure creature. And they left a space
always, till in this clear uncluttered place
lightly he raised his head and scarcely needed
to be. They did not feed him any corn,
only the possibility he might
exist, which gave the beast such strength, he bore
a horn upon the forehead. Just one horn.
Unto a virgin he appeared, all white,
and was in the silver mirror and in her.

> —*Rainer Maria Rilke*,
> Sonnets to Orpheus, *"The Unicorn"*

Rainer Maria Rilke is generally considered the most influential
German poet of the twentieth century. His work has caught and

reflected some of the century's major concerns. This poem about the unicorn is one of the central readings in the concept café that my colleague and I run for business leaders. I think that it adds important new dimensions to discussions of the servant-leader concept. More than that, I think these are particularly quantum dimensions, and the servant-leader concept is vital to understanding quantum leadership.

As I understand the term, servant-leadership involves practicing the essence of quantum thinking. Servant-leaders lead from that level of deep, revolutionary vision that is accessed only by the third of our three kinds of thinking. They change the system, invent the new paradigm, clear a space where something new can be. They accomplish this not just from "doing," but, more fundamentally, from "being." All this makes servant-leadership the essence of what this book is about. Such leaders are essential to deep corporate transformation. For this reason, I chose servant-leadership as the final and summary theme for my book *ReWiring the Corporate Brain*.

The unicorn has always been a special symbol in our culture. He is that most impossible creature of the human imagination, a beast conjured up by longing and the human capacity to dream. In Rilke's poem, he is conjured up by love, and given a space to be by those who dare to believe in the possibility that he might exist. In quantum science, the whole of existence is a set of possibilities plucked out of the quantum vacuum's infinite sea of potentiality. Some of these possibilities are plucked out by observers, by human beings living our lives. An awareness of our role as cocreators of existence can increase our capacity to fulfill that role. Each of us is a servant of the vacuum, a servant of the manifold potentiality at the heart of existence.

Business leaders who become aware of servanthood in this sense know that they serve more than company or colleagues, more than markets or products, more even than vision and values as these are normally understood. They serve that longing that conjures up unicorns, and through this service they build or contribute to a successful—a profitable—business that adds some new dimension both to business and to human well-being.

One independent company founder with whom I spoke told me she could see three reasons why people might start up a business. The first reason is opportunity. The would-be entrepreneur looks at the market and sees that there is an opening for some service or product, and says, "Someone needs to provide this. I *will*." The second reason is talent or opportunity. The would-be entrepreneur looks inward at personal resources and skills or outward at the local environment and says, "I *can* provide this." The third reason is more spiritual. The future entrepreneur doesn't begin by thinking about business or a career, but about a feeling of inner necessity. "This *has* to exist. This *has* to happen. I *have* to do it." I think this is the beginning of the servant-leader's business career.

There seems to me an interesting and useful interplay among these three motives for going into business, the three kinds of thinking our brains can do, and the three models of self and organization that we have looked at. The opportunity motive is very logical. I analyze the market, I see what is missing, I decide to provide it. This is the way my rule-bound, goal-oriented serial thinking operates. It's compatible with seeing myself as a Newtonian billiard ball in human form, as able to place myself in the scheme of things through manipulating and controlling the forces and bodies around me. It is management by objectives.

The skill motive is very associative. I am this sort of person with these sorts of resources, so I can see that I fit in here. This is the way the brain's parallel, networked thinking operates. Those things are most natural (those neural connections strongest) that conform to past experience, to habit, to the relationships around me. This is compatible with seeing myself in terms of my relationships to others, to what I can offer them. I find my place in some existing network. I go into the family craft or the family business. I deal locally, with familiar things and familiar people.

The inner necessity, the "I *have* to" motive, is quantum. The existing provisions, products, services, and so on, are not adequate. Something new is needed here, and I have to provide it. This is the way the brain's creative, rule-breaking, rule-making kind of thinking operates. Experience throws up things and events for which there are no previous neural connections, therefore no concepts or categories. So the brain creates new ones. It rewires itself. This is compatible with the quantum model of self where I see myself as a cocreator, as an active agent in this universe who makes things happen. If I want the world to change, I have to change it. If this product or service should exist, I have to provide it.

We've seen, both in the brain and in life's experiences, one reason why quantum thinking kicks in: there is a crisis. We have little motive to change our neural wiring or our paradigm if the existing one is doing its job. Such crisis is common in the shift from normal or conservative science to revolutionary science. It often plays a role in the making of servant-leaders. In their case, this is often a spiritual crisis, some threat to their usual self-esteem, to their usual framework of meaning and value, some longing for something more.

Real Servant-Leaders at Work

I have had the good fortune to know three such leaders personally and to know a bit about their stories. I want to share brief episodes from each because they throw light on those deeper dimensions of servant-leadership that I think are associated with the vision of the new science.

Juliette's Story

This is a true story, but the names have been changed at the request of its subject. The leader I will call Juliette Johnson owns a small but growing business, Juliette's Fashion Studios. The founding studio is located in southeast England. She is in her early forties—a French immigrant to the United Kingdom who is married to an Englishman. It was Juliette who outlined the three reasons why someone might start up a business.

In France, Juliette was an opera star. She is a large woman with the broad chest and wide neck that are usually associated with a successful singing career, and she was successful. She had her success, a husband, two teenage children, and a wide circle of friends. She dabbled in spiritual quest, but not seriously. Then, within the space of a year, her husband left her, her children decided to join their father, and her friends became critical and distant. "I was devastated," she says. "I didn't know what had happened. I didn't know where to turn."

On the advice of associates in England, Juliette signed up for a six-month extensive study course at a spiritual community in Scotland. She studied the writings of an eleventh-century Sufi mystic, Ibn Al'arabi, and those of ancient Eastern and more modern Western mystics, all of whom used their work to celebrate the unity of existence. Life at the community was quiet, disciplined, and reflective. Juliette was thrown back on herself and on a quest to discover what really mattered to her. During the course, she met her future husband, an Englishman, and they moved on to the south of England.

Living in a small flat above a shop, and supported through state welfare funds, Juliette had no clear sense of career direction. Then a friend asked her to help with a handmade dress. Juliette had done sewing ever since her early teens, and the dress she now made for her friend awakened something. She made a few others and felt that in her original designs she saw an expression of the passion she had felt during her study course in Scotland, a passion to celebrate the unity of existence and the true reality that lies behind the human form. She felt that she *had* to make more dresses, whether or not anyone wanted to buy them. But people did buy them. Her designs were fresh; they brought out some special, deeply feminine quality in any woman who wore them. She consciously designed in a way that made bodily shape and size unimportant. "All bodies are beautiful," she says. "Every woman should be able to feel good about her body. She should feel happy about herself."

In fact, Juliette's clothes flatter something beyond the body, something even beyond the feminine. She smiles and says, "Yes, of course. It's a celebration of that source from which all form arises." The passion, and the vision it inspired, led to more designs, to the opening of a large shop, to the growth of a promising business. "It *had* to be a business," she says. "I had to show that I could serve something sacred *and* that I could do this inside a business. I wanted my business to be an act of service." Nonetheless, she is loath to describe herself as a servant-leader. It seems too grand, too lacking in humility. Quoting the mystic who inspired her, she says, "Just say what you know. Don't say how you got there."

Andrew Stone's Story

Andrew Stone is extremely well read but has had little formal education. As he puts it, he left school "in disgrace" at age fifteen with only five "O"-level exams, one of which was in woodwork. He began to live by his wits, as they say in England, and by the age of seventeen was a spiv in the street markets of Cardiff in Wales. A spiv is a seller of "dubious" goods. He had his own market stall where he could offer these wares, and he made a good living from it. "I had a car, a flat, and some good mates who, admittedly, were in the criminal world. I could pull any bird I wanted. I thought I was a very big deal."

Stone is from a Jewish family, though that had meant little to him. Still, in 1967, when the Six Days War broke out and friends chided him that if he was really such a big deal, he would go to Israel and fight, he went. As so many of us of that generation found, the war was over by the time he got there, but he decided to stay on for a while. But Israeli life didn't live up to his expectations—at least, he felt his own life didn't live up to Israeli standards.

"I was used to pulling birds with a flashy car and fast line and a big wad of pound notes," he says. "Israeli girls could not have cared less. They wanted philosophical conversations about Jewish destiny and the meaning of life. They were attracted to war heroes and guys who wanted to dedicate themselves to something. I felt like shit. I felt I was a total nothing, a germ that ought to be eradicated." He spent a year in Israel, feeling this way, until he suddenly felt that he *had* to be of service. He couldn't justify living otherwise. "Even when I was a spiv," he says, "I wanted to make my customers happy. I always wanted to get them a good deal. Now I felt I had to play that out on a wider stage."

Stone wrote to his father, also a Jewish street trader, back in Wales, about his new feelings, saying he wasn't sure how to act on them, what to do next. "My father reminded me of my skills at retailing and told me about the principles of Marks & Spencer, an idealist Jewish firm with a vision of serving the community. He said it was rare to combine in one person an intense belief in caring principles and knowledge of how to buy and sell profitably. There are do-gooders who can write and talk. There are traders who can turn a profit. But a great challenge would be to work for Marks & Spencer and try to carry on to the next generation this combination of great retailing done in a socially responsible way. I was inspired by this."

Stone went back to England and applied for a job at Marks & Spencer (M&S). He took the standard recruitment test and failed on every point. The recruitment officer at that time was David Sieff, son of the then chairman, and today director of community affairs at M&S. Sieff told Stone that by any of the normal criteria, he was unemployable. But at the same time, M&S at that time was aware of the growing dangers of its size and a tendency to become bureaucratic and institutionalized. They wanted to retain the skills of the entrepreneur that had built the company. "I have an instinct about you," Sieff told Stone. "I'll try you out for a year." The rest is company history.

Katsuhiko Yazaki's Story

Katsuhiko Yazaki is a Japanese businessman in his early fifties. He owns a global mail-order company named *Felissimo,* with offices in Japan, Europe, and North America. His story is told in his 1994 book, *The Path to LiangZhi.*

As a very young man, Yazaki had inherited a "storeless business" from his father. Goods were sold door to door, by word of mouth, through the network. Over the years, he built this up to a successful mail-order business that left him very wealthy. By his mid-forties, he had everything that he thought he wanted: success, wealth, esteem in the community, a family. But something was missing. Some friends showed him a book about Zen and told him of a Master Kido Inoue who taught it.

Yazaki went to Master Inoue's monastery for a week of meditation. He found it difficult, at times painful, but liberating. "One moment," he says, "I felt as if I had found peace, another moment I felt like a prisoner of my delusions. I was astonished at the realization of what I had been calling 'me.' This was the first time I realized how many delusions were within myself. It was also the first time I realized how many delusions I had that were causing ups and downs in my daily life. Until this point, I had never confronted realities about myself so directly."

Yazaki emerged from his monastery cell after a week "to see the beauty of the world for the first time." He realized that he had been living his life in shadow and that the world itself was being damaged by human shadows. "Humans," he wrote, "by separating the world from the self, nature from humanity, and the self from others, trap themselves in delusions to protect the ego. They inevitably enter a frightening scenario of hypocrisy and self-righteousness."

After these insights, Yazaki rededicated his business life. He wanted to use his company to do something for the earth's environment and for future generations. He renamed the company *Felissimo,* which means "happiness" in Spanish and Italian, because his vision of the proper role of business became to increase the sum of human happiness. He formed his new concept of the "ultra store," a store that can "gather value over a wide area" by transcending the limits of geographical space and present time. He felt that he could help his customers to realize images of their future selves and to imagine more fulfilling future lifestyles by marketing his goods globally, thus expanding service and awareness at a more universal level. He attended the Rio Earth Summit Conference and dedicated himself and much of his money to saving the earth's environment. He started a foundation to study the needs of future generations and to back needed educational projects. "I believe," he says, "that these international activities flowed from the development of our business as an ultra store and from my rethinking as a business owner." He readily quotes one of his heroes, Kazuo Inamori (founder of the Kyocera Corporation), who said that what he had done as a business owner was "to continue to raise the level of my ideology every day."

The Concept of Servant-Leadership

Western businesspeople who have been discussing the servant-leader concept do mean by this a leader who has a sense of deeper values and a leadership style that involves conscious service to these values. But we don't always mean the same thing when we speak about values. The usual Western corporate values, at their best, speak of things like excellence, fulfilling one's potential and allowing space for others to do so, achievement, quality of products and services, commitment to never-ending growth. In the East, traditionally, deep values have centered around things like compassion, humility, gratitude, service to one's family and community, service to the ancestors, or to the ground of Being itself. Traditionally, the East has emphasized cooperation and trust; the West, competition and control. A "good man" in the East has a quality of *being*. In the West, a "good man" is usually measured by his quality of *doing*.

Robert Greenleaf, who wrote the original paper on servant-leadership, had something more Eastern in mind. Indeed, he used the example of a Nepalese Buddhist monk. And in his recent book, *Synchronicity,* Joe Jaworski emphasizes the importance of *being* before *doing* in corporate leadership. He uses dialogue practice extensively as a way of helping leaders access the level of being within themselves. Jaworski's own life was turned around during an interview with David Bohm about the thinking in the new science. I deeply believe the conceptual structure of this new science can give us a more solid underpinning for understanding the true meaning of the servant-leader—and a deeper understanding of what that leader serves.

As someone trained in physics at MIT, I know well from my own educational background the role that science and the wider spirit of Newtonian mechanism have played in widening the gulf between values associated with doing and those associated with being. Newtonian science is preoccupied with objects, obsessed with analysis and measurement. It draws a sharp divide between spirit and matter, between humans and nature. And it gives us a concern with the here and now, a view of truth as black or white, a preoccupation with achievement and progress as measured by doing and acquiring. These are not the values that have inspired the three leaders whose stories I have cited.

We have seen that the new science of this century has a very different philosophical and conceptual basis. Quantum science tells us that the world is all of a piece, holistic. We human beings are in and of nature, we help to make reality happen, we are free agents with a responsibility for cocreation. More than that, quantum science shows us that we are, in our essential physical and spiritual makeup, *extensions,* "excitations," of the underlying ground state of Being. As I put it earlier, a quantum view of the self shows us that we are "thoughts in the mind of God."

To qualify as servant-leaders in the deepest sense, I think that leaders must have four essential qualities. They must have a deep sense of the interconnectedness of life and all its enterprises. They must have a sense of engagement and responsibility, a sense of "I *have* to." They must be aware that all human endeavor, including business, is a part of the larger and richer fabric of the whole universe. And perhaps most important of all, servant-leaders must know what they ultimately serve. They must, with a sense of humility and gratitude, have a sense of the Source from which all values emerge.

Describing the unicorn, Rilke said, "Really it was not. Of their love they made it." The servant-leader serves from a base of love. The three whose examples I quoted do so—not from some gooey sentimental love of all humanity and wish to do good works, but out of a deep, abiding passion for and commitment to service. And that service itself is to something beyond the given: a wish to make women feel good about themselves, inspired by the underlying nature of existence; a wish to make people happy, inspired by the Jewish love of community; a wish to serve future generations, inspired by a vision of the interconnectedness of existence.

To these servant-leaders and others like them, the business of business no longer restricts itself to manipulating things and nature and people for profit. Rather, business becomes a spiritual vocation in the largest sense of that word. The brain's "spirit" (quantum thinking) integrates the abilities of the brain's "intellect" (serial thinking) and the brain's "heart" (parallel thinking). As such, it initiates and perpetuates the brain's necessary rewiring. I believe that only from such a basis of spiritual servant-leadership can really deep transformation come about in the corporate world. Without it, there can be no fundamental rewiring of the corporate brain.

Nancy Larner Ruschman was previously program director at the Greenleaf Center for Servant-Leadership. Prior to that, she had a long career in the hospitality industry, working as a manager and supervisor, and experiencing firsthand the difference between servant-led and nonservant-led businesses. This experience prompted her to pursue her master's degree in Wellness Management at Ball State University, where she researched servant-leadership in companies as the basis for her thesis. Besides her research and writing in servant-leadership, she provides coaching and consultation to businesses and business leaders.

In this essay, she definitively answers the question that many people have when they first hear about the concept of servant-leadership: It's a nice theory, but will it really work in business? As she shows, in this carefully researched article, it definitely does work in business. Several of the top ten of *Fortune* magazine's "100 Best Companies to Work For in America" practice servant-leadership and have shown unmistakable bottom-line success. Ruschman gives the details of their servant-leadership practices and culture.

10

SERVANT-LEADERSHIP AND THE BEST COMPANIES TO WORK FOR IN AMERICA

Nancy Larner Ruschman

SEARCHING FOR A LITTLE stability in this rapidly changing marketplace? You might begin by taking a look at a growing number of innovative companies that keep some basic principles in mind. These companies can be found at the top of a unique list of businesses that continue to grow in distinction because of their high-quality work practices and bottom-line potentials. Rather than scrambling to implement the next great fad to pump up the troops, these companies focus on keeping a long-term, quality workforce through sustainable practices focused on the employee, the customer, the product, and the bottom line.

The businesses I'm referring to can be found in *Fortune* magazine's yearly ranking of the "100 Best Companies To Work For in America." The "100 Best" list is quickly becoming the benchmark, the standard toward which other organizations work.

It is quite an honor (and a feat!) to appear on the "100 Best" list. What is even more interesting is that several of the top twenty companies ranked in the 2001 issue of *Fortune* magazine's 100 Best were servant-led organizations. The best part about these servant-led companies is that everybody wins! The employees have great benefits and perks, respect, more balance between work and home, a sense of community inside and outside the organization, and competitive wages. The business gains loyalty, productivity, lower turnover, greater profits, more innovation, and a highly respected standing in the community.

The three organizations on the "100 Best" list that have formally embraced servant-leadership within their corporate culture are:

1. Southwest Airlines (#4), a $5-billion airline transportation company known for its low-cost, no-frills, on-time flights (and wonderful sense of humor), based in Dallas, Texas;

2. TDIndustries (#6), a $170-million national mechanical construction and service firm headquartered in Dallas, Texas (TDIndustries has been in the top 10 of the list four years in a row);

3. Synovus Financial Corporation (#8), a multifinancial services company based in Columbus, Georgia, with over $13.7 billion in assets.

Two other businesses on the "100 Best" list—The Container Store (#1) and AFLAC (#61)—will also be discussed. The Container Store and AFLAC do not use formal servant-leadership language to explicitly guide their corporate culture, but both organizations practice a values-based leadership closely aligned with servant-leadership. The CEOs of both the Container Store and AFLAC have participated in various servant-leadership forums, and have shared stories of how they operate their organization through values- or principles-based leadership.

Essentials on *Fortune* Magazine's 100 Best Companies to Work For in America

In 1998, *Fortune* magazine collaborated with best-selling authors Robert Levering and Milton Moskowitz to compile the "100 Best" list, using methodology similar to that used for their book, *The 100 Best Companies to Work For in America.*

To be eligible for inclusion on the "100 Best" list, a company has to be at least 10 years old and have a minimum of 500 employees. Employees are randomly selected to fill out surveys that focus on company policies, programs, and philosophy, and the employees' perception of their workplace relationships with management, their job, and other employees. Research conducted by Levering and his colleagues has found that companies that have high-quality–high-performance work environments tend to be financially successful.

The "100 Best" list is chock-full of high-performance workplaces, which, in Levering's words, are companies that simultaneously deliver outstanding service and financial returns while being a great place to work. The results have been impressive:

○ Shares of public companies on the list rose 37 percent annualized over a three-year period, compared with 25 percent for the S&P 500 companies.

○ Most of the 100 Best have seen a 50 percent reduction in turnover as compared to industry standards.

○ The 100 Best enjoy a significantly increased talent pool: 397 percent applications per employee compared to 209 percent per employee of other companies—more applications per job as compared to those not on the list.

○ The 100 Best have seen a 15 percent increase in new job positions.

○ The 100 Best take more steps to engage employees in the business.

○ The 100 Best make an effort to create a supportive and inclusive company culture and environment.

○ The 100 Best give greater consideration to their employees' quality of life.

The Greenleaf Center was pleased to see servant-led and values-based organizations on the 100 Best list. In addition, over one-third of the companies on the 100 Best list were members or customers of the Greenleaf Center for Servant-Leadership.

Building the Business Case for Servant-Leadership

*The first order of business is [to begin] on a course
toward people-building with leadership that has a firmly
established context of people first. With that, the
right actions fall naturally into place.*

—Robert K. Greenleaf, from *The Servant as Leader*

The aim in writing this chapter is to further pique the interest of leaders in the business world who already believe in their hearts that servant-leadership, because of its human values and service aspects, is the right way to do business. But more to the point, by providing pertinent information not only on these servant-led organizations but also on studies conducted on values-based work practices, I hope to convey to business leaders that servant-leadership is also a logical and viable way to run an organization.

You cannot have a go at adopting the servant-leadership philosophy for the sole purpose of increasing your bottom line; it doesn't work that way. A person needs to be predisposed to these values and principles in order to attempt incorporating servant-leadership into the organization.

Servant-leadership offers new ways to capitalize on the knowledge and wisdom of all employees. It allows for the business strategy to be shared widely throughout the company rather than with only a few top executives, and it encourages individuals to grow from just doing a job into having fully engaged minds and hearts.

The following leaders pursue, in their companies, Greenleaf's vision of working toward becoming servants first:

○ Jack Lowe, CEO, TDIndustries (sixth on the 2001 list).

○ Herb Kelleher, CEO, Southwest Airlines (fourth on the 2001 list).

○ Jim Blanchard, Chairman and CEO, Synovus Financial Corporation (eighth on the 2001 list).

The subsequent information is based on interviews with key leaders of servant-led organizations, articles, and other research focusing on high-performing workplaces.

TDIndustries

Trustworthiness, which requires character and competence, can only flourish with leadership that trusts, supports and encourages. At TD we call that servant-leadership.

—Jack Lowe, CEO, TDIndustries, and
Board Chair for the Greenleaf Center

There are two basic types of folks who want to talk to Jack Lowe about business at TDIndustries. Those in the first group say they are impressed with TD's business results and want to know how they too can achieve such a successful bottom line, but they make it clear that they have no interest in the concept of servant-leadership. The second group say, "We've always wished we could run our business with these principles, but we're not sure how to go about it." "This second group," says Jack Lowe, CEO of TDIndustries, "is the group I'm interested in speaking with." Others quote Jack as making a much more blunt statement: "If you do servant-leadership for the bottom line, you've already blown it."

TDIndustries is a $170 million, employee-owned national mechanical construction and service firm headquartered in Dallas, Texas. TDIndustries has provided air conditioning, plumbing, piping, and electrical services to customers in Texas and throughout the Southwest for over 50 years. Its 1,300-plus employees are known as "Partners," and that's not a Texan idiom showing through; they *are* Partners, in every sense of the word: the way they work together, their stake in the company (Jack Lowe owns only 6 percent of the outstanding shares of the company; the rest is widely owned by the employees), the way they partner with the community.

TDIndustries attributes much of its success to servant-leadership, but servant-leadership isn't the only factor that has made the company fiscally sound and a great place to work. As Jack has explained: "Being a servant-led organization, and the trust that it engenders, provides the underpinnings of a great company. But if you don't have a solid business strategy or great customer-focused processes, you won't consistently blow away your customers.

"People try total quality management, open book management, diversity, or any other initiative you can name, and often it doesn't work. My guess is that they either didn't try hard enough or they didn't have a solid foundation of trust."

Training and Retention at TDIndustries

TDIndustries maintains extensive training and development efforts, and has no limit on its training budget. This support enables TD Partners to take personal responsibility for their own learning. The company's lasting investment in its Partners is reflected in its practice of promoting from within. Because Partners are encouraged to continually build their skill set, many who are hired into entry-level positions eventually attain managerial roles.

This, in turn, has an effect on employee retention at TD. It is difficult to find turnover percentages for the construction industry; most companies don't track turnover. Many in the industry hire people for a specific job, then let them go after the work is complete; therefore, turnover is constant. TD hires people for *careers,* not for one or two jobs. Turnover is unheard of at 15 percent.

Some Unique Benefits

TDIndustries pays an average of 70 percent of the health care coverage provided to its Partners. The health care premiums are indexed to pay with an overall cap—the less one earns, the less one pays for health care coverage. This enables all Partners and their families to afford excellent health care coverage, regardless of their pay. It has also resulted in a healthier workforce. Here are a few more of TD's benefits:

○ Partners may receive paid time off for volunteer work they do.

○ TDFair Day: The job site is shut down for two entire mornings. Breakfast is served to all, and Partners browse through information booths on retirement planning, financial counseling, a blood drive, smoking cessation information, and more.

○ Participation in Mentium, an exchange executive development program for women.

○ Work/Family: TD is working on plans to provide a child care tax credit program and to hire a work/family life coordinator who will head up a quality team to investigate a number of work/family life issues such as parenting seminars, child care resource and referral services, adoption resource and referral services, sick/emergency child care, child care center discounts, a dependent care spending account, paid paternity leave, and other family issues.

Contributing to the Community

Here is a brief listing of community programs that TDPartners participate in:

○ Hearts and Hammers—building houses for the disadvantaged.

○ Heat the Town—providing heating for the disadvantaged.

○ Meals on Wheels; TD is a distribution point for the community.

○ Founding member of the Dallas Servant Leader Institute.

○ Service to community groups/organizations: School Boards; Little League; Boy Scouts of America; United Way; Salesmanship Club; Greenleaf Center.

Through the years, servant-leadership has continued to be the linchpin of TD's engaging culture. TDIndustries' servant-leaders celebrate daily the basic values of building trusting relationships, having concern and belief in each other, fairness, honesty, responsible behavior, and a high standard of business ethics in all their work relationships.

Southwest Airlines

> *We are trying to find out what people are like at the center of their being—whether they have a sense of humor, whether they have a servant-leadership attitude and mentality, whether they have the capability of being leaders too. You hire somebody for one job, but we're looking for the capability and the leadership qualities that will enable them to rise through the ranks.*
>
> —Herb Kelleher, CEO, Southwest Airlines

When Southwest Airlines, a $5 billion airline transportation company, opened its doors in 1971, it touted its low-cost, on-time, no-frills, humorous approach to flying. Southwest's distinct strategy has helped the company to soar above its competitors, and to carve out three decades of prosperity—a highly unusual achievement for the airline industry. Southwest embodies the practical applications of servant-leadership in its daily operations. Front-line employees are empowered to solve customers' problems; pilots and executives load baggage and clean planes; and Culture Committees keep the spirit alive among its 30,000 employees.

Some Statistics on Southwest

- ○ Southwest regularly achieves the highest level of on-time arrivals, the lowest number of complaints, and the fewest lost-baggage claims per 1,000 passengers.
- ○ Southwest's fares are from 50 percent to 70 percent lower than competing fares in its market niche.
- ○ Southwest often deplanes and reloads its flights in 20 minutes or less.

- Southwest has about 40 percent more pilot and aircraft utilization compared to other airlines.

When I asked Libby Sartain, VP of People, and Ginger Hardage, VP of Public Relations, what Southwest's key strategy is, they responded that Southwest is employee-driven. "If you focus on your employees, they will treat the customers well. If you serve your internal customers (the employees) well, they will in turn serve the external customers well, which will also serve the shareholders well."

The overall culture at Southwest supports people. Whenever possible, the company hires for attitude and behavior rather than skills, and recognizes and rewards achievement. Leaders of Southwest treat people as they would want to be treated, value people as individuals, and promote from within.

Making a Difference in the Internal and External Community

Southwest strives to be the hometown carrier in all the cities it serves, and it focuses its efforts in volunteering within those communities in various ways:

- Fund-raising and providing meals for Ronald McDonald House. Since 1986, Southwest employees have raised and donated over $3.7 million.
- "Adopt a Pilot" program, which focuses on local schools. Pilots work with fourth- and fifth-grade children, teaching them geography, math, and science (making it fun, of course).
- Southwest encourages employees to embrace their favorite cause in the community where they live and to rally fellow workers to support that cause.
- Southwest Employee Catastrophic Fund—funded by employees for employees who have experienced a tragedy or disaster in their lives.

Southwest ensures that the internal community is being served well by requiring leaders to do "Days in the Field" once a quarter.

This means loading baggage, working at the reservation counter, or performing other everyday tasks. The leaders at Southwest believe you cannot serve your internal customers well if you are in an office day in and day out.

Maintaining the Famous Southwest Culture in the Midst of High Growth

Because more than 50 percent of the employees have been with Southwest for only five years or less, I asked Libby and Ginger how they continue to keep their strong culture intact. Each Southwest city has its own culture committee, which oversees everything from orienting new employees to the Southwest culture to organizing fund-raisers within the local community, to volunteer efforts. Southwest as a whole has "Spirit Parties" in various Southwest cities throughout the year. They usually take the shape of cookouts or parties that are not related to a special occasion or holiday. They offer an opportunity to celebrate with one other.

Keeping a High-Caliber Workforce

Researchers at the Harvard Business School believe the internal quality of the workplace is a major contributor to employee satisfaction. Internal quality is measured by employees' feelings and attitudes toward their job, the company, their colleagues, and how each area serves another area.

This is right in line with Harvard's Service-Profit Chain. In 1994, *Harvard Business Review* (March–April) published "Putting the Service Profit Chain to Work," an article that focused on several highly successful service-oriented companies, including Southwest Airlines. The service-profit chain establishes relationships among employee satisfaction, customer loyalty, productivity, and profitability. The researchers found:

○ Employee satisfaction originates primarily from high-quality support services and policies that enable employees to deliver results to the customers.

○ Customer satisfaction is largely influenced by the value of services provided to customers.

○ Loyalty is a direct result of customer satisfaction.

○ Profit and growth are stimulated primarily by customer loyalty.

The bottom line is that satisfied, loyal, and productive employees create value. Southwest seems to have taken notice of the service-profit chain by making employee satisfaction its first priority. In most service jobs, the real cost of turnover is the loss of productivity and decreased customer satisfaction. In some of Southwest's locations, satisfaction levels are so high that turnover rates are as low as 5 percent.

Synovus Financial Corporation

Great leaders are responsible for creating work
environments in which people care about each other,
share pride in a common goal, and celebrate the successes
of all. For this atmosphere to flourish, we have to realize
that, though we can't change everyone around us, we can
change ourselves, and make a difference.

—Jim Blanchard, Chairman and CEO,
Synovus Financial Corporation

Based in Columbus, Georgia, Synovus Financial Corporation is a multifinancial services company with over $13.7 billion in assets. The Synovus family of companies includes 39 community banks in Georgia, Alabama, Florida, and South Carolina, and *pointpathbank,* an online financial center for engaged and newlywed couples; an ownership of over 80 percent of Total System Services, Inc., one of the world's leading processors of payment transactions, servicing over 182 million cardholder accounts; DotsConnect, a wholly owned subsidiary of Total System Services, Inc., specializing in e-payment exchange; Synovus Wealth Management, for brokerage, trust, and insurance services; Synovus Leasing Services; and Synovus Mortgage Corporation.

Synovus puts people first. The company seeks to deliver superior customer service, to practice conservative financial policies, and to treat people with courtesy and respect. Its 11,000 Team Members (Synovus's preferred term for "employees") say their corporate ethic is a "culture of the heart," where the work and spirituality of employees are encouraged and celebrated. The leaders of Synovus believe in servant-leadership, community-building, and promoting the growth and well-being of the firm's associates.

A Noble Calling or a Great Business Strategy?

Jim Blanchard, Chairman and CEO of Synovus, is convinced that a business can be both successful and moral. Blanchard has stated that treating employees with dignity and respect is not a means to an end, but an end in itself. It is "a noble calling . . . as well as a great business strategy."

Synovus is largely organized around its shared values rather than around corporate policies. In a talk to business leaders at Emory University, Blanchard explained how shareholder value could not be improved by focusing solely on shareholder value. It can only be improved by tending to the heart—the people—of a business. Tending to the heart for Blanchard, and for Synovus, means:

- ○ Communicating to each team member his or her intrinsic worth.
- ○ Offering team members the opportunity to make a difference.
- ○ Providing team members with the chance to be part of a winning team.

To convey this "Culture of the Heart," Synovus created the Leadership Institute at Synovus, which offers leaders weeks of intensive training sessions each year. The sessions focus on various management practices, such as servant-leadership, systems thinking, personal development, teamwork, conflict resolution, and strategic leadership planning.

Blanchard believes that servant-leadership and keeping a servant's heart of humility are essential for those training for top-level positions. The greatest barrier to having a successful business and a great place to work is arrogance. Arrogance violates the Synovus values chain; it also makes for poor business strategy.

Making a Difference in Local and National Communities

Everything Synovus does for the community falls under the banner of REACH: Recognizing and Encouraging an Atmosphere of Community and of Hope. Some ongoing efforts include:

○ Working extensively, on local and national levels, with Habitat for Humanity, United Way, and the Boys and Girls Clubs of America.

○ Hosting Olympic athletes. In 1996, athletes were taken to schools and visited classrooms to teach children how they too can be winners and leaders.

○ Participating in The Great Gift Exchange, which involves team members in an internal Christmas gift exchange and in donation of toys or canned goods to local distribution agencies throughout the community. Over 12,000 gifts were distributed in 2000.

The Internal Community

○ Synovus offers adoption assistance to team members wishing to begin a family through adoption.

○ Family Education Leave allows 20 hours of paid time off per year to attend special events for children or grandchildren— soccer games, plays, teacher meetings, and other school activities.

○ Synovus provides a stock purchase program in which the company contributes 50 cents for every dollar a team member contributes.

Synovus, Southwest Airlines, and TDIndustries have taken the application of servant-leadership to a higher level. They have created new benchmarks with their intent to maintain high employee and customer satisfaction levels, quality products, and services *along with* being profitable companies.

The Container Store (First on the 2001 "100 Best" List)

In 1978, cofounders Garrett Boone, CEO, and Kip Tindell, President, opened up The Container Store, a retail store devoted entirely to storage and organizing. Based in Dallas, Texas, this retail operation has a unique corporate culture that empowers employees to use their own intuition and creativity to solve problems. The Container Store prides itself on selling service, and its customers do receive unparalleled, knowledgeable service. The employees have incredible business literacy; from cashier to manager, they are expected to know or find the answer to any Container Store question posed to them.

The Container Store's approach has cultivated fierce loyalty through its training and other employee programs. The average retail industry turnover approaches 100 percent or more annually. With its emphasis on a values-based culture, the Container Store's turnover is less than 10 percent. In addition to hundreds of hours of training, and great benefits, Container Store employees receive wages higher than the industry average, a 40 percent merchandise discount, and encouragement to build a future within the company. Communication abounds. Everything, from daily sales information to company goals and expansion plans, is shared with all employees.

The hiring process is a critical link in the strength of the Container Store chain. Elizabeth Barrett, Director of Human Resources, is steadfast in her hiring practices. With customer service as Container Store's core competency, she hires people who are highly self-motivated, have great attitudes, and are team-oriented. She sometimes takes as long as three months to find just the right person for a position. Her persistence has paid off. Retail sales have increased at an average of 20 to 25 percent a year. In 1999, sales were $194 million, and sales were projected to reach $287 million by 2001.

The Container Store also takes care of its internal and external community. From generous community outreach programs to Fun

Committee activities and to creative growth and interaction between employees, Container Store's spirit, pride, and camaraderie are evident.

AFLAC

A Fortune 500 Company, AFLAC (American Family Life Assurance Company) was sixty-first on the 2001 "100 Best" list. Founded in 1955, it is the principal subsidiary of AFLAC Incorporated, an international holding company. President and CEO Daniel P. Amos has seen the company become the leading provider of supplemental insurance sold at the work site in the United States, and the largest foreign insurer in Japan, where it insures over 40 million people located worldwide. Headquartered in Columbus, Georgia, AFLAC's annual revenues top more than $9 billion, and its assets total nearly $40 billion. In addition to being named on the "100 Best" list, AFLAC has been ranked, two years in a row, as the number-one insurance company to work for.

AFLAC's family-friendly corporate culture blends sound business and customer service practices with quality employee benefits. It provides an enriching and rewarding workplace for its employees. One of the more unique benefits AFLAC offers to its employees is an on-site childcare center that accommodates nearly 300 children and grandchildren of employees. It also offers all employees stock options, which, at this writing, had appreciated 52 percent since 1998. Its caring for the community is evident by the many ways AFLAC and its employees enthusiastically assist in making the community an even better place to be. What seems to be most evident in all these organizations is that loyalty, superb leadership, and a serving-others attitude are elements that have allowed these outstanding companies to flourish.

The Key: Keeping a Good Workforce

By the year 2008, there will be an estimated 161 million jobs for 155 million workers. This means that keeping good people will be more important than ever. The new economics dictates that customers and employees will need to be the center of management concern, or these same customers and employees will find work and products elsewhere. The research at Harvard (mentioned earlier) shows that satisfied, loyal, and productive employees create value by keeping the customer loyal, which tends to create a healthier bottom line. Keeping good employees pays off.

It is also important to be able to measure and manage the drivers of employee and customer satisfaction, in order to identify and close the dissatisfaction gaps. Discovery of these gaps provides the starting point for fostering deep change through practicing servant-leadership.

Is Servant-Leadership Right for Your Organization?

> *Traditionalists have long argued that business's only*
> *social obligation is to maximize profit. The new social*
> *contract between business and society inverts that principle:*
> *In the new century, companies will grow their profits*
> *only by embracing their new role as the engine of positive*
> *social and environmental change.*

—Bennett Daviss, author and journalist

TDIndustries and the other companies highlighted here try to attain a balance within several areas: internal service quality (how to serve employees and how they treat each other), external service quality (how to serve customers, purveyors, community, etc.), profit, and growth. You need to ask yourself: Are we committed to becoming a servant-led organization and everything that goes along with this decision, ultimately making systemic changes in the way we currently operate?

Some of these changes may include compensation changes to encourage and reward a servant attitude and teamwork and discourage focusing on competition and each-person-out-for-himself/herself attitudes. Perks may need to change, to reflect more balance between work and family; concern for the community may take on a new focus through the company's modeling this change and encouraging employees to volunteer in community development projects. A company may also need to look at the way it develops, designs, sells, and markets a product in order to become more service-oriented to the customer. These and issues such as quality initiatives and strategic planning are only some of the changes that would need to be made to create an integrated service experience within the organization.

At first glance, servant-leadership seems like an easy concept. The simplified version is "Be nice to your employees and customers and they will be happy, and the money will come in." But servant-leadership is much more than a feel-good concept; it is an integrated way of serving all people involved within an organization. It takes a good deal of risk-taking and tenacity, and a high degree of trust, to make the changes that will foster a servant-led organization.

Many believe it is worth making the change. Going back to Robert Levering's research, the advantages of being a great place to work include higher productivity, lower turnover and retention costs, higher-quality products and services, more highly qualified employees, and more innovation.

For those who are already predisposed to embrace the servant-leadership concept—and being predisposed is nearly a prerequisite in making this concept viable—you have nothing to lose and everything to gain.

Dr. Ann McGee-Cooper is internationally recognized for her pace-setting work as a brain engineer. Her Dallas-based consulting firm, Ann McGee-Cooper and Associates, Inc., has worked with a wide range of clients, including TXU, Fluor Daniel, AT&T, TDIndustries, and Southwest Airlines. Dr. McGee-Cooper is the author or coauthor of several books, including *Time Management for Unmanageable People,* and *You Don't Have to Go Home from Work Exhausted!*

Duane Trammell is managing partner of Ann McGee-Cooper and Associates, Inc., and coauthor of the two books listed above. Before becoming a popular business facilitator and conference leader, he served as a classroom teacher and was the recipient of the Dallas Teacher of the Year Award and the Ross Perot Award for Excellence in Teaching.

Ann McGee-Cooper and Duane Trammell contrast the traditional hero-as-leader model—the champion who constantly comes to the rescue, putting out fires and saving the company—with the servant-as-leader model. Using systems-thinking and learning organizations' perspectives, they present a good case for developing servant-leadership in an organization in order to fully tap the brain power and joy that traditional leadership models miss. Ann McGee-Cooper is a scheduled keynote speaker at the Greenleaf Center's 2002 annual international conference.

11

FROM HERO-AS-LEADER TO
SERVANT-AS-LEADER

Ann McGee-Cooper and Duane Trammell

AN ORGANIZATIONAL AND SPIRITUAL awakening is currently taking place. On the cusp of the new millennium, more and more people are seeking deeper meaning in their work beyond just financial rewards and prestige. The desire to make a difference, to support a worthwhile vision, and to leave the planet better than we found it, all contribute to this new urge. Whom we choose to follow, how we lead, and how we come together to address the accelerating change are also shifting.

Organizations must pay attention to these transitions because of (1) the radical reduction in the numbers of workers currently available for jobs and (2) the movement into our working ranks of a new generation of employees with totally different values and expectations. If companies want to attract and keep top talent, the old ways of recruiting, rewarding, and leading won't get them there. A different kind of leadership is required for the future.

Traditional Leadership Models

What are the roots of the leadership models that brought us to this point in organizational development? During the Industrial Revolution, hierarchies were the norm. At that time, businesses depended on the completion of many repetitive tasks in the most efficient way possible. To that end, factories, railroads, mines, and other companies followed a top-down view of leadership in which those at the top gathered the information, made the decisions, and controlled the power. Those at the bottom—the "hired hands"—were rewarded for conformity and unquestioning obedience. In addition, business moved much more slowly than it does today.

Our approach to preparing new leaders over the last 50 years has sprung from these roots. Leadership training in MBA courses has been based on the case-study method, through which learners study patterns of how others solved their business problems. The assumption has been that if you learn enough about the successful case studies, you will be prepared as a leader—you will be able to go forth, match your new challenges to the case studies of the past, and superimpose a similar solution on the problems of today.

Yet change is accelerating, and we are now in a time when many companies view a traditional education as more of a negative than a positive. They even consider an MBA a detriment, because graduates must *unlearn* their reliance on the past in order to see new, more complex patterns emerging. Some observers have said that this shift has turned the pyramid of power on its head.

The Beginnings of Servant-Leadership

Servant-leadership is one model that can help turn traditional notions of leadership and organizational structure upside-down. Robert K. Greenleaf came up with the term "servant-leadership" after reading *The Journey to the East* by Hermann Hesse. In this story, Leo, a cheerful, nurturing servant, supports a group of travelers on a long and difficult journey. His sustaining spirit helps keep the group's purpose clear and morale high until, one day, Leo disappears. Soon after, the travelers disperse. Years later, the storyteller comes upon a spiritual order and discovers that Leo is actually the group's highly respected titular head. Yet, by serving the travelers rather than trying to instruct them, he had helped ensure their survival and bolstered their sense of shared commitment. This story gave Greenleaf insight into a new way to perceive leadership.

Greenleaf was reading this book because he was helping university leaders deal with the student unrest of the 1970s, a challenge unlike any they had faced before. In the spirit of trying to understand the roots of the conflict, Greenleaf put himself in the students' shoes and began to study what interested them. It was from this reflection that the term "servant-leadership" first came to him. To Greenleaf, the phrase represented a transformation in the meaning of leadership.

Servant-leadership stands in sharp contrast to the typical American definition of the leader as a stand-alone hero, usually white and male. As a result of this false picture of what defines a leader, we celebrate and reward the wrong things. In movies, for example, we all love to see the "good guys" take on the "bad guys" and win. The blockbuster *Lethal Weapon* movies are a take-off on this myth and represent a metaphor for many of our organizations. Our movie "heroes" (or leaders) act quickly and decisively, blowing up buildings and wrecking cars and planes in high-drama chases. Although they always win (annihilating or capturing the bad guys), they leave behind a trail of blood and destruction.

This appetite for high drama can fool us into believing that we can depend on one or two "super people" to solve our organizational crises. Even in impressive corporate turnarounds, we tend to look for the hero who single-handedly "saved the day." We long for a "savior" to fix the messes that we all have had a part in creating. But this myth causes us to lose sight of all those in the background who provided valuable support to the single hero.

Seeing the leader as servant, however, puts the emphasis on very different qualities. Servant-leadership is not about a personal quest for power, prestige, or material rewards. Instead, from this perspective, leadership begins with a true motivation to serve others. Rather than controlling or wielding power, the servant-leader works to build a solid foundation of shared goals by (1) listening deeply to understand the needs and concerns of others; (2) working thoughtfully to help build a creative consensus; and (3) honoring the paradox of polarized parties and working to create "third right answers" that rise above the compromise of "we/they" negotiations. The focus of servant-leadership is on sharing information, building a common vision, self-management, high levels of interdependence, learning from mistakes, encouraging creative input from every team member, and questioning present assumptions and mental models.

How Servant-Leadership Serves Organizations

Servant-leadership is a powerful methodology for organizational learning because it offers new ways to capitalize on the knowledge and wisdom of all employees, not just those "at the top." Through this different form of leadership, big-picture information and business strategies are shared broadly throughout the company. By understanding basic assumptions and background information on issues or decisions, everyone can add something of value to the discussion because everyone possesses the basic tools needed to make meaningful contributions. Such tools and information are traditionally reserved for upper management, but sharing them brings deeper meaning to each job and empowers each person to participate more in effective decision making and creative problem solving. Individuals thus grow from being mere hired hands into having fully engaged minds and hearts.

This approach constitutes true empowerment, which significantly increases job satisfaction and engages far more brain power from each employee. It also eliminates the "That's not my job" syndrome, as each person, seeing the impact he or she has on the whole, becomes eager to do whatever it takes to achieve the collective vision. Servant-leadership therefore challenges some basic terms in our management vocabulary; expressions such as "subordinates," "my people," "staff" (versus "line"), "overhead" (referring to people), "direct reports," "manpower," all become less accurate or useful. Even phrases such as "driving decision-making down into the ranks" betray a deep misunderstanding of the concept of empowerment. Do we believe that those below are resistant to change or less intelligent than others? Why must we *drive* or *push* decisions down? Something vital is missing from this way of thinking—deep respect and mentoring, a desire to lift others to their fullest potential, and the humility to understand that the work of one person can rarely match that of an aligned team.

A New Kind of Leadership

Traditional Boss	Servant as Leader
Motivated by personal drive to achieve.	Motivated by desire to serve others.
Highly competitive; independent mindset; seeks to receive personal credit for achievement.	Highly collaborative and interdependent; gives credit to others generously.
Understands internal politics and uses them to win personally.	Sensitive to what motivates others and empowers all to win with shared goals and vision.
Focuses on fast action. Complains about long meetings and about others' being too slow.	Focuses on gaining understanding, input, buy-in from all parties.
Relies on facts, logic, proof.	Uses intuition and foresight to balance facts, logic, proof.
Controls information in order to maintain power.	Shares big-picture information generously.

(continued)

A New Kind of Leadership *(Continued)*

Traditional Boss	Servant as Leader
Spends more time telling, giving orders. Sees too much listening or coaching as inefficient.	Listens deeply and respectfully to others, especially to those who disagree.
Feels that personal value comes from individual talents.	Feels that personal value comes from mentoring and working collaboratively with others.
Sees network of supporters as power base and perks and titles as a signal to others.	Develops trust across a network of constituencies; breaks down hierarchy.
Eager to speak first; feels his/her ideas are more important; often dominates or intimidates opponents.	Most likely to listen first; values others' input.
Uses personal power and intimidation to leverage what he/she wants.	Uses personal trust and respect to build bridges and do what's best for the "whole."
Accountability is more often about who is to blame.	Accountability is about making it safe to learn from mistakes.
Uses humor to control others.	Uses humor to lift others up and make it safe to learn from mistakes.

Phil Jackson, former coach of the world champion Chicago Bulls basketball team [and now coach of the world champion Los Angeles Lakers], described this notion well in his book *Sacred Hoops.* He wrote: "Good teams become great ones when the members trust each other enough to surrender the 'me' for the 'we.' As [retired professional basketball player] Bill Cartwright puts it: 'A great basketball team will have trust. I've seen teams in this league where the players won't pass to a guy because they don't think he is going to catch the ball. But a great basketball team will throw the ball to everyone. If a guy drops it or bobbles it out of bounds, the next time they'll throw it to him again. And because of their confidence in him, he will have confidence. That's how you grow.' " Phil Jackson drew much of the inspiration for his style of coaching—which is clearly servant-leadership—from Zen, Christianity, and the Native American tradition. He created a sacred space for the team to gather, bond, process, and learn from mistakes.

A servant-leader is also keenly aware of a much wider circle of stakeholders than just those internal to the organization. Ray Anderson, chairman and CEO of Interface, one of the largest international commercial carpet wholesalers, has challenged his company to join him in leading what he calls the "second Industrial Revolution." He defines this new paradigm as one that finds sustainable ways to do business that respect the finiteness of natural resources. His vision, supported by his valued employees, is to never again sell a square yard of carpet. Instead, they seek to lease carpeting and then find ways to achieve 100 percent recycling.

A servant-leader thus does not duck behind the letter of the law but asks, "What is the right thing for us to do to best serve *all* stakeholders?" He or she defines profit beyond financial gain to include meaningful work, environmental responsibility, and quality of life for all involved. To quote Robert Greenleaf, "The best test, and difficult to administer, is: Do those served grow as persons; do they, while being served, become healthier, wiser, freer, more autonomous, more likely themselves to become servants? And, what is the effect on the least privileged in society; will each benefit, or at least not be further deprived?"

Supervisors often believe that they don't have time to make a long-term investment in people. When an individual's primary focus is on doing everything faster, he or she becomes addicted to the constant rush of adrenaline. To feed this craving, the person neglects proactive tasks such as coaching, mentoring, planning ahead, and quiet reflection to learn from mistakes. Instead, the brain sees only more *problems*—reasons to stay reactive and highly charged. Servant-leaders spend far less time in crisis management or fire fighting than do traditional managers. Instead, they use crises as opportunities to coach others and collectively learn from mistakes.

The Power of Internal Motivation and Paradox

So what does it take to become a servant-leader? The most important quality is a deep, internal drive to contribute to a collective result or vision. Very often, a servant-leader purposely refuses to accept the perks of the position and takes a relatively low salary because another shared goal may have more value. For example, Southwest Airlines (SWA) chairman Herb Kelleher has long been referred to as the most underpaid CEO in the industry. Herb was the first to work without pay when SWA faced a serious financial threat. In asking the pilots' union to agree to freeze their wages for five years in exchange for stock options, he showed his commitment by freezing his own wages as well.

Big salaries and attractive perks are clearly not the main motivators for Southwest's leadership team; the company's top leaders are paid well below the industry average. Rather, they stay because they are making history together. Their vision is a noble one—to provide meaningful careers to their employees, and the freedom to fly to many Americans who otherwise could not afford the convenience of air travel. SWA's leaders love to take on major competitors and win. Beyond that, each finds fulfillment in developing talent all around him or her. Servant-leadership has become a core way of being within Southwest Airlines.

A second quality of servant-leaders is an awareness of paradox. Paradox involves two aspects: the understanding that there is usually another side to every story, and the fact that most situations contain an opposite and balancing truth (see "The Structure of Paradox: Managing Interdependent Opposites," by Philip Ramsey, *The Systems Thinker,* Volume 8, Number 9). Here are some of the paradoxes that servant-leadership illuminates:

- We can lead more effectively by serving others.
- We can arrive at better answers by learning to ask deeper questions and by involving more people in the process.
- We can build strength and unity by valuing differences.

○ We can improve quality by making mistakes, as long as we also create a safe environment in which we can learn from experience.

○ Fewer words (such as a brief story or metaphor) can provide greater understanding than a long speech. A servant-leader knows to delve into what is *not* being said or what is being overlooked, especially when solutions come too quickly or with too easy a consensus.

A Time for Transformation

We are moving away from a time when a strong hierarchy worked for our organizations. In the past, we gauged results in a far more limited way than we do today—financial and other material gain, power, and prestige were viewed as true measures of success. Other, more complex measures, such as the impact of our businesses on society, families, and the environment, have not been part of our accounting systems. Yet now, as we move into the Information Age and a new millennium, we've come to recognize the limitations of the traditional "bottom line."

A servant-leadership approach can help us overcome these limitations and accomplish a true and lasting transformation within our organizations. To be sure, as we envision the many peaks and valleys before us in undertaking this journey, we sometimes may feel that we are alone. But we are not alone—many others are headed in the same direction. For instance, in *Fortune* magazine's (1999) listing of the "100 Best Companies to Work For in America," three of the top four follow the principles of servant-leadership: Synovus Financial (#1), TDIndustries (#2), and Southwest Airlines (#4). In addition to providing a nurturing and inspiring work environment, each of these businesses is recognized as a leader in its industry.

On a personal level, as many of us begin to come to terms with our own mortality, our desire to leave a legacy grows. "What can I contribute that will continue long after I am gone?" Some yearn to have their names emblazoned on a building or some other form of ego recognition. Servant-leaders find fulfillment in the deeper joy of lifting others to new levels of possibility, an outcome that goes far beyond what one person could accomplish alone. The magical synergy that results when egos are put aside, vision is shared, and a true learning organization takes root is something that brings incredible joy, satisfaction, and results to the participants and their organizations. For, as Margaret Mead put it, "Never doubt the power of a small group of committed individuals to change the world. Indeed, it is the only thing that ever has." The true heroes of the new millennium will be servant-leaders, quietly working out of the spotlight to transform our world.

Practicing Servant-Leadership

1. *Listen without Judgment.* When a team member comes to you with a concern, listen first to understand. Listen for feelings as well as for facts. Before giving advice or solutions, repeat back what you thought you heard, and state your understanding of the person's feelings. Then ask how you can help. Did the individual just need a sounding board, or would he or she like you to help brainstorm solutions?

2. *Be Authentic.* Admit mistakes openly. At the end of meetings, discuss what went well during the week and what needs to change. Be open and accountable to others for your role in the things that weren't successful.

3. *Build Community.* Show appreciation to those who work with you. A handwritten thank-you note for a job well done means a lot. Also, find ways to thank team members for everyday, routine work that is often taken for granted.

4. *Share Power.* Ask those you supervise or team with: "What decisions am I making or actions am I taking that could be improved if I had more information or input from the

team?" Plan to incorporate this feedback into your decision-making process.

5. *Develop People.* Take time each week to develop others to grow into higher levels of leadership. Give them opportunities to attend meetings that they would not usually be invited to. Find projects that you can co-lead, and coach the others as you work together.

James D. Showkeir is a partner in Henning-Showkeir and serves as a Greenleaf Center adjunct facilitator. He brings to his work more than 25 years of experience in education and organization development. Professionally, he gained experience at the Buick/UAW Employee Development Center, EDS, TRW, and Ford Motor Company, in various management and organization development positions. He served as president of the Autism Society of Michigan and was Dean of the School for Managing and Leading Change, which provides in-depth, long-term learning experiences where distributing power is the basis for managing, organizing, and structuring successful businesses.

In this essay, Jamie Showkeir makes a compelling business case for servant-leadership. He says herein: "While I am all for making the world a kinder and gentler place, I am also not so naïve as to think that anything in business will get a fair hearing without dealing with the marketplace issues." The necessity for distributing power and accountability is thoroughly examined, and this argument is presented with the conviction that when fully informed, businesspeople will choose the better way.

12

THE BUSINESS CASE FOR SERVANT-LEADERSHIP

James D. Showkeir

"The Servant-Leader is servant first—as Leo was portrayed.
It begins with the natural feeling that one wants to serve first.
Then conscious choice brings one to aspire to lead."

"The best test, and difficult to administer, is: Do those served
grow as persons? Do they, while being served, become healthier,
wiser, freer, more autonomous, more likely themselves to become
servants? And, what is the effect on the least privileged in society;
will they benefit, or, at least, not be further deprived?"

—*Servant-Leadership*, Robert Greenleaf, 1977

CENTRAL TO SERVANT-LEADERSHIP is power and its use. Robert Greenleaf writes about power and the difference between persuasive power and coercive power. *Persuasive power* creates opportunities and alternatives so individuals can choose and build autonomy. *Coercive power* is used to get people to travel a predetermined path. The servant-leader practices persuasive power and walks a fine line in most people's minds. This is a wise and useful insight, but in practice it is, for many, a bit like trying to grab a handful of smoke.

153

Organizational power, on the other hand, is concrete. In his book, *The Future of Staff Groups,* Joel Henning defined organizational power as consisting of five elements, all of which are necessary to impact the marketplace:

1. *Accountability*—choosing personal responsibility for the success of the whole organization.

2. *Business literacy*—knowing the financial and market picture of the organization and how each unit contributes to it.

3. *Choice*—granting exceptions and making promises on behalf of the organization.

4. *Competence*—learning, performing, and managing skills in the core processes.

5. *Access to resources*—having access to the time, people, money, equipment, and support needed to carry out the requirements of the business.

Those who possess greater degrees of these elements are more powerful than those who possess lesser degrees. "Management," in most organizations, describes a class of people who are more powerful because they possess greater degrees of organizational power.

If one is going to meet the "best test" for servant-leadership, then it is essential to actively and intentionally distribute organizational power. Distributing organizational power will satisfy all of the requirements of the test and build the capacity of the business for attaining greater marketplace results. It will also meet with resistance from others in management, as well as from those doing the work. Distributing organizational power, at times, may seem more like grabbing a handful of hornets than smoke—at least you know you have hold of something!

Distributing organizational power requires focusing attention on the culture, management practices, and architecture of the organization. It also requires a solid business argument that reconciles the attainment of unequivocal business results (profit, market share, and so on) with the need and longing for individual meaning and purpose at work. Neither is sufficient—both are necessary for success.

Much of the writing on servant-leadership to date has centered on personal traits, concepts, and techniques. Most of the resistance

I hear is that servant-leadership is too soft and touchy-feely; it does not have enough business focus; it has too many religious overtones; it is not for companies under financial strain; or it is good when times are good, but, under stress, "business as usual" prevails. This indicates a serious misunderstanding of the connection between servant-leadership and attaining business results.

While I am all for making the world a kinder and gentler place, I am also not so naïve as to think that anything in business will get a fair hearing without dealing with the marketplace issues. The aim here is to begin making the business case for servant-leadership, in the hope that others will be attracted by it and will find ways to extend its use and practice.

The Marketplace and Building Organizational Capacity

The days of stability in the marketplace have disappeared, regardless of the organization. Increased domestic and global competition, the information explosion, the demand for long-term financial growth measured quarterly, cross-cultural interdependencies, and the integration of complex and rapidly changing technologies with constantly changing lifestyles all contribute to the complexity. As organizations work to create greater possibilities for customers in this environment, they must be able to manage four key business demands:

1. Being profitable (creating greater value; cutting costs; and so on).
2. Improving quality and reliability.
3. Reducing response and cycle time.
4. Providing unique and understanding responses to customers and the market.

Traditionally, these demands are managed one at a time or are traded off one against the other. For example, when quality initiatives were beginning, there was a great deal of conversation about the hit profitability would take because of the expense. There is some truth to this, but framing the issue this way shows the trade-off mentality. In today's marketplace, this will not work. Improving these demands must be done *concurrently*—all four demands must be satisfied at the same time. If a business cannot learn to deal with these demands concurrently, its future prosperity—even its survival—is at stake. The marketplace will decide.

Successful organizations also develop the ability to *continuously reinvent* themselves as frequently as the marketplace changes. They create conditions that are *derived from and through* the way they operate. The organization must possess the ability to:

1. Rapidly develop, and continuously integrate, new learning and knowledge to serve the business and the marketplace.

2. Create circumstances within, where people are passionate about the business and choose accountability for its success.

3. Act quickly and smartly on the demands of the marketplace.

Reinvention is seen as part of the "real work" and is integrated into it.

The *capacity* of the organization is the extent to which it can concurrently manage the business demands (quality, profitability, cycle time, and unique response). Simply put, an organization with a high capacity does a superior job with the concurrent management of the demands; an organization with a low capacity does not. High capacity uses all the human, technical, and management capability available to the business. Running the business, serving the marketplace, *and* building capacity are all part of the game.

Organizational power directly impacts capacity. How business literacy, choice, resources, competence, and accountability are dealt with either builds or detracts from capacity. The use of organizational power starts with a set of beliefs and intentions that are manifest in methods, practices, policies, and structure. Also, the methods of deliberation and the content of conversations support the beliefs and intentions and yield a clear understanding of what is occurring. By examining the methods and intentions, the servant-leader can assess the value of distributing organizational power.

Traditional Organizations Consolidate Power

Historically, we have intentionally separated the managing from the doing of the work. When Frederick Taylor determined that planning should be separated from the shop floor, the die was cast for the next hundred years. The consolidation of organizational power had its beginning. We have purposefully continued constructing organizations to ensure and refine this thinking and its innate compliance. Within our organizations, we live out these credos and values:

- ○ Consistency.
- ○ Alignment.
- ○ Predictability.
- ○ Playing it safe.
- ○ Holding others accountable.
- ○ Denying self-expression.
- ○ Keeping relationships instrumental.
- ○ "No surprises, please."
- ○ "Management is a class of people."
- ○ "Change is an engineering task."

Culturally, from this point of view, each of us exchanges our freedom, and our accountability to contribute, for the unfulfillable wish that the organization will take care of us and provide safety. We are all betting that enforcement of compliance will lead to success. The conversations we engage in are parent/child. This leads to "holding others accountable," to ensure compliance. Business literacy and information are distributed on a "need-to-know" basis. Difficult news, layoffs, business downturns, and so on, are kept secret as long as possible and are softened so people will not get too anxious or upset. Individuals meet in small groups and decide how to tell others the results of their meeting so the information can be "communicated" in the right way. In short, we treat each other as if we were adversaries rather than partners.

The policies, procedures, and management practices we design reinforce and support parent/child relationships, control, and compliance. Performance appraisals are still done by the boss. Even 360-degree reviews are done with the intent and practice of holding *others* accountable. Management training is for managers. Budgeting, goal setting, resolving conflict, granting exceptions to customers, levels of signature authority, and many other practices are controlled tightly by policies that send a clear message about who is in charge and responsible. Generally the answer is: "Not I."

Architecturally, staff groups enforce policy and provide oversight, jobs are pieces of entire processes, and people are grouped by function and role and are trained for job-specific requirements—all because this approach is easier to monitor and control. We even pay more to those who watch and monitor—a true indication of the meaning we attach to holding others accountable.

All this together sends one clear message about our intentions regarding organizational power: It is *consolidated* in the hands of a few specialists, managers, and executives. The traditional belief is that, for the organization to succeed, organizational power should be entrusted to only a few at the top of the organization. The rest of the organization should comply with their directions and suffer the bureaucracy, even if it inhibits serving the customers. Limited business literacy, choice, authority, accountability, and resources mean that unit members must comply with circumstances that often do not make sense to them and have little to do with serving the customer and doing the work. We continue to believe that what Taylor created is good for business and will lead to success. If we did not, we would change more readily, more drastically, and more rapidly. It seems clear that this thinking and practice do not support the best test for servant-leadership.

Compliance is not commitment. Compliance does not create passion. Compliance does not make individuals wiser. Compliance does not encourage choosing accountability. Compliance does not lead to creativity, flexibility, differentiation, and speed. Compliance does not create meaning and purpose. Compliance does not breed freedom. Meaning, purpose, and freedom ensue from struggle, risk, and engagement; compliance cuts us away from these. If, in fact, the business does not need any of these things, then compliance is a reasonable answer. Servant-leadership is much more than putting a compassionate face on compliance.

Servant-Led Organizations Distribute Power

Servant-leadership requires a revolution in thinking, intentions, and practices applied first to oneself. Essential to this revolution is:

- Changing the underlying assumptions we hold about human capability and individual contribution.
- Changing our beliefs and expectations regarding organizing human effort.
- Changing how we value individual contribution.
- Changing how we see those who populate our organizations.
- Changing our beliefs about what and who is responsible for morale and motivation.

In rethinking intentions, servant-leaders must value different things. Values that support a new intention are:

- Innovation.
- Diversity of thought.
- Individual commitment.
- Self-managing.
- Freedom and accountability for service.
- Teaching and learning as central issues.
- Embracing risk.
- Staying personal.
- Courage.

Here, choosing personal accountability to the whole business is exchanged for freedom of choice in serving the marketplace. This means choosing to be accountable and responsible for the entire business, embracing the incumbent risks, and being free to choose how to serve. These intentions place the bet that individuals will choose for accountability and responsibility for serving the business when given the opportunity, literacy, and support. Placing this bet means we choose to believe that this will lead to success. It means making a leap of faith. It means placing faith in a new system for success, and forsaking our faith in a traditional system that has out-lived its usefulness and continues to disappoint us. Our faith in the traditional system of compliance is so strong that we ignore or jus-tify its failures and even blame individuals for its shortcomings.

Some major cultural differences exist. With servant-leadership, business literacy and information are accessible to all. There are no secrets about the business, marketplace, financials, and similar in-formation. People tell each other the truth about the business, even when it is difficult. Conversations are adult/adult and recognize that adults lead complex lives and are capable of facing difficulty with re-solve and optimism. Cynicism, helplessness, and withholding com-mitment are recognized as choices and are confronted as such. People speak with the voice of the business, not the voice of their expertise. Deliberations occur in larger groups, across organizational bound-aries and hierarchies. Those who do the work have a critical and equal voice.

Policies, management practices, and procedures are redefined to support these intentions. Performance management becomes the re-sponsibility of the individual. Each person schedules, invites, and manages participation and input into his or her own appraisals. Bud-geting and goal setting become inclusive processes and cut across traditional boundaries; allocations are accomplished for the good of the whole organization. Managing conflict is the responsibility of individuals and groups, and speaking with the voice of the business is the rule for resolution. Most of the existing management practices are candidates for reinvention because they were formulated and evolved with a completely different set of intentions in mind.

Architecturally, individuals are responsible for whole work processes. They organize the work in the way that best suits their marketplace and customers. Structure is designed to give *customers* the most complete and easy access that is possible. Staff groups be-come repositories of capacity-building expertise that is transferred to benefit their clients' business results. Reward systems are de-signed to support sharing in the risk and rewards, and some por-tion of everyone's pay is tied to marketplace success.

In today's marketplace, the major problem with the traditional system is that it consolidates organizational power in places that have the least marketplace and customer contact. *Those with the most contact are the least powerful.* When competition was not so stiff and things were not changing so rapidly, this made sense and worked. Today, organizations deal with complex marketplace situations that cut across the boundaries of the traditional organization. For example, assume an organization produces a wide variety and number of consumer goods that are manufactured in many different locations around the country. A major retail customer that uses hundreds of these products decides it wants single invoicing and integrated delivery of products. Resolving this situation requires great flexibility. A situation like this cannot be managed adequately from the top alone. Manufacturing, warehousing, distribution, accounting, and information systems must give a coordinated and unique response. The individuals doing the work must understand the business, the marketplace, and the financials if they are to make appropriate decisions that satisfy the customer *and* benefit the whole business. Organizations in which power is widely distributed are much more capable of delivering the necessary response.

Creating this type of organization through servant-leadership is not an easy task. It requires revolutionary thinking and evolutionary patience. The main reason for such an undertaking is: *The business demands it.* Innovation, diversity, flexibility, speed, differentiation, and quality are all necessities for survival today. These results cannot be delivered by an organization in which the rules for engagement are compliance-oriented. Organizations cannot afford any longer to have a few deciding while the masses wait. Distributing organizational power builds individual capacity. Building individual capacity creates greater organizational ability for concurrently managing the business demands.

Distributing organization power also greatly contributes to individuals' creating meaning and purpose at work, for themselves and others. Generally, people will not commit to and choose accountability for something they do not understand. Distributing business literacy creates understanding, and although understanding does not create commitment, it does create a clearer picture of the choices the individuals face. Some will choose not to commit, and that is fine— not everybody is on the same page at the same time now.

After the marketplace situation and the differences between the traditional strategy and what is possible are examined, a reasonable explanation must be made in support of such a significant change. Here are some factors worth remembering:

○ Customers have ever-increasing choice about products and services; our competition would love to have our customers.

○ Customers are no longer interested in "one size fits all"; they want a unique and understanding response.

○ The marketplace, customers, suppliers, and regulators come in contact with the organization primarily at its boundaries—not where the power is located.

○ Core workers have the most impact on the products and services.

○ Compliance will not result in commitment, personal accountability, flexibility, or speed.

If these factors are critical to an organization, they will raise questions for the individuals who work there. The questions deal directly with whether to continue consolidating organizational power or to begin distributing it. These four questions seem particularly important:

1. Does it make sense to continue trying harder with a system and beliefs that have basically outlived their usefulness?

2. Which way of believing and managing will support getting the greatest business intelligence at the point where it is needed most?

3. Which system of managing, organizing, and structuring provides the greatest opportunity for individuals to find the meaning that is necessary and sufficient for the organization to get superior results by all measures?

4. What am I waiting for? What am I afraid of? What is stopping me from pursuing a new way?

These questions push us to examine our view of people, human capacity, commitment, and ourselves. If I see others as unwilling or unable to choose accountability, then I will not see the value in distributing organizational power. On the other hand, if I see others more like I see myself—capable of and willing to make a contribution and to commit to something of value—then distributing power becomes far more attractive. It follows that I am the only one capable of changing how I see others; there is no doubt that faith is involved. Of course, when I begin to think of making this change, I am reminded of how often others have disappointed me and let me down. I also remember how often I have let others down—sometimes without even knowing it. I can begin to see how much alike we are. This is what makes servant-leadership so difficult. I must first find the courage to confront myself and change the person in the mirror. I must find compassion and goodwill for others and myself. I would much rather deal with the illusion of being able to change *you*.

Changing the Membership Requirements and Inviting Participation

In order to serve first, I must declare what I am serving and what I am trying to create. I do this to put myself out there and exhibit my own choice for accountability, not to enroll others. Making the business case for distributing organizational power provides the rationale for my declaration. Defining a cultural context in which I choose to engage is useful to those around me. Organizations have implicit and explicit membership requirements—things I abide by in order to be a part. Some are stated, like dress codes, codes of conduct, rules of operation, and the volumes written in the human resources manuals. Some are not stated. I deny self-expression or risk being labeled a nonteam player. I comply with those above or risk being insubordinate. I do not talk about how I feel for fear of being labeled as flaky and weak.

Beginning to think of membership requirements in terms of individual rights and responsibilities makes sense. Everyone has rights, and along with them come responsibilities. Keeping these rights and responsibilities simple and few adds clarity and helps engagement. For example, we could say that everyone has the right and responsibility to:

○ Embrace the marketplace risk and choose accountability to serve it and the business.

○ Be literate about the business, customer, market, and core work processes.

○ Create individual and shared meaning and identity.

○ Manage and do the work.

○ Learn and teach skills that serve the business.

○ Deal with his or her own issues of morale, motivation, commitment, and optimism.

○ Seek common ground in order to serve the whole organization.

○ Have a point of view and make it public.

○ Tell the truth with goodwill.

Simply conveying the new membership requirements is not enough, and trying to demand adherence only engenders compliance as the response. Instead, it is necessary to engage individuals and invite them to participate. Stating a strong and truthful business case for the change is necessary, but the message must be an invitation. Inviting others to join and engaging conversations about their choice explicitly honors that with which only they can deal—their choice and their free will. It also encourages them to wrestle with the difficult issues for themselves, and thus to give meaning to their involvement. Some will choose not to accept; leave them alone. For a commitment of "yes" to have meaning, "no" has to be a legitimate and acceptable option.

Dissent is highly undervalued in organizations. Of course, when culture, practices, and architecture are formed with compliance in mind, our beliefs about dissent are clear. Dissent represents our choice for freedom and individuality, which are considered detrimental to organizational effectiveness and efficiency. Consolidation of organizational power is the perfect remedy for this. Distributing power encourages freedom, creativity, flexibility, individuality, and the creation of widespread business intelligence—all of which are necessary in today's marketplace. Distributing organizational power encourages and gives value to dissent; and from dissent spring creative, superior answers to marketplace dilemmas.

For those who withhold their commitment, claim helplessness, or have little optimism that things will work out, I compassionately confront their stance for the *choice* it is. They are choosing how they view this change, and only they can change their view. Confronting their choice, standing firm with goodwill on my choice, and inviting them to examine their stance more closely over time is the best I can do. Getting on with my pursuit of distributing organizational power is as good as it gets. Trying to barter the commitment of others, or to sell them on the data, will not work in the long run. As soon as they experience disappointment again (and they will), they will feel free to withdraw because of the conditional nature of their commitment. They must choose optimism in the face of the certain disappointment—this is where commitment comes from. Also, it is useful to remember that I, too, am a cynic, a victim, and a bystander, so sometimes their voice speaks for me. We cannot create a culture of consent and commitment by forcing compliance—even to a more attractive set of values.

My wish here is to ground the best test for servant-leadership in building the capacity of the organization by making a business case. It matters not whether the organization is engaged in community service or for-profit commerce. The goal is the same: enabling those "being served, (to) become healthier, wiser, freer, more autonomous, more likely themselves to become servants." To do so requires distributing power. This requires change and evolution away from traditional business strategy.

Admittedly, it is difficult, but no individual or organization can create for its customers, clients, and constituents what it cannot create for itself. Meeting the best test means making others more powerful in order for them to be more autonomous and accountable for their own choices and future. If organizations are going to contribute to the greater possibilities of their markets, they must internally be able to increase the capability of everyone to concurrently manage the demands of the marketplace. They need to invite and engage participation, not demand compliance. Distributing organizational power concretely brings us to this end: it gives each of us—who are the pure essence of the organization—accountability and responsibility for serving the business. This leads to an organizational capacity for concurrently managing the business demands, attaining greater marketplace results, and creating the individual meaning we long for in our work.

John C. Bogle founded The Vanguard Group, Inc., in 1974, and served as CEO and senior chairman of the Board of The Vanguard Group and of each of its mutual funds until his recent retirement. The Vanguard Group, with current assets totaling more than $500 billion, is one of the two largest mutual fund organizations in the world. John Bogle is also the author of *Bogle on Mutual Funds: New Perspectives for the Intelligent Investor* and *John Bogle on Investing: The First 50 Years*.

This essay demonstrates the relevance of the servant-as-leader principle to the business world. The author shows how treating customers as human beings and serving them well go hand-in-hand with marketplace success for a major company, The Vanguard Group.

John Bogle was a keynote speaker at the Greenleaf Center's 1998 annual international conference.

13

ON THE RIGHT SIDE OF HISTORY

John C. Bogle

I WANT TO MIX SOME corporate history and some personal philosophy, and try to impart some sense of how the idealistic vision of the servant as leader, and of the leader as servant, can have—and has had—an impact on the pragmatic, dog-eat-dog competitive world of American business. I'm going to use as my example the burgeoning mutual fund industry—next to the Internet, I suppose, the fastest-growing industry in the United States—and The Vanguard Group, its fastest-growing major firm.

What is of interest, I think, is not our mere *success*—a word so elusive in its connotations that I use it here with considerable reluctance—but the fact that, whatever we have achieved, it has been by marching to a different drummer. Our unique corporate structure has fostered our single focus on being the servant of our fund shareholders, our disciplined attitude toward the costs that they bear, and our conservative investment strategies and concepts (many of which we created *de novo*). In remarks that I hope will be especially relevant to all of you who are interested in servant-leadership, I plan to demonstrate how so many of those concepts have served us well—implicitly, to be sure, but served us well nonetheless—in bringing us to where we stand today.

The Fund Industry and Vanguard

Hesitant as I may be to do so, I must establish my *bona fides,* as it were, by drawing a brief sketch of the mutual fund landscape today and identifying Vanguard's position in the scene. The mutual fund industry is booming:

- ○ Its asset base has swelled to $4.7 trillion, compared to just $50 billion a quarter century ago—a 90-fold increase, equivalent to a compound growth rate of 20 percent annually.

- ○ Cash *inflow* from investors is running in the range of $500 billion per year, compared to an *outflow* of $290 million in 1974. Mutual funds have become the investment of choice for American families at the moment, accounting for 100 percent of net additions to the financial assets of our households.

- ○ Twenty-five years ago, the market was tumbling; the Dow Jones Industrial Average was on its way to a 12-year low of 578. Today, the Dow is at the 9000 level. While the *relative* returns of the average managed equity mutual fund have fallen far short of those achieved by the unmanaged market averages, the *absolute* returns of even the most mundane funds have been little short of spectacular.

- ○ As a result of the great bull market, common stock funds are again the driving force of the industry with 53 percent of its assets, although money market funds have had their turn as the industry's largest component (75 percent of industry assets in 1981), followed by bond funds (37 percent of assets in 1986). This is a market-sensitive industry!

- ○ The character of the industry has changed rather radically. As investors have become better educated, more aware, and more self-reliant, the no-load (no sales commission) segment of the mutual fund industry has become its largest component—surging from just 15 percent of industry assets in 1979 to 35 percent currently. In fact, the industry's two largest firms, and five of its 10 largest, offer primarily—often solely—no-load funds.

Using the conventional measuring sticks, Vanguard, a firm that did not even exist 25 years ago, is emerging as the industry leader. We have by far the fastest growth rate of any major firm, and as a result have become one of the two largest fund organizations in the world. A scattering of measures makes the point:

○ Assets recently topped $400 billion, up from $1.4 billion in the mutual funds for which we assumed responsibility at our inception in 1974—a near 300-fold increase, equivalent to a compound growth rate of 27 percent.

○ Cash inflow is running at a $50 billion annual rate, compared to an outflow of $52 million in 1975, an even more extreme turnabout than the industry has enjoyed.

○ Typical of the industry, Vanguard funds carried sales loads at the outset. However, we abruptly made an unprecedented switch to no-load distribution in 1977, less than two years after the firm began operations. We led the industry shift to no-load dominance, and are today that segment's largest unit.

○ Our market share has risen from 2 percent of industry assets in 1980 to 8 percent today, and from 9 percent of no-load assets to 24 percent—one dollar of every four invested in no-load funds.

○ Driven by our preeminence in money market funds, bond funds, conservative stock funds, and index (market-matching) funds, we currently account for fully 50 percent of the net cash flowing into no-load funds. Our three nearest rivals account for 15 percent, 7 percent, and 6 percent, respectively.

My point in presenting you this context is not merely to illustrate, with what I hope is not false pride, our position in the industry, but to set the stage for how and why this situation has developed, and what it says about the important principles of business ethics—so closely aligned with the principle of servant-leadership—we have established for ourselves. Most important of all, I want to strike an important and optimistic keynote in this essay: that it is possible to do well by doing good, to succeed by serving others, to lead by having principles hold sway over opportunism. Indeed, it is my deeply held conviction that our principles, by creating a corporate environment that encourages us to do the right things in the right way, have placed us on the right side of history.

Turning Back the Clock

Let me now turn back the clock. In 1925—nearly three-quarters of a century ago—an aging professor said to his university class, "There is a new problem in our country. We are becoming a nation that is dominated by large institutions—businesses, governments, universities—and these businesses are not serving us well. I hope that all of you will be concerned about this. But nothing of substance will happen unless people inside these institutions lead them to better performance for the public good. Some of you ought to make careers inside these big institutions and become a force for good—from the inside."

Those words could have as easily been said today. But, as some of you will surely recognize, they were in fact the words that inspired a college senior named Robert K. Greenleaf to cast his lot with business as a career. On graduation, he joined American Telephone and Telegraph Company, an important measure because it was then the largest employer in our nation. He described himself as one who knew how to get things done and as a pursuer of wisdom, and his objective was to work on organizational development for the company. He worked there for nearly 40 years, until he retired in 1964.

I have no way of knowing about the influence that Robert Greenleaf exerted on the AT&T organization. But the work he did after his retirement, beginning with his brilliant 1969 essay, "The Servant as Leader," has surely brought much-needed wisdom and insight to the subject of corporate and institutional leadership in the United States. And I salute with admiration the leadership of the

Greenleaf Center for its extraordinary accomplishments in carrying on his crusade.

Remarkable Relevance

I must acknowledge that I did not read "The Servant as Leader" until the early 1980s, well after it had become one of a series of a dozen related essays published in book form under the title *Servant-Leadership*. But as I read his words then, and as I reread them again in preparing these remarks, I was thunderstruck by the power and relevance of his philosophy. Not merely to the great world out there, beyond my ken, but to me. To me, directly and personally, as if this man of my own parents' generation had placed me in the crosshairs of his telescopic sight, and would not rest until he captured the mind of his quarry.

Now, I hope—and, indeed, I suspect—that many others who have shared in his concepts feel the same way. And that acceptance, that feeling of revelation, more than anything else, suggests the force of his mind and the power of his ideas. In this sense, then, the fact that he speaks to me with such relevance may be far more important than if he had in fact been directly responsible for inculcating in me the values and principles of the enterprise I founded in 1974, years before the uncanny yet powerful reinforcement I received from his accumulated wisdom.

I want to directly quote, at reasonable length, some of the words that Robert Greenleaf has written (taking only the most minimal liberties in paraphrasing them), and then describe the extraordinary parallelism their spirit holds with the spirit of Vanguard. I hope in this way that I can persuade you that his dreams of long ago can not only find their way into the hard reality of the world of business, but can form the basis for a corporate success story.

I'm going to touch on five areas: (1) his essay, "Building a Model Institution"; (2) the linkage between foresight and caring; (3) his reflections on the superior company and on the liberating vision; (4) a series of powerful parallel phrases; and finally, somewhat poignantly, (5) his "Memo on Growing From Small to Large." In each case, I'll then follow with examples of how directly Robert

Greenleaf's wisdom has spoken to me, and has fortuitously been manifested at Vanguard.

Building a Model Institution

In August 1974, Robert Greenleaf spoke about building a model institution. Interestingly, he was speaking not about a business, but about Alverno College, a women's college affiliated with a religious order, at the celebration of its one-hundredth anniversary. His blueprint identified the four cornerstones.

> First, a goal, *a concept of a distinguished serving institution* in which all who accept its discipline are lifted up to nobler stature and greater effectiveness than they are likely to achieve on their own or with a less demanding discipline.
>
> Second, *an understanding of leadership and followership,* since everyone in the institution is part leader, part follower. If an institution is to achieve as a servant, then only those who are natural servants—those who want to lift others—should be empowered to lead.
>
> Third, an *organization structure* (or *modus operandi*) focusing on how power and authority are handled, including a discipline to help individuals accomplish not only for themselves, but for others.
>
> Fourth, and finally, *the need for trustees,* persons in whom ultimate trust is placed, persons who stand apart from the institution with more detachment and objectivity than insiders can summon.

As it happened, Vanguard was a month away from its creation when Mr. Greenleaf spoke to this century-old institution. But our resemblance to his model is striking. Our original concept, for example, was to transform the very focus of a mutual fund business from serving two masters (something *Matthew* describes as, well, impossible): the fund shareholder and the owners of the funds' external manager-adviser alike. We would be the servant of the fund shareholder alone, since the mutual funds—and thus their shareholders—would own our funds' manager, and would operate at cost. In effect, our fund shareholders would become the beneficiaries of the entrepreneurial rewards that managers traditionally arrogate to themselves. While I happen to believe that this concept lifts a fund enterprise to nobler stature, the fact that no others have chosen to follow down "the road less traveled by" suggests a profound disagreement with that assessment. So be it.

But it is a fact that our concept of an institution that serves solely its own investors has provided measurably greater effectiveness. The combination of our focus on conservative equity funds, on bond and money market funds of high-quality securities within specific maturity ranges, and of stock and bond market index funds—of which we were the pioneering creators—has worked effectively. Our at-cost operation is now producing annual expense savings to our investors of—think of it—nearly $3 billion. Together, these successful strategies and these minimal costs have provided virtual across-the-board superiority in the long-term returns we have earned for the shareholders of the funds we serve, relative to their peer funds with similar objectives.

While I cannot in all honesty say that we began with an understanding of leadership and followership (the second Greenleaf rule for a model institution), I can say that I've spent much of my career developing similar concepts. For example, in one of my early talks to our tiny 28-person original crew, I said, "I want every one of us to treat everyone here with fairness. If you don't understand what that means, stop by my office." I constantly stressed the values that I wanted to distinguish Vanguard—above all, the need to recognize that both we who serve and those whom we serve must be treated as "honest-to-God, down-to-earth human beings, with their own hopes, fears, ambitions, and financial goals."

Over the years, I have come to love and respect the term "human beings" to describe those with whom I serve and those whom we at Vanguard together serve. I even gave a talk at Harvard Business School on how our focus on human beings enabled us to become what they there call a "service breakthrough company." I challenged the students to find the term "human beings" in any book on corporate strategy that they had read, but as far as I know, none could meet the challenge. (Surprisingly, I do not believe that I've seen that term in any of Mr. Greenleaf's vast writings, but I'm certain that he'd love it too.)

Organization structure, or *modus operandi,* was also integral to our new model of an investment institution. Power and authority would rest not with the managers, as is the mutual fund industry convention, but with the fund shareholders. Of necessity, to be sure, much of the power would be delegated to the managers, but the ultimate authority would be vested in the collective power of those we serve. One rule set forth in modern-day business books is: "Treat your clients as if they were your owners." It is a good rule, but it is particularly easy for us to observe it: Our clients are our owners.

It was obvious, of course, that our managers would require more direct oversight than a large mass of widely dispersed investors, most with moderate holdings in our funds, could provide. So we quickly determined that we needed truly independent trustees, who, as in Mr. Greenleaf's fourth and final requirement for a model institution, would be able to provide objectivity and detachment, and in whom the ultimate trust would be placed. Ever since, at least eight of our 10 trustees have been unaffiliated with Vanguard in any way other than in the capacity of directors of our funds. In all, the Greenleaf model, described for a venerable institution, was to closely resemble a model created for a new company, with a new concept, that, as he spoke, was just coming to birth.

Linking Foresight and Caring

I now want to single out two subjects that, perhaps surprisingly, Mr. Greenleaf seemed to link: foresight and caring. He led into his subject with a few words about great leaders.

> Edwin M. Land, founder of Polaroid, spoke of the opportunity for greatness—not genius—for the many: "Within his own field (be it large or small, lofty or mundane) he will make things grow and flourish; he will grow happy helping others in his field, and to that field he will add things that would not have been added had he not come along." But greatness is not

enough. Foresight is crucial. The lead that the leader has is his ability to foresee an event that must be dealt with before others see it so that he can act on it in his way, the right way, while the initiative is his. If he waits, he cannot be a leader—at best, he is a mediator.

Foresight is the central ethic of leadership. Foresight is the lead that the leader has. Leaders must have an armor of confidence in facing the unknown. The great leaders are those who have invented roles that were uniquely important to them as individuals, that drew heavily on their strengths and demanded little that was unnatural, and that were right for the time and place they happened to be.

Caring for persons, the more able and the less able serving each other, is the basis of leadership, the rock upon which a good society is built. In small organizations, caring is largely person to person. But now, most caring is mediated through institutions—often large, complex, powerful, impersonal, not always competent, sometimes corrupt.

To build a model institution, *caring* must be the essential motive. Institutions require care, just as do individuals. And caring is an exacting and demanding business. It requires not only interest and compassion and concern; it demands self-sacrifice and wisdom and tough-mindedness and discipline. It is much more difficult to care for an institution, especially a big one, which can look cold and impersonal and seem to have an autonomy of its own.

While in 1986 I had not read the essay by Robert Greenleaf from which those paragraphs were excerpted, I had read an earlier speech which may have been the source of his inspiration. It was a speech given in 1972 by Howard W. Johnson, chairman of the Massachusetts Institute of Technology. It inspired me profoundly, and as 1986 drew to a close, I quoted it amply in my speech to our crew. Note the similarity:

There is always a time when the longer view could have been taken and a difficult crisis ahead foreseen and dealt with while a rational approach was still possible. How do we avoid such extremes? How can sustainable growth be achieved? Only with foresight—the central ethic of leadership—for so many bad decisions are made when there are no longer good choices.

If foresight is needed to protect an institution, what are the requirements necessary to make it work? First, the sense of purpose and objective. Second, the talent to manage the process for reaching new objectives. Finally, and let me surprise you by emphasizing this third need, we need people who care about the institution. A deep sense of caring for the institution is requisite for its success.

The institution must be the object of intense human care and cultivation. Even when it errs and stumbles, it must be cared for, and the burden must be borne by all who work for it, all who own it, all who are served by it, all who govern it. Every responsible person must care, and care deeply, about the institutions that touch his life.

My 1986 speech was but one of many times when I spoke of the importance of caring. Then, I reminded the crew that "only if we truly care about our organization, our partners, our associates, our clients, indeed our society as a whole, can we preserve, protect, and defend our organization and the values we represent." Again, I emphasized our responsibility "to faithfully serve the honest-to-God human beings who have trusted us to offer sound investment programs, with clearly delineated risks, at fair prices. We must never let them down."

Five years later, in 1991, I returned to the same theme in a talk entitled "Daring and Caring." I illustrated daring by using Lord Nelson's victory at the Battle of the Nile on August 1, 1798. That battle is part of our corporate history for Nelson's flagship was *HMS Vanguard*. Only weeks before the firm was incorporated in 1974, I had fortuitously learned of the battle, and, inspired by Nelson's remarkable triumph, chose Vanguard as our name.

At Vanguard, I reminded the crew, we dared to be different: in our unique corporate structure, in our unprecedented switch to commission-free distribution, in our decision to provide candid information to investors, and in forming the first market index fund—an idea considered so, well, stupid, that it wasn't even copied by anyone else for a full decade.

But caring quickly took center stage in my talk. I emphasized that caring must be "an article of faith," pointing out that each of those daring decisions that I had mentioned was driven by a philosophy of caring for our clients. And I reinforced the concept that caring must be also accorded to our crew, even then urging a spirit of "cooperation and mutual courtesy and respect," and reminding them that while we were so large as to require a policy manual, "it will never replace our own selves as the ultimate source of a caring attitude." Yes, a great deal of the spirit of Robert Greenleaf (and Dean Johnson, too) had found its way into our young business enterprise.

The Superior Company and the Liberating Vision

I now want to spend a few moments on Robert Greenleaf's views on the superior company and the liberating vision. Here is what he said:

> What distinguishes a superior company from its competitors is not the dimensions that usually separate companies, such as superior technology, more astute market analysis, better financial base, etc.; it is *unconventional* thinking about its dream—what this business wants to be, how its priorities are set, and how it organizes to serve. *It has a radical philosophy and self-image.* According to the conventional business wisdom, it ought not to succeed at all. Conspicuously less successful competitors seem to say, "The ideas that company holds ought not to work, therefore we will learn nothing from it."
>
> In some cases, the company's unconventional thinking about its dream is born of a liberating vision. But in our society liberating visions are rare. Why are liberating visions so rare? They are rare because a stable society requires that *a powerful liberating vision must be difficult to deliver.* Yet to have none is to seal our fate. We cannot turn back to be a wholly traditional

society, comforting as it may be to contemplate it. There must be change—sometimes great change.

That difficulty of delivery, however, is only half of the answer. The other half is that so few who have the gift for summarizing a vision, and the power to articulate it persuasively, have the urge and the courage to try. But there must be a place for servant-leaders with prophetic voices of great clarity who will produce those liberating visions on which a caring, serving society depends.

I leave to far wiser—and more objective—heads than mine the judgment about whether or not Vanguard meets the definition of a superior company. Of course, I believe it does. But I have no hesitancy in saying it is the product of unconventional thinking about what we want to be, how we set priorities, and how we organize to serve our clients. And surely our competitors—even the most successful of them—look with a sort of detached amusement and skepticism at our emergence as an industry leader. We have dared to be different, and it seems to be working just fine.

I cannot responsibly describe the ideas on which I founded Vanguard as part of a liberating vision. But I can tell you that, way back in 1951, I was writing my senior thesis on a little-known industry, which *Fortune* magazine described as "tiny but contentious" in the 1949 article that first aroused my interest in an industry about which I had never before heard. In my thesis, I sketched out my ideas of how a better industry—if not a model institution—might be built. Nearly a half-century ago, I called for a fairer shake for investors, urged lower sales commissions and management fees, cautioned against claims that mutual funds' managements could produce miracles, warned that unmanaged indexes had proved tough competition for active managers, and ended up with a ringing call for fund managers to focus, not on the peripheral diversions of the business, but on the duty to provide prudent stewardship. "The principal function of investment companies," I concluded, "is the management of their portfolios. Everything else is incidental to the performance of this function."

If all of that sounds much like Vanguard today, so be it. But it was not a dream that easily became a reality. And it was most certainly not a deterministic series of linked events. Rather, it was really a long and random series of happy accidents that led from 1951 to 1981, when the essential structure of today's Vanguard was finally put in place.

But it is, I think, remarkable how the original, if crude, dream hinted at in that Princeton thesis about the need to serve a single master—our investor-owners, now more than 10 million human beings in the aggregate—has to this day determined our basic corporate strategies. I've often emphasized that "Strategy follows structure," a relationship that has logically led to business decisions that are shaped around our unique shareholder-owned structure. It is what makes our enterprise work. Belying the competitors to whom Greenleaf referred when he pictured them as saying "It ought not to work," putting the shareholder in the driver's seat "ought to work." And it does.

For example, as nearly all now concede, cost is a factor in shaping long-term investment returns. If a firm achieves low-cost provider status, its bond and money market funds can follow lower-risk strategies and still offer higher yields than their peers. If low cost is the key to a successful index fund (and it obviously is), index funds can appropriately be a major focus of development. If money spent on marketing consumes shareholder assets while offering no countervailing benefit, it would seem foolish to spend much money on marketing. And all of these things are what aware investors should want. *It turns out that they do.* In the world of investing, in fact, it turns out that a superior company can be built on these strategies, all of which flow from a structure in which service to shareholders is the watchword.

Powerful Parallel Phrases

I've now touched on three broad areas of commonality between Robert Greenleaf's thinking and my own—building a model institution, foresight and caring, and the superior company and the liberating vision—as I've tried to manifest them in Vanguard's development. In this fourth section, I want to briefly describe some particularly powerful phrases that I observed in his writing that paralleled those that I have used at Vanguard forever, or so it seems. I do so because it suggests once again that his idealistic visions can in fact be successfully incorporated into a caring, sharing, serving business.

"Everything begins with the initiative of an individual." So reads the second subhead in "The Servant as Leader." "The very essence of leadership," Mr. Greenleaf says—and I am confident that he was referring, not only to a sort of grand idea of corporate leadership, but to the infinite number of tasks where less sweeping forms of leadership are required if an enterprise is to succeed—"is going out ahead to show the way, an attitude that is derived from more than usual openness to inspiration. Even though he knows the path is uncertain, even dangerous, a leader says: 'I will go, come with me.'"

Almost uncannily, my words about the importance of the individual leader convey the same idea. "Even one person can make a difference" has become a Vanguard article of faith, and is in fact engraved on the Awards for Excellence that we make each quarter to individuals who have met the highest standards of service, initiative, and cooperation. And even as Mr. Greenleaf defines individual initiative as "showing the way," Vanguard's very name suggests the same idea, for the motto on the *HMS Vanguard* ship badge is "leading the way."

And then there is the matter of the dream. Greenleaf speaks of the need for a leader to state and restate the goal, using the word goal "in the special sense of the overarching purpose, the visionary concept, the dream. Not much happens without a dream. And for something great to happen, it must be a great dream. Much more than a dreamer must bring it to reality, but the dream must be there first."

And I've talked often about Vanguard's dream. In particular, my 1975 speech to the crew was entitled "The Impossible Dream." In it, I said:

> The issue, it seems to me, is no longer how to make Vanguard a bigger company, but rather how to make Vanguard a better company, provide greater convenience and enhanced investment performance, all in the name of better service for the human

beings who have turned over to us the responsibility for their investment assets. A dream it may be—getting bigger only by being better—even an impossible dream, but a thrilling dream. And we must reach for it. In the marvelous musical play *The Man of La Mancha*, Don Quixote puts it this way:

> To dream the impossible dream.
> To fight the unbeatable foe
> To strive when our arms are too weary
> To run where the brave dare not go.
>
> This is our quest, to follow the star
> No matter how hopeless, no matter how far . . .
>
> And the world will be better for this
> That one man, scorned and covered with scars
> Still strove, with his last ounce of courage
> To reach the unreachable star.

I don't mind at all being a bit of a dreamer, if I can share the attribute with the likes of Robert Greenleaf.

Finally, I was struck by a third powerful parallel, nautical in derivation. Mr. Greenleaf gave this advice: "No matter how difficult the challenge or hopeless the task may seem, if you are reasonably sure of your course, just keep on going!" Leaving aside the obvious similarity with the words from "The Impossible Dream" ("no matter how hopeless, no matter how far"), his words come remarkably close to my often-repeated theme, "Press On Regardless," which was in fact the subject of a speech I gave to a graduating class at Vanderbilt University. But "just keep on going" is also a statement of what may well be the most universal of all the nautical themes we use—and sometimes perhaps even abuse—at Vanguard: "Stay the Course." It is wonderful advice for a career, superb wisdom for a project, and probably the best single piece of investment advice ever offered: "Establish a sound balance of bond funds and stock funds in your portfolio. Then, no matter what the financial markets do, *stay the course.*"

Memo on Growing from Small to Large

In about 1972, Robert Greenleaf wrote this memorandum at the request of the head of a small company that had achieved a reputation for unusual quality of products and service, had grown rapidly to its present size, and was in the process of becoming a distinguished large institution:

> The line that separates a large business from a small one might be drawn at that point where the business can no longer function well under the direction of one individual. If the company has been built largely on one person's drive, imagination, taste, and judgment, as yours seems to have been, it may be difficult to recognize when that point has been reached. The greatest risk may be that the company cannot grow and keep its present quality.
>
> I suggest that you begin to shift your personal effort *toward building an institution* in which you become more the manager of a process that gets the job done and less the *administrator of day-to-day operations*. This might be the first step toward the ultimate optimal long-term performance of a large business that is *managed* by a board of directors who act as trustees and *administered* by a team of equals who are led by a *primus inter pares*—first among equals. The result would be an institution that would have the best chance of attracting and holding in its service the large number of able people who will be required to give it strength, quality, and continuity if it is to continue to do on a large scale what you have been able to do so well on a smaller scale.
>
> I am suggesting that a person like you who has been so successful in taking a distinguished business from a small size to large size might, at your age, find an even more exciting challenge in transforming a one-person business into an institution that has autonomy and creative drive as a collection of many able people, one that has the capacity for expansion without losing, and perhaps even enhancing, the claim to distinction it has already achieved.

To say that I found this memorandum both relevant and poignant when I first read it just two weeks ago, as I was preparing these remarks, would be quite an understatement. For what struck home to me was that, while there was much that I thought of when I decided in 1996 to relinquish my position as head of Vanguard, I had not seriously considered abandoning the traditional route of simply recommending to the directors a qualified successor to replace me. The directors agreed without hesitation, perhaps in part because my weak heart was quickly deteriorating and because of my age (I was 67 at the time), and, in fairness—although they did not suggest this—perhaps because they had tired of my leadership style.

In any event, within a year I had undergone a remarkably successful heart transplantation, miraculously receiving an infusion of new energy and confidence that had to be seen to be believed. A second chance at life is not to be taken lightly! But my decision had been made, and only time will tell whether it was the correct one. But whatever the case, I have no doubt that the service-caring-ethical principles of Vanguard will remain in place for as far ahead as one can see.

In the Vanguard structure, of course, the entrepreneur is not the owner. (The stock in the company is held by the funds for *their* shareholders.) When one leaves office, then, power devolves to another. And, as Robert Greenleaf wrote:

> In an imperfect world, some abuse of power will always be with us. In 1770, William Pitt said to the House of Commons, "Unlimited power is apt to corrupt the minds of those who possess it." One hundred years later, more famously, Lord Acton (in opposing the doctrine of papal infallibility) said, "Power tends to corrupt and absolute power corrupts absolutely." That corruption is reflected in arrogance. For example, the head of a large corporation, when asked what made his job attractive, listed first, before monetary reward, prestige, service, and creative accomplishment, "The opportunity to build power."

The power-hungry person, who relishes competition and is good at it (meaning: he usually wins) will probably judge the servant-leader to be weak or naïve or both. But if we look past that individual to the institution which he or she serves, what makes that institution strong? I believe the strongest, most productive institution over a long period of time has the largest amount of voluntary action toward the goals of the institution. The people who staff the institution do the right things at the right time because the goals are clear and comprehensive and they know what ought to be done, and do the right thing without being instructed. It takes a strong leader to put the people who serve first, but that is the way to insure that they will deliver all that people can deliver—and to insure that the business will continue to lead in its field.

Vanguard, in my view, has been built on an extraordinary crew—now 8,000 strong—"who know what ought to be done, and who have done the right things at the right time." And while my strong leadership may well have been described as power-driven, my drive (I think) was focused on intellectual power—to devise sensible investment policies, an efficient structure through which to offer them, and a sensible strategy for their delivery—and moral power—to make certain that both structure and strategy were founded on a sound ethical base. Those kinds of powers do not vanish when one leaves office. But other kinds of power do, including the power of the purse, the power to direct people, the power to reshape values, even the power to change what lies firmly in place. But I hope and believe that our crew and my successors will continue to hold high what we have built, its structure and strategy, and the ethical foundation that is Vanguard's rock.

Where History Comes In

Vanguard has had the marvelous opportunity to test, in the real-world marketplace, the concept that serving is the essential ingredient of true success, and that servant-leaders—and leader-servants—can successfully dedicate their careers to serving the human beings who depend upon their services. All of that may sound idealistic—it is!—but we live in an era of consumerism (in the best sense) in which business has no recourse but to make a determined effort to build a new level of trust in consumer products and services alike. In the world of finance, if we are going to make the United States a nation of investor-capitalists, we'd best give our citizens the maximum possible proportion of the fruits of investing, rather than consuming large portions of those returns with excessive costs.

The fact is that "the Vanguard way" works. Not because our principles give us some divine right to success, but because we are creating extra value for investors. And, as the numbers I presented at the outset illustrate, the growth that Vanguard is enjoying relative to our peers makes clear that investors have clearly recognized that value advantage.

Yet it is a curious fact of competitive life in the mutual fund world that, while our investment policies—most notably in index funds and in bond funds—are being copied (albeit often with little enthusiasm), our low-cost philosophy and our focus on management rather than marketing are not. But as the investing public makes known its preferences, this industry will finally change. To use a computer analogy, all mutual fund organizations have pretty much the same software—common ways to invest in securities—but the industry must adopt a new operating system: serving the fund shareholder first.

I have no way of knowing whether the coincidence of Robert Greenleaf's philosophy and my own is merely fortuitous—a happy accident, random molecules bumping together in the night—or powerful evidence of the mysterious universality of a great idea. Perhaps it is a little of each. But in the mutual fund industry, the central idea of serving is being proven in the marketplace by tens of millions of investors. I've long thought that servant-leadership is on the right side of evolving corporate history. And so too, in that small but growing corner of the financial world that is the U.S. mutual fund industry, the policies and principles that Vanguard adopted a quarter century ago—which we continue to treasure today—are on the right side of history too.

PART THREE

SERVANT-LEADERSHIP IN THE COMMUNITY

Dr. John Carver is the world's most published author on the governing board role, having authored or coauthored four books and over 160 articles on the subject. As creator of the groundbreaking Policy Governance® Model, he is widely considered the most provocative international authority on governance. Carver has consulted with business, nonprofit, and governmental boards on every populated continent.

John Carver posits that the chair is a servant-leader of the board, and the board is the servant-leader of the ownership. The chair is, therefore, servant-leader of the servant-leaders. This essay explores this unique double servant-leadership role of the board chair.

John Carver was a keynote speaker at the Greenleaf Center's 1998 annual international conference.

14

THE UNIQUE DOUBLE
SERVANT-LEADERSHIP ROLE
OF THE BOARD CHAIR

John Carver

IT IS COMMON KNOWLEDGE that the position of board chairperson is an important position, indeed. Its importance is due, of course, to the considerable authority wielded by the governing board being chaired. I believe that the chairing is not so crucial a topic as that which is chaired. If I am correct, any discussion of the chair's role must rest upon a prior discussion of the board's role. It is my pleasure today to address you on the intriguing topic of "The Unique Double Servant-Leadership Role of the Board Chairperson." In short, I want to make the case that the role of board chairperson is, if I may say so, "servant-leadership squared." But to do that, I must begin with the play in which the chair is merely an actor: the setting called governance.

Governance can mean a number of things, but, for the moment, it will be defined merely as the kind of leadership appropriate for a governing board, that is, defined as a governing board's proper job. I have some peculiar ideas about what "proper" means in the board context, ones that radically challenge the conventional wisdom, a "wisdom" that is actually a hodge-podge of tradition-blessed practices with little managerial respectability and no conceptual coherence. The governance job is the weakest link in enterprise, the least well designed, the least studied, the least modeled.

But I don't stand alone with that sad diagnosis. Consider a few brutal comments. Peter Drucker said in 1974 that all boards have one thing in common—they don't function. In 1984, Harold Geneen complained that the boards of 95 percent of America's top 500 companies are not doing what they are legally, morally, and ethically supposed to do and couldn't, even if they wanted to. A Danforth Foundation report in 1992 charged that many school boards are an obstacle to—rather than a force for—fundamental education reform because of their tendency to become immersed in the day-to-day administration. In a gentler vein, a 1994 article in Canada's *Maclean's* magazine noted that the time is long past when corporate directors can remain imbued with what a British judge once characterized as "lovable dimness."

But, in fact, *Maclean's* is wrong. The time is neither long past, nor even recently past. The time is with us still. To be sure, you and I have seen a few bright moments, for sometimes boards do rise to leadership. But it is an inescapable conclusion that standards for governance are appallingly low, that mediocrity is the norm. Trivia and empty ritual abound. What should give us pause is: If the most powerful role in enterprise is not up to its task, what hope can we have for our institutions?

Robert Greenleaf beat me to that distressing opinion. Unfortunately, my Policy Governance model and my 1990 book came into existence without the benefit of knowing about Robert Greenleaf. I would love to have known his work and even to have shared my emerging governance model with him. That is my loss.

In *Trustees as Servants,* he observed that there is "an abundance of literature on contemporary institutions, but most of it is concerned with 'fine tuning' within the limits of conventional language and wisdom." He eschewed merely helping "trustees do just a little better with their roles as now defined." In the parlance of today, we would call his aim a full paradigm shift, for he said his vision was not boards as we know them, but "*a substantially new institution* [italics mine], one that serves society much better, far ahead of anything that now exists or that is now dreamed of as possible."

Transformation toward "a Substantially New Institution"

I'd like to examine with you the role of the chairperson as that shows up within my vision of effective governance. This vision, which I have codified as the Policy Governance® model of board leadership, applies to any governing board of anything anywhere. That is, it is a generic model applicable in nonprofits, business, and government . . . of large or small organizations. This broad applicability has been tested in quite a few parts of the world.

But allow me to position Policy Governance with respect to Greenleaf's work. Peter Senge has observed that "recent books on leadership have been about what leaders do and how they operate." "By contrast, Greenleaf," Senge says, "invites people to consider a domain of leadership grounded in a state of being, not doing." The choice of servant-leadership, he explains, is "not something you do, but an expression of your being." Policy Governance is an operational definition (in its scientific meaning) of leadership in a specific setting—that of the governing body. In some ways, the difference Senge points out is like that between philosophy and strategy or between basic research and technology.

If the judgment of history is kind, the Policy Governance model may merit being seen as a technology of servant-leadership. At any rate, it is a carefully crafted prescription for how boards can operate—boards that are committed to being servant-leaders.

My consulting practice using this model has been largely confined to the United States, Canada, Britain, and The Netherlands, though it has also extended in a very limited way to every populated continent. It has been applied in widely varying cultures, from North American aboriginal tribes to Dutch colleges and independent schools in Australia. While today's discussion of the chairperson's role could focus equally well on city councils, trade

associations, foundations, business corporations, professional societies, or airport authorities, most of my references will be to the
public or quasi-public domain. So let's look more closely at what
the model sets out to do and, in good time, how that relates to the
servant-leadership role of the board chairperson.

Greenleaf's dream of a substantially new institution cannot be
achieved by cosmetic changes to the kind of governance we all
know so well. Such a lofty goal calls for a true paradigm shift. This
endeavor isn't a matter of improving our personnel committees,
sprucing up the agenda, getting more fund raisers on the board, or
getting board members more involved in the organization's work.
Nor is it addressed by more board training—an exercise often best
described as teaching boards how to do the wrong things better.
No. Leadership, as said so well by A. Bartlett Giamatti, late President of Yale, is essentially a moral act—one of moral courage, vision, and intellectual energy.

John Gardner asked us a compelling question: "Do we have it in
us to create a future worthy of our past?" It is embarrassing that the
answer is not so evident. Tom Peters, in his trademark in-your-face
style, has said that "we must move beyond change and embrace
nothing less than the literal abandonment of the conventions that
brought us to this point. Eradicate 'change' from your vocabulary.
Substitute 'abandonment' or 'revolution' instead. . . . Much of what
ails corporations today is traceable to a failure of nerve in every
part and at every level of the organization." Making that leap from
yesterday's trapeze to tomorrow's, however, requires not only innovation, but boldness and risk.

Governance has been long overdue for a theory. But even if Kurt
Lewin tells us "There is nothing so practical as a good theory," in-
troducing a new order will not be easy, for familiar poison grabs at
every weakness in our confidence. So until the new order grows familiar enough to be the new old order—at which time we'd better
get started on its successor—fundamental change will be an uphill
battle. Many counter any new vision of how things can be with a
tired appeal to human nature. I am sure that at some point the idea
that a court system would be largely free from bribery, or that a

population could actually choose its own leaders, were preposterous ideas, patently "contrary to human nature." And before Roger Bannister, so was the four-minute mile. "Some . . . say that, human nature being what it is, the recommendations here are too idealistic and therefore impossible. They should be reminded that we got where we are by doing the impossible, and future progress in the quality of our major institutions, which is both inevitable and imperative, will be by the same route!" Those aren't my words; they belong to Robert Greenleaf.

When I was engaged in creating the Policy Governance model 25 years ago, I wasn't sure what to do with lofty sentiments like those. But I was sure of one thing: Leadership, particularly leadership at a high level, must be concerned with—perhaps I should say *obsessed* with—values: the importance of life, the commitments of life, and, yes, the swap-offs of life. Leaders must be able to speak the language of values and, if there is no such language, they must create one that connects our sometimes rather soft and fuzzy insides with hard and precise operational utility. For the organizational context, there has long been a need for a technology of values. And, in fact, making a successful marriage of the seemingly oxymoronic juxtaposition of "technology" and "values" is exactly what is demanded to connect *who we are* to *what we can do.*

For governing boards, the context in which those values would be sought out, explicated, debated, and decided would have to be a context of trusteeship. For boards, as traders in values, do so not for themselves, but for others. The creed expressed in the short phrase "on behalf of" is integrally attached to every motion, every debate, every vote. If the board fails to act powerfully, it cheats those for whom it is in trust of a voice. If it acts self-servingly, it fails to act in their behalf. It must be powerful and deferential at the same time, for both timidity and high-handedness defraud the trust. The contemplation of and theory-building for governing boards—these vessels of leadership—must recognize that *proper governance is a logical impossibility if it does not include the concept of servant-leadership.* Let's look a bit more closely at the nature of a board's servanthood.

Where Servanthood Begins: Fidelity to the Ownership

The governing role of any board is not to administer an institution, but to be an owner-representative. Whether the owners are shareholders, trade association members, or a political constituency, the governing board stands in for them. The board is a microcosm of the ownership. That is true even when the ownership is only a convenient fiction, such as when the general public is the ownership of a local mental health center or family planning clinic. Indeed, in the case of most public or quasi-public organizations, most owners do not even know they are owners.

I have stubbornly insisted on using the term "ownership" in dealing with such boards simply because it forces consideration of an important role, a role either omitted from the usual governance equation or defined without the clarity or forcefulness that befits its importance. We do this, for example, by diluting it in the popular, but less specific, "stakeholder" concept. After all, if a board is operating on someone's behalf, it is rather crucial to know who the someone is. In the absence of a compelling concept of ownership, pretenders to that crown move in to fill the vacuum. Many public organizations, for example, operate as if the staff owns the enterprise more than the public. In other cases, a vocal consumer group grasps that high ground when a cowardly board bends to its every wish. These phenomena are not rare, but routine. They can be observed every time a city council pays more attention to the few insistent citizens who demand the council's collective ear than it does to the other 99 percent of citizens who do not descend upon the council chambers or tie up officials' home phone lines each evening.

In any event, the ownership for a board to concern itself with may well be a moral rather than a legal matter. In my own missionary zeal as a reformer, I have coined the term "moral ownership" to underscore the nature of owners in the public and quasi-public sectors, occasionally confusing people who thought my term had something to do with moral majority or, in a more serious vein, that I simply meant "stakeholder." No—on both counts. The ownership to which I refer is a very special subsection of stakeholders. It is the legitimacy base that closely parallels the role of shareholders for an equity corporate board, the membership for an association or federation board, or the municipal residents for a city council. So let me place that important group into an accountability scheme.

Although we are accustomed to using the board-staff relationship as the point of departure in describing the board's own peculiar role, it is really the wrong place to start. The board's role is more properly described from the other direction: The board is an organ of ownership. Its relationship with owners should be the more intimate relationship and the one it spends more time on, not its relationship to staff.

And from that vantage point, the board forms an important link between owners and operators. For that link to have accountability, the board must actually use its authority, not default upon it as nonprofit boards rather commonly do. As the great psychologist Rollo May taught us, failing to lay claim to the power we have is a certain path to irresponsibility in its use. Power must be used. But, as we have been warned by Lord Acton, and as every day's newspaper proves, power corrupts. Only servanthood tempers the power and makes it incorruptible. Servant-leadership, in other words, enables incorruptible power. To get ahead of my story, that protection is further represented in a properly construed chair's role; but more on that later.

So the board is servant to the owners. Of course, the servanthood of a board is neither weak nor passive, for the board is also a leader with respect to the owners. The board of a health clinic may be servant to the public, but it is also obligated to inform, educate, and lead that public with respect to the issues of health. The trade association board is servant to the membership, but must also lead the membership to confront issues of the trade, trends not to be ducked, and even the duties of responsible ownership. Leading those to whom one is first a servant is, experience shouts at us, tricky business. Let's look at one familiar aspect of this phenomenon.

A board's role as servant to the ownership requires that the board find out what owners want before it decides what the institutional outputs shall be. Goal-setting, in other words, is not a closeted activity, emerging full blown from board members' own foreheads.

Knowing this, boards frequently reach out for input by using public hearings, polls, and surveys. But being a proper servant does not
mean the board is a mere poll-taker. If it were, we would not need
boards; we would only need polls and pocket calculators.

Owners have a right to expect a board operating in their behalf to know more than the owners themselves do about the subject matter of the board. For example, a school board operating
on behalf of citizens of a jurisdiction should know more about
what is possible in education, what the future holds, and what
knowledge young persons are likely to need 20 years from now.
Therefore, while by no means unmindful of ownership opinions,
the board is obligated to bring specialized judgment to the situation. I hasten to add that this is not necessarily professional judgment nor is it an uninformed judgment. As Greenleaf said, it is
"not a *lay* judgment. It is a unique thing, *trustee judgment,* and it
stands on a par in importance with any other judgment within
the institution." It is on behalf of the owners, but more informed
than the owners. That quality can easily become elitism, if not
tempered with considerable stewardship. A Texas legislator put it
this way: "I vote the way my constituents would vote if they knew
what I know."

Tricky though the task might be, the board as a group is both
servant and leader and has no responsible choice to be otherwise.

The Discipline of Leadership

Using one's judgment on behalf of someone else introduces what
legal scholars would call the problem of agency—the difficulty of
an agent subjugating his or her own needs in the service of the principal. Board members, frail humans all, have a special authority to
act on behalf of the interests of an ownership that they rarely see.
Board members do not hold their considerable trust in order to get
perks, or to "be involved," or to engage in whatever they'd like to
do. A given board's role, in other words, should not be defined as
the laundry list of trustees' individual interests. It is a job. Like any
real job, it has obligatory outputs and disciplines, though in the absence of a coherent model, those outputs and disciplines are more

a product of anecdotal experience than a conceptually sound wisdom. And those elements must amount to the board's behavior being always in the service of the ownership it represents, not the service of board members' own personal needs.

So we ego-driven, flawed individuals must somehow rise to the occasion of fulfilling a bigger-than-life role wherein the mantle we take on is that of many. We speak for hundreds or even millions. When board members take their seats, a transformation must take place wherein they become the vessels through which the multitudes dream, form intentions, debate, and decide. If not mystical, this phenomenon is, at the very least, impressive and inspirational. Robert Bellah explains de Tocqueville's experience of this transformation. Citizens, he found, got involved in local civic associations out of self-interest, yet the resulting mindfulness of public responsibility caused them to transcend that very self-interest.

Any approach that we design for the governance task must aid in making this transformation that de Tocqueville either observed or idealized. It is common, however, to speak of board strategies that cater to board members' individual interests rather than to the satisfaction of their servanthood obligation. Staffs are known to turn flips trying to find ways to keep the volunteers happy, or keep them involved, or satisfy their individual needs to partake in one or another part of the organization's work.

A question I confronted recently is illustrative of this "please-the-board-members" phenomenon. A journalist called to interview me about a number of governance articles being run in the inaugural issue of a new Canadian magazine—an issue focusing on my work. In her research, she uncovered some criticisms of my work and called to give me the opportunity to respond. That is an opportunity I always love, partly because I love to explain governance, but also because, after this many years, there aren't many questions I haven't heard. But one question surprised me. She said one source thought the Policy Governance model is flawed in that it doesn't allow some board members to do what they want to do. That is, the board job as I have defined it may not be of interest to every board member. The discipline required would not allow all board members to follow their specific interests.

It speaks volumes about how we have trivialized and cheapened this pivotal servant-leadership role in our society that a significant number think that the job of a governance model is to enable current board members to use their platform of trust as a protected province for following their own interests—or in more than a few cases I have encountered—to use the privilege of board position to provide a permissive playground. An example from last month: A questioner recounted his board's struggle with whether to allow board members to volunteer within the staff organization, that is, to be operational volunteers at the same time as being governing volunteers. They ultimately decided to allow it, in part because they felt it would be wrong to "deny board members the opportunity to participate as volunteers!" The distressing aspect of that position is not that it came up or even that it won the day in this particular board. The distressing aspect is that so many boards' members— as well as those who work for them, write about them, and consult to them—would not notice anything awry about it!

One would have hoped, for this board and all others, that the first consideration, perhaps the obsessive one, be: "What is our governance obligation to those who morally own this organization?"— a question I believe must be answered in servant-leadership terms. Then the board might have asked what must we do and be to fulfill that trust as a board, and what behaviors, processes, or failures of discipline will jeopardize our fulfillment of that trust. But this board showed itself more concerned about trustee rights than about right trusteeship.

As an aside, many of our so-called "voluntary" organizations are at risk from the damaging confounding of volunteer roles. It is common for persons active in voluntary health organizations, for example, to "graduate" to a governing board level because of their years of conscientious service. Robert Greenleaf, a quarter of a century ago, was prescient and bold enough to say that volunteers who govern should stay out of operational work. Rather less boldly than he, I have warned only that they should be scrupulous in wearing these two very different hats separately. The problem is obvious. Board members inappropriately drag their operational interests, proclivities, and ways of thinking into the board room, dooming governance to a short-term mentality, to interference in staff work, and to fragmentation of that all-important big picture. Operational details are not inconsequential if one is in operations. But they certainly are if one is on the board.

A character in a novel by Lee Gruenfield put it well: "It's human nature, this propensity in the face of the profound to be distracted by the trivial." Since "trivia" in the board room can consist of merely dealing with topics that are perfectly appropriate in an operational setting, failing to make the transition from operations to governing virtually cripples board leadership. Greenleaf felt that making the necessary switch would be difficult, in part because "one is apt to make any position one holds fit one's habitual way of working." Board members whose interpretation of board leadership consists largely of dragging operational behavior into the board room remind me of the old saw about a kid with a hammer: everything comes to look like a nail. Long-term conceptual problems are met with short-term operational solutions.

When discussing the mix of conceptual and operating skills and talents, Greenleaf observed: "Leadership, in the sense of going out ahead to show the way, is more conceptual than operating." So trustees must be conceptual people, persons capable of envisioning a world that isn't, rather than of being captured by a world that is. But beyond their intellectual and visionary equipment, those who would be our leaders at the board level must have a commitment to discipline, for the board job is a real job, not just a ceremonial position. And, of course, their commitment must be one of servant-leadership. A proper governance model, then, is merely a structure for fulfillment of the servant-leadership obligation of intelligent, caring, committed persons.

Let me add here that the tradition-blessed practice of reserving a board position for an accountant, a lawyer, a public relations person, a human resources person, or, in some cases, a physician, an educator, or other specialty, also falls into the same trap. If an organization is quite small, these provisions may make some sense. But in an organization large enough to have a CEO and active staff organization, the practice is outmoded and dysfunctional. It persists because boards feel it is their responsibility to furnish experts to guide their staff in staff work. Board-as-expert-collection is quite different, however, from board-as-responsible-servant-leader for an ownership.

Don't get me wrong on this point, please. Lawyers, accountants, physicians, and others can be wonderful governing board members—if, in fact, that is what they are charged to be. But they will not be if they are recruited so that the board can load on to them responsibilities that should have been shouldered by the full board. With the entire group taking responsibility, it can entertain whatever wisdom should be heard, make appropriate policies using that wisdom, then have something of substance to delegate to the CEO. (At that point, if the CEO wishes to use experts from any source to help him or her fulfill the board's expectations, that is completely the CEO's business.) How commonplace is the refrain: "Our fiduciary responsibility is too complicated for us; we have Sally, a CPA, on the board to take care of that for us."

What would I say to Sally? You are a board member first and an accountant second. You may bring your knowledge and wisdom to the table for the board to use in accomplishing its job. But never save the board from being the board. Leave pigeonholes to pigeons. Your portfolio is the same as all other board members': to participate in the group responsibility of governance. What would I say to the board? To fulfill your responsibility, you must learn to use experts to *inform* your wisdom, never to substitute for it.

But—back to the role of a conceptually coherent framework to embrace this thing we call governance. My point is that a respectable governance model is not designed to make trustees happy—though their happiness is by no means a bad thing—but to see to it that trustees, taken as a body, fulfill their trusteeship responsibly. Board members who can only meddle might just have to leave the board. Board members who can only rubber-stamp might be left behind. This job of governing isn't for everyone. We need to define the job and let the chips fall where they fall, not define the job to fit board members as they have, by accident of history, been appointed in the past. "There are able people," Greenleaf said, "who ought not to be trustees." He was comfortable that a better approach would "more quickly and sharply expose those who should not be in institutional leadership at all."

From Responsible Individuals to Responsible Boards

But as important as it is that trustees be capable servants, being so *individually* is not good enough to transform this institution of governance—not sufficient to the task of creating a servant-leadership group. Boards can easily be incompetent groups of competent people, untrustworthy groups of trustworthy people, and, far more often than even I sometimes imagine, cruel groups of good-hearted persons. The transformation of responsible individuals into a responsible group is not an automatic product of good people with good intent. Greenleaf noted that the servant-leadership role of the board is optimized only if the board learns to act as a *unitary* body. He said, "If trustees . . . (are) to be influential in raising the performance of the institution to the optimal . . . they confront a difficult problem: how to carry that role *as a group*. It is one thing to carry a trustee role as an individual. It is quite another to function effectively as part of a group process." The board *as a body* has the authority to act on behalf of the ownership, not trustees taken one at a time. Another way to say this is: No one board member has any right at all over the organization governed.

No one argues with this in theory. But, in practice, this tenet is violated regularly. Staff members can be seen scrambling to do what one board member wants done. Individual board members can be found expressing criticisms of staff performance against criteria the board has never stated—criteria that emanate from the one trustee alone. Subgroups of the full board—committees—regularly do the same things. In practice, boards have rarely learned to discipline themselves in this regard. As a consequence, the leadership of most boards is seriously flawed because the integrity of group authority is not strictly maintained. (Existing popular and reputable expert sources actually teach governance methods designed with these flaws built in.)

Let me assure you that my allegation that "most boards" are caught in the pervasiveness of this phenomenon is not lightly made.

I have personally dealt with thousands of boards directly and tens of thousands indirectly through their members' participation in my workshops. I truly mean, given experience that is admittedly not "research" in a scientific sense, *most* boards. Try a simple test: Any board that truly means its authority will be exercised only as a group will tell its CEO that "when we speak as individuals in or out of board meetings, you never have to pay attention to any of us." Try to find such a board.

Perhaps this is a good place to point out that proper exercise of the board's group challenge enables the board to delegate cleanly and powerfully to a CEO. There is never a need for the board chair to be in that loop. The chairperson helps the board get its job done, but does not interfere between the employer (the board) and its employee (the CEO). Contrast this with the common practice in which boards allow or even require their chair to "supervise" the CEO or, similarly, to require that certain CEO actions have chair approval, and other such dilutions of the CEO's role. Each dilutes the board's integrity as a body and seriously weakens the board's ability to hold the CEO accountable to it and to it alone. A properly construed chair role has virtually nothing to do with CEO activities, decisions, or performance. In fact, the only excuse for the chair's becoming, if you will, the super-CEO, is the board's failing to do its own job—that is, to make governance decisions as a group so crafted that delegation to the CEO is direct and unobstructed by any intervening authority, including that of a chair or of committees.

This is to say that the board's relationship with the chair is circular, while its relationship with the CEO is linear. Consider two scenarios: Number one, I meet with my personal physician, accepting that I am responsible for my own health, but enlisting my doctor in helping me do that well. Number two, as owner of my manufacturing business, I tell the plant manager what I want, after which he or she instructs the shift managers, who in turn instruct their various supervisors.

Allow me to amateurishly misappropriate from physics and hypothesize a "plasma" that flows in these relationships, a plasma composed of both instructing and "acting upon," quite apart from the more familiar concept of feedback. Mindful of the difficulty of group discipline, the board charges the chair with the task of keeping his or her boss on track, *not* with becoming the boss himself or herself. The "flow" of governance plasma, if you will, is back and forth between the board and the chair, a closed system, two-party interaction that does not go beyond the dyadic. In contrast, mindful of the impracticality of the board itself accomplishing the organization's work, the board charges a CEO with the task of getting that job done, *not* with keeping the board on track. The flow of executive plasma is from board to CEO to sub-CEO staff—a linear progression that may have as many parties as the organizational size accommodates.

An analogy in more familiar management terminology can be found in the concepts of "line" and "staff." Although there is some variation in the way the words are used in the management literature, I will define them in this way. *Line* positions are those on a direct line that can be drawn from the highest authority through to the lowest person engaged in producing the organization's output to customers or clientele. Thus, the board, the CEO, the plant manager, and the product installer all hold line positions. *Staff* positions, on the other hand, assist or counsel one or more line positions; their authority is always granted and controlled by some line position, and they have no direct-command authority of their own over line positions. As an aside, violating this principle results in dismaying problems in many nonprofit organizations when, for example, a programmatic head is expected—in practice if not on the organizational chart—to work for the finance officer.

At any rate, given this distinction between line and staff that management tradition has given us, it can be seen that the board chairperson is *staff,* while the CEO is *line.* The board chairperson is staff to the board, much as the finance officer is staff to the CEO. This highly visible staff position, no matter how important it is to the board, can have no legitimate authority over line personnel— including the CEO and his or her employees.

Whether you find it more convenient positing a fictional plasma or seeing things in terms of line and staff, it is inescapable that the role assigned here to the chairperson is impossible if the board is incapable of speaking with one and only one voice. It must be so, for the chairperson's authority can only derive from a group decision—and the chair's obligation is, similarly, to group expectations. "One voice" in this context does not imply unanimous votes, but does require the mindset that if the board hasn't spoken as a group, it hasn't spoken at all. Contrary to common belief, the great impediment to this one-voice simplicity is not that some boards have members who differ widely and almost violently. The impediment is simply lacking the discipline to say that, until a motion passes, the board exercises absolutely no authority over anyone.

Quite often, however, boards are not sufficiently committed to their trusteeship to require this discipline of themselves. But nature abhors a vacuum, including the vacuum of leadership. When the board as a group fails to be the originating seat of leadership, the vacuum gets filled anyway. Sometimes, of course, boards fly off in all directions—so that the vacuum is filled with uncoordinated individual actions—but, more commonly, they settle into the indolent comfort of letting someone just tell them what to do.

That someone might be the chair. But, even more commonly, it is the board's employed executive who moves into that vacuum. Ask any board where its last agenda came from. Although our rhetoric celebrates the board as the source of vision and strategic leadership, it has to have someone else tell it what to talk about at the next meeting! I submit that the only reason this phenomenon doesn't sound absolutely daft is because it has historical momentum on its side. Board agendas being provided by management is just the way we've done it. It is common for a board to expect its CEO to be more responsible for at least the appearances of governance than the board is. And, credit to their cordiality more than their judgment, CEOs oblige.

As illustration of the unquestioning acceptance of this inversion, almost every article on boards that appears in the popular periodical *Nonprofit World* tells CEOs how to see to it that their boards do the right things. No one ever publishes about how vice-presidents should make their presidents do the right things. Governance can only have the needed integrity when boards, not their CEOs, assume the responsibility for governance. Wouldn't it be a breath of fresh air if board meetings truly became the board's meetings, not the CEO's meetings for the board?

The Chairperson: Servant-Leader to the Servant-Leaders

But how can a leaderless board determine its own agenda, its own role, its own discipline? It can select a chairperson who can help the board be what it means to be. But in this familiar practice lies a trap. Boards can easily default to their chairs rather than delegate to them. For chairs can help rob a board of its group strength quite as quickly as CEOs can. The traditional "strong" chair might run a tight ship, but does not develop a strong board. In fact, it is not uncommon for a strong chair to become more the board's boss than its servant. Yet strength is needed, so how is the dilemma to be settled?

The solution, of course, is servant-leadership. The chair, in fact, works for the board. If we remember that the organizational authority begins with the board as a group, then no one can have any authority that the board as a body has not given out. That includes the chair quite as much as it includes the CEO. The board begins by accepting that it, and it alone, has the responsibility to govern—there is no whining that holds up at this point. Failure to govern well can never be blamed on the CEO or the chair or a committee. The buck truly stops with the group. Understanding this, the board then admits that fulfilling its role will be difficult without enlisting someone to help it stick with the task.

The CEO is a very bad choice for that job, hence the role for one of the board's own: a chairperson. But the logical sequence is crucial. In the beginning was the board. There is no chair until the board empowers a chair, which means the chair works at the pleasure of the board and has whatever authority the board chooses to give. And the "value added" assigned to this newly created servant is the job of leadership! "Lead us to be what we've decided to be. Lead us to produce what we've decided to produce. Impose upon us the discipline we've committed ourselves to." The authority of the chair, in other words, comes from the board. The visible, dynamic, sometimes insistent leader is, first, a servant.

You may have come across a greeting card that reads: "A friend is someone who learns the words of your song, then sings them back to you when you forget." That is a beautifully simple description of the role of board chair at its best. And in this role, the chairperson can be inspiring, encouraging, enlightening, challenging, and often cajoling—all within the servanthood that calls for just this kind of tough-love leadership.

But while I am describing a good chair, let me warn against the problem I am myself, at this moment, exacerbating. Charging the chair with responsibility for meeting-by-meeting and even minute-by-minute board discipline risks letting other board members off the hook for that discipline. Group responsibility is tricky business, and negotiating its unfamiliar twists and turns is not second nature to us yet. Let me put it this way: If board hegemony is to make sense, the point of departure must be the board's *group* responsibility for governance, including the discipline necessary to make governance work. The board exercises that responsibility in three ways. It first *describes* the discipline to which the board *as a body* will be committed. Second, it pins the fulfillment of that discipline on the chairperson, simultaneously granting the chairperson the authority over themselves that will be necessary to keep discipline on track. Third, the board also prescribes for itself the discipline that *individual trustees* are to observe—this can take the form of a code of conduct that goes beyond the usual conflict-of-interest provisions.

As the real work of board meetings takes place, the chairperson plays a role we might describe as the board's "point person" for discipline. The term is borrowed from the old army term "point man." Everybody will get shot, but the point person will get it first. Although the chairperson has been given authority to keep the board in line, and should do so, board members must not be released from their individual responsibility to object if the board is not on track. In other words, any time a board is doing things it said it wouldn't do, making decisions it said it would leave to the CEO, judging the CEO on criteria it never set—or any of a myriad strayings from its stated discipline commitment—*every* board member whose hand does *not* go in the air to correct the straying *is culpable.* In other words, waiting for the chair to be responsible is not itself responsible.

There is irony in group responsibility wherein the group charges and empowers one of its own to help it be true to its self-defined responsibility. Your experience and mine is that who the chairperson is makes a big difference to board effectiveness, the tone of interpersonal interchange, the board's relationship with its staff, and, yes, the board's relationship with the ownership. But we have garnered that experience in the environment of traditional governance. The irony to which I refer is this: The more a board really learns how to embrace group responsibility and to express that responsibility through a coherent governance model, the less it makes any difference who the chairperson is!

I am not convinced that the most perfect board composition and board process will ever be *completely* unaffected by who the chairperson is. The powers of personal modeling and inspiration are too great for me to see that far ahead—if, indeed, that perfection does lie ahead. And I certainly do not want to take the chance that we are closer to that nirvana than we are. So, I too have a list of personal qualities I believe will lead to a chair's being able to fulfill the "servant-leadership squared" role I have described.

○ *Personal integrity.* It is important that the chair deal straightforwardly with trustee relationships and commitments. He or she neither engages in interpersonal games nor plays favorites. This person's conduct is guided more by principles than politics.

○ *Ability to leave the CEO alone.* A good chair candidate must have no need to interfere with chief executive prerogatives granted by the board. A chair who covets the type of executive authority vested in the CEO may well encroach upon that role. Although chair intervention between the board and its CEO can satisfy a board's anxieties in the short term, it inevitably causes deterioration in the proper board-CEO relationship.

○ *Intelligence and conceptual flexibility.* Because board members should all be leaders, it is hard to imagine a chair who can lead their process but is not their intellectual caliber. Because of the especially conceptual nature of leadership at this level, the ability to deal with concepts and constructs and principles is crucial.

○ *Mindfulness of group process.* Living by principle, however, need not mean unawareness of interpersonal and political realities. A candidate for the chair should be comfortable with group process, especially the ability of a group to capitalize on the talents of its members. This capability should extend to dealing calmly and appropriately with the occasional group process that goes awry. When Kipling wrote of keeping "your head when all about you are losing theirs and blaming it on you," he spoke to board chairs.

○ *A disposition of servanthood.* The chair is servant to the board and must never forget it, particularly when tough times call upon the chair to lead. The chair can never forget in whose behalf he or she works and by whose grace he or she exercises authority. The chair's compelling ambition is only to influence the board toward greater integrity and leadership.

○ *Ability to confront and lead.* The chair must be able to act with the authority the board has granted; not to do so cheats the board process. That includes the ability to confront individuals and the group with their or its own behavior. "We committed ourselves to do X, yet we at this moment are doing Y. We must either stop or change our commitment. Which shall it be?" I alluded earlier to the analogy of learning the board's song, then singing it back when board members forget. I suppose that the most effective "singing" might, on some occasions, better be described as bellowing!

These characteristics are those of a person who is capable of being *modestly in command.* The task of board chairperson calls for leadership that is both compassionate and compelling, as self-disciplined as it is obliging others to be self-disciplined. It means servant-leadership practiced by a highly capable person. It means fulfilling what Robert Greenleaf conceptualized so purely for us: The most morally justifiable leadership is founded in, legitimized by, and, yes, even sanctified by, servanthood.

Summary

The chair is servant-leader of the board. The board is servant-leader of the ownership. The chair is, therefore, servant-leader of the servant-leaders. The chair thus holds a unique twofold servant-leadership role. The woman or man in this role is ideally situated to make servant-leadership work, for this role is crafted to be an institutionalized embodiment of servant-leadership, a visible and practical model for others.

This kind of chair is guardian of group integrity, not worker of his or her own agenda. This kind of chair nurtures the ability of his or her boss—the board—to truly be and stay the boss. This kind of chair is a reflector of board discipline, like the moon shining by a light no less spectacular because it is only reflected. This kind of chair never forgets that the conductor doesn't make the music.

Dr. Ruth Mercedes Smith served as president of Highland Community College, in Freeport, Illinois, from 1991 until her death in September, 2001. Prior to 1991, she was president of Mountain Empire Community College in Virginia, and held leadership positions at Genesee Community College, in New York State, and at Waukesha County Technical College in Wisconsin. She was an active community leader and a member of numerous boards locally and nationally, including the board of the Greenleaf Center for Servant-Leadership.

Dr. Kent A. Farnsworth has been president of Crowder College, in Neosho, Missouri, since 1985. Prior to coming to Crowder, he served as dean of students at Muscatine Community College, in Muscatine, Iowa, and as director of admissions at Truman State University, in Kirksville, Missouri.

These authors bring a long history of personal servant-leadership convictions and institutional implementation of servant-leadership at their respective campuses. In this essay, they share stories of how the philosophy and practice of servant-leadership has impacted the structure and culture of their schools and of their communities at large. Both Dr. Smith and Dr. Farnsworth have attended the Greenleaf Center's Leadership Institute for Higher Education and have shared the results of their servant-leadership work with attendees at subsequent institutes.

15

SERVANT-LEADERSHIP IN
COMMUNITY COLLEGES

Ruth Mercedes Smith and Kent A. Farnsworth

Highland Community College, Freeport, Illinois

"I dwell in possibilities" is a quote by Emily Dickinson that hangs on my office wall. These words have been a guiding principle for me over the years as I worked for different community colleges in a variety of positions. This statement reminds me to plant the seeds of opportunity and then watch them grow across the campus and the community as others nurture them. It also makes it clear that while one must believe in possibilities, one cannot make things happen by oneself.

In fact, one of the most exciting things about administrative leadership is not knowing exactly how an idea will come to fruition and not having to be the only one to make something happen. My natural inclination is to develop a *task timeline* for major projects. The caveat is that the original timing and tasks will change because others will soon begin to take the opportunity in new directions.

So, while one must be organized (says my mind), one must also hang loose (says my heart) and let things happen outside of the original plan.

Thus it was with servant-leadership at Highland Community College (HCC). Some of the seeds were even planted before it was clear that this was a philosophy that would capture the hearts of many. In 1991, the college was funded by a local bank to develop a community leadership program. We included servant-leadership as one of the components of the curriculum. Then, in 1993, HCC was selected to participate in the Phi Theta Kappa Leadership project. Interestingly, servant-leadership was a piece of this course as well, so our college students became aware of the power of these concepts.

Several years later, in 1996, the board chair and I attended the first Leadership Institute for Higher Education developed by the Greenleaf Center and funded through the W. K. Kellogg Foundation. That was the point at which we realized that this philosophy could be the cornerstone for how Highland Community College would approach its work with consistency in mind and spirit.

After the retreat, several things happened that were planned according to my original task timeline: the Board of Trustees adopted a servant-leadership philosophy; information and training on the concepts were provided to various groups across the campus; an annual servant-leadership award was established; and a spring servant-leadership reception was held to recognize students, faculty, and staff who were servant-leaders.

As part of the original plan, I visited our freshman orientation classes to talk about the college. During those visits, I explained the servant-leadership concepts and helped students to understand our philosophy. Actually, many of us take this opportunity as we teach and as we speak to various groups. Also, in the summer of 1997, the college was honored with a grant from the W. K. Kellogg Foundation to develop a servant-leadership program for high school students from across the College's four-county area. This program, which included high school juniors and their adult mentors, involved the students in service projects for their communities.

After that, the timeline no longer mattered. The seeds were planted on and off campus, and many people embraced the concepts and began to not only "talk" the language but to "live" it as well. How exciting it was to sit in a Cabinet meeting at the college and discuss how we had learned to listen better or had worked on having empathy for others. As a result, many of us truly recognized that servant-leadership begins with the desire to change oneself, and we actually tried to change ourselves, which, we all know, is difficult to do. However, by working together, this challenge was manageable and the results were evident.

We were surprised to find that the 1999 Greenleaf Center summer conference on servant-leadership was of interest to many of our employees and to others in the community. At that meeting, we had HCC faculty, administrators, and support staff, plus two citizens from other Freeport agencies. This group was so energized and inspired by this conference that an informal community servant-leadership group was formed. It now calls itself the Northwestern Illinois Center for Servant-Leadership. Another seed was planted. It will be nurtured by many and will lead to new and exciting possibilities.

After this conference, another interesting thing happened on campus. The support staff member who attended decided that this was a concept that could be helpful to her colleagues. She proceeded to share information with them, and the interest grew. As a result, some of us were invited to do some additional training and exploration with them at their summer retreat. This seed, too, will take root and grow across the campus in new and different ways.

In the spring of 2000, the college sponsored a Servant-Leadership in Education workshop, led by Julie Beggs from the Greenleaf Center. Participants, who came from across the college district, left with many ideas for applying these principles in their organizations. These seeds, too, will be nurtured by others; the results cannot yet be predicted. One of the most inspiring events for us is the annual May celebration by the high school servant-leadership students. Each year, they talk about their service projects, what they have learned, and how they have applied these principles in their lives. Once again, we know the seeds have been planted and they will be growing, across the college district and beyond, as these students go to college and enter the workforce.

For me, the concept of building community in the workplace became extremely important. Most organizations function well, and the people who work in them feel okay about their work. Our dream was to become a place where people actually wanted to come to work and felt connected with each other and our students. Although that is not true for everyone, at this point I do believe that most of us feel that sense of community and know that others care about us and want to help us do our best. We are all in this together.

I see evidence of this on and off our campus. When I roam about the college, it is not unusual to see faculty members or support staff members engaged in meaningful conversation with each other or with students. People seem to be at ease, and there are many smiles. Students tell me that administrators, faculty, and staff are very helpful to them. They feel comfortable and valued by others on campus.

When I am off campus, I also have this belief verified. In the grocery store, a mother will stop me and tell me how much people at the college helped her child grow and reach goals. Recently, while I was eating breakfast in a local restaurant, a former adult student came over to tell me that she is now nearing completion of her master's degree. She has attended four educational institutions, including Highland, and she stated that HCC was the best for both education and a caring, supportive attitude.

One more interesting thing has happened as the servant-leadership concepts are being shared across the college district. Both of our local newspapers sometimes print articles that include servant-leadership information. The daily newspaper frequently carries articles about local high school students. Often, these students are members of our high school leadership program and reference is made to the program and the service projects conducted by the students. Our weekly paper also prints a monthly business issue. Recently, it began including an article about servant-leadership in each issue. This has been very exciting. Thus, the concepts are being spread through the media, and more people are becoming interested. With the help of local media, the servant-leadership message is reaching more businesses, more community members, and a greater number of homes. This is especially rewarding in a time when most coverage is given to violence and destructive actions. It is truly heartwarming to pick up the paper and read about the good things that are being done by local servant-leaders who are making a difference.

Yes, the servant-leadership philosophy has made a difference at our college. Much of my proof is subjective, but there is validation from an outside source. Two years ago, we applied for a Lincoln Award, the Illinois version of the Malcolm Baldrige Award. When the external team visited our campus, they were surprised that whenever they asked about our servant-leadership philosophy, they received clear and enthusiastic answers. It was evident that our employees knew what it was and what it meant to them.

Looking back on the evolution of servant-leadership at Highland, I see a web being spun, much like *Charlotte's Web*, with various pieces becoming connected over time. In the end, it is clear to me that the whole is much stronger than the parts. We now speak a common language internally—and often externally as well. As a result, our college functions even more effectively, and our communities' organizations work with us and understand the concepts as well. Using servant-leadership principles as our guide, we are building a stronger college, and, together with our communities, we continue to "dwell in possibilities" because we know that many wonderful things can and do happen every day in northwestern Illinois.

Crowder College, Neosho, Missouri

If asked to describe her responsibilities at Crowder College, Jan York is likely to provide a brief description of her duties as Records

Manager, then add, "Oh, and I serve on the Curriculum Committee." Having an hourly employee on a key academic committee is not at all unusual at this Missouri community college, where a secretary to one of the deans sits on an important committee reviewing insurance policies, and the payroll clerk cochairs the college's professional development committee.

At Crowder College, we take Robert Greenleaf's servant-leadership concept of *primus inter pares*—first among equals—very seriously. Although we realize that education, professional preparation, and job responsibilities establish distinctly important roles for members of the college family, if we are going to serve well, every person's contribution is critical and must be viewed as important.

Crowder's journey toward applying principles of servant-leadership took its first steps almost two decades ago in the imagination of the college's Board Chairman, Jim Tatum, after he heard the 1983 inaugural address of Stephens College's newly appointed president, Patsy Sampson. Her references to Greenleaf and servant-leadership so intrigued Tatum that, after returning home, he called Robert Greenleaf, a call that began a long and intimate friendship.

Over the next several years, Tatum systematically exposed the rest of the Crowder board to Greenleaf's leadership philosophy and cultivated an administrative team whose personal leadership interests mirrored principles of servant-leadership. When I came to Crowder in the mid-1980s, I was firmly committed to the belief that leadership is an act of service, and that the greater the leadership responsibility, the greater the obligation to serve. At Tatum's urging, I studied Greenleaf's writings, attended Greenleaf Center workshops with other members of the administrative team, and found in servant-leadership an approach to institutional governance that complemented my own interests in broad-based participation and a service-oriented working environment.

To be honest, I initially had some difficulty finding a practical handle with which to grip and apply Greenleaf's concepts. He describes leadership exactly as I think it should be exercised, but finding ways to build organization around his concepts was a challenge. I discovered some of those handles in the writings of nineteenth-century management theorist Mary Parker Follett. Though Follett was born in 1868, in the introduction to a collection of her writings, Peter Drucker credits Follett with having "struck every single chord in what now constitutes the 'management symphony' " (*Mary Parker Follett: Prophet of Management,* 1996). Educated in economics, government, law, and philosophy, she spent her early professional life in social work, immersed in a very practical side of organizational behavior. This experience and a keen understanding of human nature directed Follett's interests toward a study of organizational dynamics and shared governance. This led to the publication, in 1924, of what is generally considered her most important work: *Creative Experience.*

Two Follett principles fit hand-in-glove with the philosophical base established by Greenleaf. She referred to them as *creative conflict,* and *power with* rather than *power over.* Follett viewed organizational conflict as inevitable, but believed it served a useful purpose by illuminating areas of disagreement or misunderstanding which could then be used to foster consensus. Conflict arises either when employees do not identify with organizational goals, or when these goals are differently understood by employees and the leadership. In either case, conflict acts as an opportunity to identify which of these deficiencies exists. When resolution of the conflict is approached objectively, the result can be a creatively "integrated" solution that strengthens the organization and each person's commitment to mission and values.

The keys to finding this solution are: complete candor and openness among those involved in the conflict, plus the opportunity for as many as possible to thoroughly examine the problem. This broad involvement is the basis for the second important Follett principle applied at Crowder College: the concept of *power with* rather than *power over. Power over* is coercive and manipulative; *power with* is integrating—it considers the desires of all who are concerned with finding solutions. It assumes that the collective "we" has the power to satisfy all or most of our desires through serious examination of our interests and specific attention to where they appear to be in conflict.

I recognized in these Follett principles a means by which the college could pursue Greenleaf's goal of insuring that all served became "healthier, wiser, freer, more autonomous, more likely themselves to become servants." To develop a deliberative, "power-with" decision-making process, the college adopted, in the early 1990s, a unique approach to employee status and institutional involvement. Crowder faculty are not tenured and do not have faculty rank. All employees (including the President) are annually evaluated and are on annually renewable contracts. All administrators have teaching responsibility, and professional staff are compensated based on the same salary schedule that is used for faculty. At the beginning of the 1990s, the college divided itself into six functional areas called Planning and Institutional Improvement Groups, affectionately known on campus as PIIGs. Every person working at the college belonged to a PIIG. Membership was designed to provide variety in gender, job responsibility, and experience. PIIG groups of approximately 20 to 25 persons identified and evaluated issues related to Instruction and Curriculum, Student Services and Satisfaction, Marketing and Community Relations, Fiscal and Physical Management, Personnel and Organizational Issues, and Institutional Assessment and Evaluation. PIIGs reported to a Steering Committee consisting of the PIIG chairs and the college administrative team. During the first two years of the college's experience with the PIIG model, each employee went through team-building training presented by a regional hospital that has a long and successful history of team-based management.

As experience with the "Six PIIG" model grew, a number of shortcomings became apparent. During the 1999 academic year, college-wide meetings evaluated and modified the organizational plan. With the assistance of outside facilitators, the entire college community evaluated how the process might be improved. Though employees uniformly agreed that they appreciated input into decision making, three important shortcomings of the model were identified through this process.

1. Planning was being done across broad functional areas, without the specific departmental planning that unit managers needed to evaluate success.

2. PIIGs were not remaining equally active. Some were having regular assignments and productivity; others were floundering.

3. Assignments to PIIGs were too broad-based and lacked sufficient definition, time lines, and results expectations to provide the needed direction.

Based on these observations and a series of follow-up planning sessions, the college community determined that universal involvement needed to remain a priority, but planning activity should be moved from the six generic PIIGs to smaller action units. "Project Implementation and Improvement Groups" (PIIG-II) were developed to replace the cumbersome PIIGs of the past.

To ensure that all members of the Crowder family continued to be involved in decision making, each employee was asked to indicate his or her participation interest areas, and the commitment to assign people to only one group annually was continued. Under the existing model, as departments need data or identify areas of desired improvement, small PIIGs are formed as "action teams." Membership is drawn from the interest lists, and emphasis is again on diverse representation. These action teams have clearly defined projects and time lines, and are disbanded after their work is completed. Consistent with the exercise of *power with,* there is no guarantee that every recommendation will be implemented, but there is an assurance that every view will be considered and valued. During the first year with the new system, 70 percent of full-time employees were part of a project team, and no recommendation was rejected.

Each year, all employees at Crowder College are invited to evaluate the President's performance, and the college conducts a general assessment of institutional climate. Feedback indicates that
employees working within this system feel empowered and appreciated. One hourly staff member wrote in her comments: "It's nice
to know that what I think about issues at the college is listened to,
just like everybody else." Another commented: "This really is a
place where everyone feels valued."

Despite these expressions of satisfaction, we acknowledge that
servant-leadership requires a mindset about leadership that many,
including a few within the Crowder family, view as uncomfortable. To be an effective servant-leader, the leader must yield significant power to others, and until they are sufficiently prepared,
those others may not wish to share in that power. One faculty
member wrote on his evaluation: "I wish the administration
would just make the decisions, and leave the rest of us out of it."
Yet the leader must believe that the only reasons for holding exclusive power is to exercise control over others, or to compensate
for lack of trust. When trust is a major objective and control is
not, power must be shared.

Servant-leadership also means more work—or at least a significantly more involving kind of work. It means participating as
a peer on some occasions, as a facilitator on others, and as a director in still others. It means understanding the organization in
a complete, holistic way so as to have a sense for where the institution is not serving as it should. It means getting in early and
staying late, becoming infinitely patient and increasingly tough-
skinned. Unlike the authoritative models in which the boss isn't
questioned, it invites constant review and evaluation of the leader
and his or her actions.

Servant-leadership does not mean, however, that the leader is ab-
solved of final responsibility for the effectiveness and success of the
organization. Some decisions, for legal or confidentiality reasons,
cannot be shared widely. Others, where consensus cannot be
reached, require a final judgment. Servant-leadership simply means
that whenever possible, every effort is made to hear each voice. It

accepts that good people, if they are given good information and share common vision and values, will make good decisions for themselves and for the organization. It also assumes that when time constraints, legality, confidentiality, or failure to reach consensus force the decision to the leader, the judgment then made reflects the leader's best effort to serve all concerned.

Dr. John C. Burkhardt is a professor of higher education and the director of the Kellogg Forum at the University of Michigan in Ann Arbor, Michigan. From 1993 to 2000, he served as program director, Leadership and Higher Education, at the W. K. Kellogg Foundation. Earlier, he held leadership positions at the University of Detroit Mercy and at Eastern Michigan University. He is coauthor of *The Guide to Student Success* and *Leadership in the Making,* and a contributing author to *Leadership Reconsidered.*

Larry C. Spears has served as CEO of the Robert K. Greenleaf Center for Servant-Leadership since 1990. Before that, he held positions with the Greater Philadelphia Philosophy Consortium, the Great Lakes Colleges Association's Philadelphia Center, and *Friends Journal.* He has edited or coedited six books on servant-leadership (see the *Recommended Reading* section of this book), as well as the contemporary essay series, *Voices of Servant-Leadership.*

In this essay, Burkhardt and Spears examine the moral responsibilities of philanthropic institutions by focusing on the application of servant-leadership characteristics in the philanthropic milieu. In the process, they pose some questions that challenge us to reconceive and reframe the work and attitudes of philanthropic organizations.

16

SERVANT-LEADERSHIP AND PHILANTHROPIC INSTITUTIONS

John Burkhardt and Larry C. Spears

CONSIDER THE FOLLOWING LIST of leadership authorities: James Autry, Warren Bennis, Ken Blanchard, Peter Block, Stephen Covey, Max DePree, Peter Drucker, Frances Hesselbein, Joe Jaworski, Jim Kouzes, M. Scott Peck, Peter Senge, Peter Vaill, Margaret Wheatley, and Danah Zohar. What do these authors have in common? All of them have been explicitly or implicitly influenced by the writings of Robert K. Greenleaf, and, like many other leadership authors, they are increasingly calling attention to the growing influence of Greenleaf's concept of servant-leadership.

The concept of servant-leadership sounds so paradoxical. What is it, and how can it enhance our understanding and practice of philanthropy in this new century? Over the past decade, we have experienced a significant trend toward values, ethics, and service-based leadership within many philanthropic organizations. A growing number of leadership education programs now focus on servant-leadership. A few of the notable advocates of servant-leadership in philanthropy and fund-raising include: James Gregory Lord (author, *The Raising of Money*), John Lore (former board chair, National Society of Fund Raising Executives), Milton Murray (Philanthropic Service for Institutions), Betty Overton (W. K. Kellogg Foundation),

Robert Payton (The Center on Philanthropy), the late Henry Rosso (The Fund-Raising School), Janet Haas (William Penn Foundation), James Shannon (Council on Foundations), and Susan Wisely (Lilly Endowment).

Today there are many signs that some outdated styles of leadership are slowly giving way to a better model—an approach which is based upon teamwork and community; one which seeks to involve others in decision making; one which is strongly based in ethical and caring behavior; and one which is enhancing the growth of people, while at the same time improving the caring and quality of our many institutions. We call this emerging approach "servant-leadership."

Understanding Servant-Leadership

The concept of servant-leadership originated in the 1970 essay by Greenleaf entitled *The Servant as Leader.* Bob Greenleaf was born in Terre Haute, Indiana, and spent most of his organizational life in the field of management research, development, and education at AT&T. Following a 40-year career at AT&T, he enjoyed a second career, which lasted another 25 years. During this time, he served as an influential consultant to a number of major institutions, including MIT, the Ford Foundation, and Lilly Endowment, Inc., to name but three. In 1964, he founded the Center for Applied Ethics, which was renamed the Robert K. Greenleaf Center in 1985.

Greenleaf distilled his observations in a series of essays and books on the theme of the servant-as-leader. The idea of the servant-as-leader came partly out of Greenleaf's half-century of experience in working to shape large institutions. But the event which crystallized his thinking came in the 1960s, when he first read Hermann Hesse's short novel, *Journey to the East.* Hesse's book is the story of a mythical journey by a group of people on a spiritual quest. The central figure of the story is Leo, who accompanies the party as their servant, and who sustains them with his caring spirit. All goes well with the journey until one day Leo disappears. The group quickly falls apart, and the journey is abandoned. They discover that they cannot make it without the servant Leo. After many years of searching, the narrator of the story stumbles upon Leo and is taken into the religious order that had sponsored the original journey. There he discovers that Leo, whom he had first known as a servant, was in fact the head of the order, its guiding spirit, and a great and noble leader (Hesse, 1956).

After reading this story, Greenleaf concluded that the central meaning of it was that the great leader is first experienced as a servant to others, and that this simple fact is central to his or her greatness. True leadership emerges from those whose primary motivation is a deep desire to help others (Greenleaf, 1970).

Since 1970, over a half-million copies of Greenleaf's books and essays have been sold worldwide. Slowly but surely, Robert K. Greenleaf's servant-leadership writings have made a deep and lasting impression upon people who are concerned with issues of leadership, management, philanthropy, service, and spiritual growth.

Who is a servant-leader? Greenleaf said that the servant-leader is one who is servant-first. In *The Servant as Leader* (1970), he wrote: "It begins with the natural feeling that one wants to serve, to serve first. Then conscious choice brings one to aspire to lead. The best test is: Do those served grow as persons; do they, while being served, become healthier, wiser, freer, more autonomous, more likely themselves to become servants? And, what is the effect on the least privileged in society; will they benefit?" (p. 4).

Greenleaf goes on to say that authentic leaders are chosen by followers, and that the ability to lead with integrity depends on the leader's skills for withdrawal and action, for listening and persuasion, and for practical goalsetting combined with intuitive foresight. Servant-leadership is an idea that begins with the self, but leads to concrete action (Greenleaf, 1970).

The term "servant-leadership" was first coined in 1970, but it is clearly a belief with roots that stretch back through thousands of years of both religious and humanistic teachings. Many people are increasingly calling attention to Bob Greenleaf as being one of the earliest proponents of today's emerging approach to management and leadership.

All of us are both leaders and followers in different parts of our lives. Servant-leadership encourages everyone to balance leading and serving within their own lives. It reminds people who are in leadership positions that their primary responsibility is in serving others. It encourages those in follower positions to look for situational opportunities to provide leadership. The end result of this moving back-and-forth between leading and following is: we enhance our lives as individuals, and we raise the very possibilities of our many institutions.

Characteristics of the Servant-Leader

The following characteristics are considered central to the development of servant-leaders:

1. *Listening.* Leaders have traditionally been valued for their communication and decision-making skills. Servant-leaders reinforce these important skills with a focus on listening intently and reflectively to others in order to identify and clarify the will of a group of people.

2. *Empathy.* Servant-leaders strive to understand and empathize with others. They accept and recognize others for their unique gifts and spirits. One assumes the good intentions of coworkers and does not reject them as people.

3. *Healing.* Learning how to help heal difficult situations is a powerful force for transforming organizations. Servant-leaders recognize that they have an opportunity to help make whole those people and institutions with whom they come in contact.

4. *Persuasion.* Another characteristic of servant-leaders is a reliance on persuasion, rather than using one's positional authority, in making organizational decisions. Servant-leaders seek to convince others rather than to coerce compliance. They are effective at building consensus within groups.

5. *Awareness.* General awareness, and especially self-awareness, strengthens the servant-leader. Awareness aids one in understanding issues involving ethics and values, and it enables one to approach situations from a more integrated, holistic position.

6. *Foresight.* The ability to foresee the likely outcome of a given situation is a characteristic that enables the servant-leader to understand the lessons from the past, the realities of the present, and the likely consequences of a decision for the future. Foresight is deeply rooted within the intuitive mind.

7. *Conceptualization.* Servant-leaders seek to nurture their abilities to dream great dreams. This means that one must be able to think beyond day-to-day management realities.

8. *Commitment to the growth of people.* Servant-leaders believe that people have an intrinsic value beyond their tangible contributions as workers. As such, servant-leaders are deeply committed to the personal, professional, and spiritual growth of everyone within an organization.

9. *Stewardship.* Greenleaf's view of organizations was one in which CEOs, staff members, and trustees all play significant roles in holding their institutions in trust for the greater good of society. In effect, everyone has a responsibility to be a good steward within an organization.

10. *Building community.* Servant-leaders seek to build a sense of community among those within an organization. Greenleaf said, in *The Servant as Leader:* "All that is needed to rebuild community as a viable life form for large numbers of people is for enough servant-leaders to show the way, not by mass movements, but by each servant-leader demonstrating his or her own unlimited liability for a quite specific community-related group" (p. 30).

These 10 characteristics of servant-leadership are by no means exhaustive. However, they serve to communicate the power and promise that this concept offers to those who are open to its invitation and challenge.

Servant-Leadership and the Moral Responsibilities of Philanthropic Organizations

What are the implications of Greenleaf's writings for the work of philanthropic organizations? This is not a new topic to either the servant-leadership movement or to U.S. foundations. During Robert Greenleaf's life, he served as an adviser to several U.S. foundations, and he practiced philanthropy on a personal basis as well. Not only have his writings inspired many within the field, but it is clear that many of his writings were themselves inspired by the problems, the processes, and the responsibilities of organized philanthropic work.

But the field of philanthropy is growing and changing, along with the society it seeks to serve. Philanthropic resources and efforts have expanded over the past decade, and the types of issues addressed by philanthropies, and the approaches to address them, have become more complex and, in many ways, more aggressive. Beginning in the 1980s, U.S. foundations began to take a closer look at the impact of their efforts. Program evaluation became more common and more sophisticated. Social problems that had been identified in the previous 20 to 30 years still loomed, and the trustees of philanthropic organizations began to question the efficacy of quasi-charitable investments. Within the foundation community (and within government policy circles as well), the reliance on demonstration models as catalysts for larger social change objectives came into question. Increasingly, foundations began to focus efforts on defined initiatives through which specific changes would be sought for identified issues.

This new direction, while not a universal trend, substantially describes the field. Moreover, it raises some questions about the role that philanthropic institutions play as leaders in a changing society. The trend suggests a need to examine the writings of Greenleaf and others who have thought about the roles of service and leadership as being intertwined and interdependent. Characteristics of servant-leadership hold special meaning when applied by philanthropic institutions.

Listening

It begins with listening. Greenleaf reminds us that leaders have a special responsibility to remain attentive to the voices of those they serve. Philanthropies must make extra efforts to minimize the barriers to communication that separate them from their constituencies and from the communities in which they work. This is a special challenge, given the perceptions held—and the realities, too—of the relative distribution of power in relationships with potential and current grantees.

As the work of philanthropic institutions has become increasingly focused on strategic initiatives, a great deal of effort has been placed on "getting the message out" about foundation efforts within society. To support this work, several major foundations have recruited talented individuals to serve as communication consultants, or have developed an in-house communication capacity to support their programming initiatives. Greenleaf offers us something to think about in this regard, in his essay, *The Servant as Leader*. He draws upon the prayer of St. Francis of Assisi, which says, in part: "Grant that I may not seek first to be understood, but to understand."

Listening, as Greenleaf pointed out many times, is an attitude. It is rooted in a genuine interest in the viewpoints and perspectives of those served. This observation has two very real implications for philanthropic work. One implication can be seen in the internal practices of the philanthropic process, as found in many established institutions. The other is a challenge to the role that philanthropy plays in the larger society. The process by which philanthropic organizations come to decisions is often based on a series of questions framed and raised by the institution, to which grantees are invited to respond (invited in the sense that if the grantee stops responding, the relationship is ended). Throughout this interaction, the philanthropy sets the pace and the context of the discussion, poses the questions, and evaluates the responses. If this is a process of dialogue, it hardly constitutes listening in the sense that Greenleaf describes. Instead, he challenges us ("Servant Responsibility in a Bureaucratic Society," in *Servant-Leadership*, page 301) to maintain "an openness within the widest possible frame of reference" when we are interacting with those whom we seek to lead and serve.

Philanthropies have a special responsibility that goes beyond listening for themselves: to lift up and amplify the voices of those who are unheard within society. The unique circumstances of established philanthropic organizations give them a place and a stature in American society. This privilege comes with a responsibility to make sure that the dialogue that creates our public consensus is inclusive of voices that are often lost. At the end of Greenleaf's essay, in which he speaks of the responsibilities of trustees in philanthropic organizations, he quotes Abraham Joshua Heschel: "All worlds are in need of exaltation, and everyone is charged to lift what is low, to unite what lies apart, to advance what is left behind." Or, as suggested by the Tuscarora Indian proverb, "Man has responsibility, not power."

Empathy

It is entirely appropriate that Greenleaf begins his description of servant-leadership with a discussion of the importance of listening. Only through that act can we access the other qualities important to servant-leadership—most notably, that of empathy. In his essay *The Servant as Leader,* Greenleaf combines a discussion of the importance of empathy by building a contrast with the idea of acceptance:

> These are two interesting words, acceptance and empathy. If we can take one dictionary's definition, *acceptance* is receiving what is offered, with approbation, satisfaction, or acquiescence, and *empathy* is the imaginative projection of one's own consciousness into another being. The opposite of both, the word

reject, is to refuse to hear or receive — to throw out. (*The Servant as Leader,* italics in the original.)

Philanthropic organizations are, to a large extent, organized around rituals of acceptance and rejection. Prospective grantees approach foundations with proposals, in hopes of having them accepted. Foundation officials review proposals with the responsibility to recommend either acceptance or rejection. The very word "grant" implies a relationship between foundations and their primary constituencies (grantees) that is far more closely associated with Greenleaf's observations about acceptance in contrast to empathy.

It is a matter of fact that foundations receive far more proposals than can possibly be funded, and therefore program staff and trustees are unavoidably in a position to make judgments about the relative merits associated with ideas. This occupation with judging ideas can easily (and some may say, necessarily) lead to a preoccupation with judging people. And when one is limited to seeing people solely in terms of the needs that they bring, as opposed to their values, assets, and strengths, it is predictable that one would begin to see them as self-interested, self-serving, and weak.

In a talk with faculty at Barnard College in 1960, Greenleaf spoke of the importance of maintaining an empathetic connection between those in positions of influence and those whom they are required, by circumstance, to judge. While his contextual reference is the classroom, the concept translates easily enough to the work of philanthropic organizations. Referring to the cultivation of servant-leadership under conditions in which power is unevenly distributed within a relationship, he said:

> Finally there is a developing *view of people. All* people are seen as beings to be trusted, believed in, and loved, and less as objects to be used, competed with, or judged.

As a former director of human resources at AT&T, Greenleaf spoke frequently of the importance of empathy as a quality at work inside organizations as well. He admonished organizational leaders to trust in their own employees and to organize work in ways that created conditions in which employees learned to respect, trust, and value one another. It is difficult to expect foundation staff to identify and empathize with others when they experience leaders and organizational cultures that fail to treat them as worthy and valuable individuals.

Healing

Can philanthropic organizations really make claim to a healing role in the societies they serve? Only if they enact this healing role in the context of the involvement and engaged partnership that we have described previously. Society's characterization of healing and the role of the healer often suggests, at best, a dispassionate and detached outsider whose views of health are imposed on the stricken. But worse, as Ivan Illich argues in *Medical Nemesis* (1976), the healer can be a most serious threat to health by fostering a relationship of false dependence or by contributing to "an industry of despair." Greenleaf acknowledges this risk of "giving as a potentially immoral act" in his essay on the role of trustees in foundations ("Servant Leadership in Foundations," 1973), a dynamic directly at odds with his view of leadership as service to promote the autonomy of those served, and his view of healing, as well.

Greenleaf's challenge to serve in a healing role is meant in a very different way and begins with a commitment to heal one's self. The best efforts of philanthropy to deal with racism, improve opportunity, promote peace or build community cannot succeed unless those efforts are reflected internally as well as externally. The implications for foundation hiring practices, trustee selection, strategic orientation, decision procedures, and communication approaches are obvious. Less clear, but equally important, are considerations about investment decisions, the style and location of corporate offices, and even the internal relationships and practices that create a sense of the organizational culture.

Foundations do have a unique opportunity to provide leadership in the ongoing process of reconciliation, which is the basis for a working civil society within the United States. As a society, we often debate the relative merits of *pluribus vs. unum,* as if we had a choice of being either "many" or "one." Organized philanthropy within the United States has the opportunity to bridge this false dichotomy and to promote respect for differences, while, at the same time, it builds connections among people, ideas, and resources.

Persuasion

Perhaps no servant-leadership role comes as naturally to organized philanthropy as that of Greenleaf's description of persuasion. Greenleaf uses this term to distinguish between leadership that relies on positional authority and coercion, in contrast to leadership that works through a process of influence, example, and moral power.

It is worth examining the role of philanthropy in terms of the classic theories of leadership that operated at the time of Greenleaf's career and during the period of his early writing. Leadership authority, as viewed in the prevailing models, was based on three sources of power: rational grounds, traditional grounds, and charismatic grounds (Parsons, 1947). Rational power derived from positional status within a formal (hierarchical) structure. Traditional power was rooted in cultural relationships of an "immemorial" nature. Charismatic power, the closest analog to leadership authority vested in the influence rather than the status of the leader, was reserved to a "certain quality of an individual . . . set apart from ordinary men . . . endowed with supernatural, superhuman, or at least specifically exceptional powers . . . not accessible to the ordinary person, but . . . regarded as of divine origin . . ." (Weber, 1921).

Greenleaf was entirely familiar with this formulation of leadership and used it as an organizing structure for his essay on "The Leadership Crisis" (1978). He goes beyond the Weberian construction of power and describes the concept of persuasive authority. He also introduces the concept of the persuasive power of institutions.

Consider the role of foundations in U.S. society in light of the classic conception of authority. They enjoy no direct coercive authority over government policy at any level. Corporations have greater access to formal resources and exercise a greater influence on economic and community circumstances within society. Foundations are specifically proscribed from lobbying and do not have the power of the vote. They do not enjoy the benefits of a direct constituency, have no means to directly foster civil unrest, or even, in most cases, provide direct, hands-on, and face-to-face service to anyone. Even the amount of resources controlled by U.S. foundations is generally overstated: Of all the charitable giving that occurs in the United States each year, only about 1 percent comes from foundations. By far the largest share of philanthropy originates with gifts made by individuals.

And yet few would argue that philanthropies lack influence. The means by which this influence is actualized comes, by and large, through the persuasive power of which Greenleaf writes. The tools of philanthropy are meager in some respects: demonstration models, support for promising projects, resources to the fledgling, some research, the rare but occasional bequest for a building or institute. The power to influence society comes, in part, from the ideas these efforts embody and the potential they hold. The persuasive power of foundations is rooted in many small things that take on larger significance because of the way they come into being.

Awareness

Greenleaf wrote of awareness and of the need to see things as interconnected whole systems long before the current discussion on systemic leadership was enjoined. Thought leaders in the field of "the new science" of leadership—Wheatley, Senge, Jaworski, and others—all give credit to Greenleaf's perception of the essential interdependence of events and causes, problems and solutions.

But translating the concept of individual knowledge, the process of "knowing," and the role that Greenleaf describes as the "leader as seeker" to an institutional perspective requires some adaptation. How do institutions create an attitude of awareness? How would this value and behavior be expressed on an organizational basis?

Senge's often cited description of the learning organization is probably consistent with Greenleaf's view of awareness as translated to a foundation setting. The learning organization is one characterized by openness, freedom of expression, and a focused curiosity in which learning becomes practiced as both a central value and a core competency. Foundations that systematically examine the impact of their own efforts and the environments in which they take place, and then adjust their efforts accordingly, are examples of this commitment.

Fully accepting awareness as a chosen characteristic of organizational life means coming face-to-face with uncertainty and ambiguity. These descriptors are not easily associated with the culture of U.S. foundations; in fact, often the opposite is true. If one were to plot the predisposition of foundations as we sometimes do with people, along the lines of an organizational Myers–Briggs scale, we would describe foundations as "judging" as opposed to "perceiving" in their approach to the organization of their work. Proposals are reviewed and accepted for funding, or rejected. Foundation executives and staff are often chosen and evaluated on the basis of their good judgment, as opposed to the breadth of their perceptions. Awareness is often a secondary characteristic in the foundation environment. Greater value is placed on objectivity, detachment, or expert knowledge.

Philanthropic work is absorbing, even fascinating. This fact makes it all the more important that those engaged in these efforts fight the tendency toward preoccupation with the process of making grants—or worse, an obsession with organizational issues that comes at the expense of an awareness of those who are to be served. If anything, the emphasis on strategy and alignment as the bases for effectiveness on the part of organized philanthropy can blind us to real conditions and real challenges that exist in the larger society.

Foresight

Philanthropic organizations lead a rather divided existence as relates to the concept of time. In many cases, particularly among the nation's most "established" foundations, the resources for philanthropic work derive from a decision that was made some time in the past, often by individuals (or, in many cases, a family of individuals) who are no longer involved in the active management of their benefaction. The bequests were made in a specific social context and were guided by a set of time-related perspectives and values, sometimes with a specific set of social conditions or objectives in mind. This is the way in which many of the largest foundations in the United States were created, and their names should remind us that actual, historical individuals made decisions some time ago that allowed the work of these organizations to go forward: Ford, Rockefeller, Kellogg, Carnegie, Lilly, Mott, and many others.

But these gifts, while made in the past, were given with the future in mind. At the very heart of philanthropy is the responsibility to take the past and present forward into the future. Those charged with managing the resources derived from a gift made in a previous era are also charged with trying to understand and interpret the intentions and wishes of individuals who, in most cases, had no idea of the circumstances in which the philanthropies that bear their names would operate. For this reason, it is a mistake for those engaged in this work to limit their perspective to the question of how the donor's wishes might be interpreted if he or she were alive at present. The real task is to accept the challenge that the original donor took on: Commit resources now, not with the present in mind, but with the future in mind.

Greenleaf speaks of this paradox in his essay, *The Servant as Leader.* He first articulated the idea in his 1969 lecture to the students and faculty at Dartmouth College: "Let us liken now to the spread of light from a narrowly focused beam. There is a bright intense center, this moment of clock time, and a diminishing intensity, theoretically out to infinity, on either side. As viewed here, now includes all of this—all of history and all of the future."

The mechanics of philanthropic work within our largest foundations involve great use of trend and analytic data, intended to get a fix on the current environment. Great store is placed on the ability of foundation staff and trustees to understand and interpret the challenges that face the societies they serve. Greenleaf reminds us that leadership in this field is equally a creative act, prospective in nature. "Foresight is the 'lead' the leader has," and those who fail to relate their actions to the future soon lose their ability to contribute as leaders, regardless of their endowment.

It is not too much to say that organized philanthropies have a special responsibility to represent and protect the future within U.S. society. They do not have to publish earnings reports or return profits to stockholders. They do not have to stand for reelection. In most cases, they have no need to appeal for public support. They have but one true constituency: the future. Philanthropy would do well to consider the test placed on decisions within the Native American tradition—a concern not merely for the present but for seven generations to come.

Conceptualization

The work of philanthropy takes place in a world that is increasingly glutted with information and yet starved for meaning. Greenleaf's writings were based on organizational life in a very different era; nonetheless, he expressed a belief that leaders have a unique responsibility to search for and articulate coherence for the groups they lead. True to the themes that run through his work, he argued that this is a process that is both intellectual and spiritual, and that rather than being the solitary gift of a leader working in isolation from his or her peers, the process of conceptualization is rooted in relationships and shared meanings.

If Greenleaf were writing today, we could not be certain that he would have framed the distinction between conceptual and operational leadership in just the same way that he did when he wrote his essay on *The Institution as Servant* (1972). His stated view—that conceptualization is the unique gift of leaders at the top of a hierarchical organization—has been challenged by advances in the ways in which information becomes available and is put to use, by the pace of change within organizations, and by the general trend to flatten organizational structures that are placing greater responsibility and adaptive capacity into more hands. But his central idea, that leaders effectively create the group by having a primary role in defining its central purpose, is a thought very appropriate to the current situation.

When ideas of all sorts flash through the marketplace of consciousness, the tendency is to associate no idea with much meaning, knowing that another will soon replace it. In fact, the preoccupation of the media with (literally) "news"—that is, only what is new and different—supports a culture where all ideas are transitory and hold equal nonimportance. Within this milieu, the leader's role is to help in the recognition of "a great hope held in common" (to use Teilhard de Chardin's phrase) and to literally "make meaning" with and on behalf of the group he or she leads.

This process of meaning–making is very much related to the current preoccupation, in our business and political leadership literature, with the idea of "vision." Unfortunately, vision has become identified as an attribute enjoyed by leaders, rather than a process that engages leaders and followers together. Despite Greenleaf's description of conceptualization as a "prime talent" of leaders, it might be seen in its larger context to be a "way" rather than an innate quality or even a skill—a way that binds individuals and ideas in a common commitment.

Philanthropic work is increasingly attentive to this responsibility of leadership. Where once the processes of grant making seemed reactive and distant, there are increasing attempts to engage collectively in the definition of problems and strategies. Philanthropic organizations can begin by looking at their own hierarchies and the ways in which they are infused with "common purpose," the degree to which this sense of commitment is the result of open interaction, and a shared construction of meaning, inside and outside the organization.

Commitment to the Growth of People

Robert Greenleaf offered a significant departure from most models of leadership when he spoke of leaders as servants to others. Previous writing in the field of leadership, extant at the time of Greenleaf's essays, placed the leader at the center of interaction with followers. Leaders directed, followers responded. Leaders brought unique gifts, talents, and aspirations to their interactions. Followers were agents, generally indistinguishable one from another, and valued for their compliance, not their potential. In fact, given the logic of a single leader at the top of a structured hierarchy, followers with a penchant for high achievement were potential threats in the long run.

Greenleaf turned this thinking upside down. His challenge to leaders was to put the needs of their followers first and to subject their leadership to this test: "Do those served grow as persons; do they, while being served, become healthier, wiser, freer, more autonomous, more likely themselves to become servants?"

This may be the heart of Greenleaf's message, and it is a direct reflection of the choices that Greenleaf made during his career at AT&T. He came to see his role, enacted over many years and in relationship with many colleagues, as a commitment to the growth of people. This was, to him, a high calling.

Foundations view their missions in the context of a similar commitment but are often challenged by the temptation to define themselves in terms of the issues they address or the aspirations they hold. It is a difficult discipline to consider philanthropic investments as commitments to people, not problems. Such a focus places an entirely different perspective on the conceptualization of the work. "Who is served? How? Is this the way in which they would choose to be served?"

And most troubling, "How do we measure the impact of what we do?" If our commitment is to the growth of individuals, our evaluation of impact will be guided by very different considerations. We would look for measurable improvement in the lives of individuals—in their opportunities, their capacities, the relief of their pain, and the maximization of their potential. The work of philanthropies would be changed in many fundamental ways if individual people—not social problems, not economic, political, or environmental circumstances—were at the heart of the effort.

Stewardship

One definition of stewardship, offered by Peter Block, is "holding something in trust for another." In a very direct way, this is the exact role of philanthropies in the United States, and it plays out in multiple ways.

The wealthy individuals who created our large foundations chose to place their wealth in the hands of a (literally) trusted organization that would, in turn, act on some responsibility in the founder's stead. These founders' decisions, taken at different points and by different individuals over the past hundred years, had this same fundamental intention: to establish a stewardship over the resources of the philanthropist that would outlive the benefactor. This has, and should have, a direct impact on the decisions taken by officers and trustees of foundations as they act on a historic trust in a modern context.

The concept of stewardship operates in a second, arguably more important, way. The wealth that created our nation's foundations was sheltered from further taxation by the decision to establish a continuing public philanthropy. In this regard, it is a resource that is held in trust for society every bit as much as it is held on behalf of the original benefactor. If taxed, most of the benefice provided by Henry Ford or W. K. Kellogg or Andrew Carnegie would have long been redistributed to others through tax policy. Bluntly, it would be gone—or at least impossible to find. No doubt it might have done some good, but the fact that it is still in an identifiable *corpus,* and is associated with the work of a specific organization, is the result of an intentional provision in the public law. In this interpretation, foundations operate as stewards for a public interest. They hold resources on behalf of a society.

This responsibility is complete with challenges and obligations and, as Greenleaf points out, its own moral dilemmas. In his extended parable, *Teacher as Servant,* he describes the situation of a foundation executive faced with the evidence that his organization has been less than effective and, worse yet, less than vigilant. Greenleaf makes it clear by his construction of dialogue in this lesson that the temptation to let "giving [become] a potentially immoral act" is manifest in the sin of inaction just as much as in action. The many layers of insulation that protect the foundation from its direct public accountability cannot ameliorate the moral responsibility that comes through an existential basis in stewardship.

Building Community

Even though Greenleaf spent much of his professional life in the context of one of America's largest corporations, he maintained a deep sense of the importance of community in the lives of people. Greenleaf spoke often about the influence of a sociology professor who, during his senior year in college, challenged him to get involved in one of the big institutions of society and to do what he could to turn the institution into a vehicle for service. Over the course of Greenleaf's career, he learned that no organization could be oriented to serve if it lacked its own sense of internal cohesion and purpose. Therefore, the first challenge for an organized philanthropy is to seek community from within.

"All that is needed to rebuild community as a viable life form for large numbers of people is for enough servant leaders to show the way, not by mass movements, but by each servant-leader demonstrating his own liability for a quite specific community-related group," wrote Greenleaf.

A sense of community within a foundation is not an end in itself, but rather a means of drawing upon an immediate experience in order to more plainly promote it within the larger society. The leadership that is at the heart of philanthropic work is leadership directed to the creation of community. In Greenleaf's essay, "The Ethic of Strength," he speaks of requirements for leadership that should be nurtured in the young leader. Among them is the need to ask: "Am I connected?" While the question is posed in the context of a young person's self-examination, Greenleaf's elaboration is appropriate to the modern philanthropic organization. Connectedness suggests the ability to be at once "on the growing edge of the contemporary phase of history but still connected to the main body of people and events" (*On Becoming a Servant-Leader*, 1996).

How is this accomplished? The key may be found in Greenleaf's admonition to live and operate in an integrated way. Foundations must make a determined effort to be both state-of-the-art and state-of-the-heart in relation to those they wish to lead. With access to expert staff and a world of eager consultants, they must discipline their efforts to build and honor bonds with people at all levels and from many perspectives within the society they serve. And this is only the start.

Foundations must set a vision for community that goes beyond access and contact, and approach the more difficult challenge of engagement. The sense of community envisioned by Robert Greenleaf does not tolerate much self-interest, nor provide much in the way of shelter from real relationships with real people in real situations.

Conclusion

Public interest in the philosophy and practice of servant-leadership is now higher than ever before. Many books and articles on servant-leadership appeared in the 1990s, and dozens of organizations have begun to incorporate servant-leadership internally. Servant-leadership has slowly but surely gained thousands of practitioners over the past 30 years—both inside and outside philanthropy. The seeds that Bob Greenleaf first planted have begun to sprout in many philanthropic institutions, and in the hearts of people who long to improve the human condition. Servant-leadership provides a framework out of which many people today are now working to create more caring institutions. We have written this essay for those persons and institutions who wish to accept the challenge of bringing servant-leadership more fully into the twenty-first-century world of philanthropic organizations. We invite you to reflect on this closing thought by Robert Greenleaf:

> The servant-leader may be not so much the prophetic visionary (that is a rare gift) as the convener, sustainer, discerning guide for seekers who wish to remain open to prophetic visions. The maintenance functions within all sorts of institutions may not require leaders of any sort, but seekers, of which every institution should have some, must have servant-leaders.

David S. Young is a pastor and professor who has served a number of congregations in regular and interim pastorates. Currently he serves as Congregation Transformation Specialist, National Ministries, for The American Baptist Churches, USA. He is also Intentional Interim Pastor, for Hatfield Church of the Brethren, in Hatfield, Pennsylvania. He is the author of several books relating to congregational life and church renewal, including *Servant Leadership for Church Renewal: Shepherds by the Living Spring.*

In this essay, David Young encourages us to learn to practice the art of foresight, the trait that Greenleaf called "the 'lead' of the leader." Young takes us through the process he uses to help congregations "see things whole" in order to find the focus of their work and make strategic, measurable plans. In this essay, he gives some practical suggestions on the process of discernment and learning to "move with the lead of the leader."

17

FORESIGHT: THE LEAD
THAT THE LEADER HAS

David S. Young

IN HIS ORIGINAL AND DEFINING monograph, *The Servant as Leader*, Robert Greenleaf says, "Foresight is the 'lead' that the leader has. Once he loses this lead and events start to force his hand, he is leader in name only. He is not leading; he is reacting to immediate events and he probably will not long be a leader." Foresight, according to Larry Spears, CEO of the Greenleaf Center for Servant-Leadership, is an area not frequently written about and largely unexplored in leadership studies, but it is a topic he feels is most deserving of careful attention. Using foresight in servant-leadership since the 1970s, in my work in the nonprofit sector in general and in the faith community in particular, I have found foresight to be a key component in the turnaround process for organizations.

Foresight is critical in helping organizations move from a survival outlook, reacting to the immediate events, to being proactive, moving with an incremental plan. In fact, Robert Greenleaf calls foresight the "central ethic of leadership." An art, not a science, foresight helps us to draw together the strands of factors we face, to act in that critical moment when we have the ability to do so, and then to move in some direction with a plan. In this essay, we will look at four components of foresight: (1) foreseeing the unforeseeable; (2) using the art of discernment; (3) moving with the lead of the leader; and (4) developing a creative, measurable plan.

Foreseeing the Unforeseeable

When I was exploring servanthood as a leadership style in the early 1970s, foreseeing the unforeseeable was one of the things that drew me to Robert Greenleaf's work. In any organization, it is easy just to see things as they are and fail to see their potential. This kind of myopia can be deadening. It is another thing to see beyond the present—to see how things could fit together and how institutions could be life-giving. Being a voluntary organization, my own arena of service in the church can be particularly susceptible to operating in a crisis mode. Because planning can seem to be unnecessary, we can find ourselves reacting to the problems before us—or, just as bad, maintaining the status quo. When I began pastoring, I found that I had to be able to see beyond the current reality. I knew that if things stayed as they were in my first assignment, matters would only get worse. Soon after my arrival, I met, at the back door of the church, a man whom I did not know and whom I never again saw. His message was quite dismal. "Sonny, you might as well leave. Things here are not ever going to get better." After that experience, I knew that my challenge was set. I asked myself what factors were present to see the future in a different way. I knew that to get there would take a lot of persistence.

Robert Greenleaf pushes this concept even further by calling foresight *the central ethic of leadership*. As a leader, you can see what has happened in the past and you can see what will probably therefore happen in the future. Greenleaf speaks of a "moving average" mentality where, as leader, you are very actively aware of the movement of an organization. You know the state of affairs, the evil that is brewing, the potential for the good. You can see patterns developing in the ebb and flow of events. In such a moving concept, which leadership certainly is, there is that window of opportunity in which you either act or fail to act. Foresight is what he calls a "better than average guess about *what* is going to happen *when* in the future." Failure to act at that moment, when you still have the freedom to act, is unethical because you fail to act responsibly when the moment of opportunity is available. Leading is critical here. The responsibility is heavy because you must act before all the evidence is in. As Greenleaf says, you go on faith that this is the direction to take, and you bear the "rough and tumble" in the process. Now *that* is hard work. Yes! It is risky. It is also what is at the heart of the leadership task.

In that first church I served, a church declining in a rapidly burgeoning community outside of Washington, D.C., we could either experience further decline or move forward. The people were eager to make something of their church, and that helped tremendously. By catching the decline at this stage, we still had enough resources to claim the future. I found that families, when they moved into the community, were at an optimal time to be contacted and served. As we began to look outward—to meet new families moving into the community and to serve their needs—we found that they were in fact looking to establish themselves in a church. With that information in hand, we had this moment to act, or we could fail to act. About this time, I entered a new Doctor of Ministry program in church renewal, in which the candidate implemented the program in the local church. This caused our congregation to become clearer in terms of what we were doing, to discern that our style was servanthood, and to find a way to shape the future.

We found that our approach of being servants made the critical difference. Our tradition as the Church of the Brethren has been strong in service. Historically, it has led to such actions as establishing Heifer Project International to give animals to hungry families; creating Brethren Volunteer Service, which served as one model for the Peace Corps; operating Church World Service for relief work; and helping initiate CROP walks for the hungry. But now our local church was utilizing servanthood to approach the families by listening to them and by seeing to their needs. Also we attempted to draw forth the gifts these people brought to us. In addition, the church began regular service projects—helping the hungry, and establishing a clothing room for needy families in our local community. With those values in us, we stopped reacting and began proacting. A family night arose; a spiritual renewal emphasis took hold; the youth ministry increased. We began to establish ministries that were quite well received. We began to look beyond the past and even the present; and into the future.

Foresight helps us foresee the unforeseeable. Foresight moves us into vision and into seeing things whole. Greenleaf links this latter concept with nurturing the human spirit because, in seeing things whole, you begin to connect the individual with the wider picture. Robert Greenleaf saw a major role for religious institutions in this regard. In one of his writings, he said that seminaries should be "prime generators of visions in a vision-starved society." Rather than throw up our hands, not knowing what to do—or rather than compromise who we are, in whatever organization we find ourselves—foresight helps us to see a vision and to work toward that vision. We can begin to see situations as they should be—to actually see things whole.

Practicing the Art of Discernment

Having worked with servant-leadership over a 30-year span, I increasingly find that discernment plays a central role in foresight. *Discernment* is a word that we hear a lot about today in some organizations. It means various things to various people, according to their faith tradition. Discernment arises from listening; it moves us into vision. It begins with the quality of one's inner life. To open *The Servant as Leader,* Robert Greenleaf cites the servant Leo in Hermann Hesse's novel. One operates from "in here, not out there." Discernment begins with an ability to step back, to listen, and to nurture wider awareness. One can then foresee, as is expressed in that never-to-be-forgotten line, "The servant-leader is functionally superior because he is closer to the ground—he hears things, sees things, knows things, and his intuitive insight is exceptional."

To discern is to be able to withdraw and listen to a wider voice, a more overarching purpose. For me, it is to listen to God. We see the big picture. We can become aware of the inner patterns and see how things are moving either in the direction of our core values and vision, or away from them. At the Greenleaf Center's Indianapolis conference, where these ideas were first presented, persons shared the variety of ways in which they withdraw to gain such wider awareness. The examples varied greatly, but the persons shared that they withdrew often, and the common theme was that persons prayed for wisdom. That is the prayer for discernment.

In *A Book of Hours,* Elizabeth Yates says that one of the monastic disciplines of the Middle Ages was to use the striking of the clock as a reminder to turn one's thoughts to God. In the hurry of life that seems typical of leadership, the hour often calls us to the next appointment. But great leaders draw apart. An example is Dag Hammarskjold, former Secretary General of the United Nations, who took time apart in order to guide the world through the cold war. In his book *Markings,* he offers a journal of reflections of the interface between contemplation and action.

Individuals differ in terms of how they conduct this inner time, and I respect others deeply for their spiritual convictions. In addition to spending time in daily prayer, I engage weekly in a two-hour retreat, which provides an example of contemplation leading to time for discernment. I go to a Jesuit retreat center and do four simple things during this weekly retreat. I first sit quietly and give everything over to God—all feelings, all situations, all concerns. I release the press of the urgent and begin to sense the presence of God. Secondly, in my tradition, I read a portion of Scripture, just a very few sentences, and then meditate on the thoughts, the deep themes, and the inner dynamics of life as it should be lived. Often here, I write in a prayer journal. Thirdly, I pick out some reading from a devotional classic—a short portion—and allow it to speak to me. I meditate upon its themes. In a fourth portion, called contemplation, I try to be totally still and, in my tradition, feel totally loved by God.

In this time of contemplation, I find that foresight emerges. Here I feel a deep sense of gratitude. I see creative solutions; I feel sensitivity for people and love for humanity. It is a time of rest and renewal. New energy emerges. Being a Jesuit center, this retreat place is at the heartbeat of discernment. St. Ignatius of Loyola, founder of the Jesuits, wrote the definitive words on discernment in the sixteenth century, in his *Spiritual Exercises*. Ignatius tells of the interior movement where you sense consolation or desolation. In looking at a situation, or a decision to be made, consolation is where you feel an increase of "hope, faith and charity," and "all interior joy." On the other hand, desolation is where there is "darkness and confusion," and "fear and distrust." When you feel desolation, you make no decisions. In discernment, you sense the rhythm of the intuitive that Robert Greenleaf speaks about, which leads to insight. You attempt to lead in the direction where you feel consolation.

Discernment has been crucial in my current work to establish a virtual institute for the American Baptist Churches. In this virtual institute, clusters of churches all across the nation are linked by advanced fiber-optic technology to bring renewal to the churches. The inner discipline of contemplation has helped us discern direction as we established the logistics for the model, set up the first seven centers across the nation for the pilot run, and gathered four leaders of four churches at each site. We teach servant-leadership as the style to bring transformation to churches and to communities. Foresight is key in helping churches establish a renewal plan to serve in their unique situations. Discernment helps as we look one way and sense whether there will be consolation, and then the other way to whether this will mean desolation. Discernment leads to the inner promptings that guide the work and move us to our desired goals.

Moving with the Lead of the Leader

Servant-leaders do lead. Knowing what they do, they go on out ahead and lead the way. But there is a special quality to this—the quality of service. They take others with them because of their very manner. Robert Greenleaf closed some personal correspondence in 1986 with a passage that speaks in this regard: "There is no magic, I believe, to leading. One simply has it in oneself to put top priority on building strength in other people, rather than trying to do it all oneself." In this manner of serving, servant-leaders live what is a kind of dual role of both being involved in the events of the time and going out ahead to point the way. It is in serving that they gain the respect of others who know that the servant carries their interests in mind, and that the servant-leader is working toward a supraordinate vision that is good for everyone.

As any leader knows, there are anxieties to this work. Greenleaf points out two such anxieties: (1) the anxiety of holding a decision until as much information is in as possible, and (2) the anxiety of making the decision when there really is not enough information, which he says is usually the case in crucial decisions. Here is where you must trust your own inner senses and have faith, as Greenleaf frequently said. The lead comes in listening, foresight, putting together the team, and creatively moving as goals are kept ahead of us and within us. Leadership is not a passive role or a job to be worked out of. Leo, in Greenleaf's work, showed that leadership is an often silent but very active role.

Servant-leadership has played a significant role in creating the virtual institute that I spoke about earlier. Leadership has meant listening to the various strands of interest while also respecting the mission and heritage of the American Baptist Churches, which includes Martin Luther King in its more recent past. Using servant-leadership, I worked to formulate a theme that would serve as a supraordinate vision. I listened to the felt desires of church leaders—some to have renewal; some, transformation; and some, revival. I searched the sacred book of the church, the Scriptures, to find a vision that would gather up the strands. The result was to test a theme: "Rekindle the Gift, Fan the Flame, and Keep It Burning!" Could not each individual and each church be challenged at some point of that progression? Leading has meant to go on to design a pilot run, enlist the efforts of individuals, and establish a plan.

A key tool in such leadership is listening. Such a lead comes in the listening. Robert Greenleaf speaks about the natural servant as automatically responding to any problem by listening first. This causes him to be viewed as a servant. This builds strength in other people. Our view of leadership can be very verbal, like the boss who gives all the commands. Actually, servants listen first, then speak. We have already seen how important listening is in discernment. Listening also plays a crucial role in sensing those patterns that are so much a part of any endeavor. Listening helps us to go to the depth in order to sense the lift that comes as leadership forges the way. From listening, we get the insights and creative thoughts to lead.

Finally, the lead of the leader is the ability to keep that vision before the group. Then we serve the vision. For our American Baptist work, the longer vision statement has been shortened to *Rekindle!* That word, with a flame aside it, provides a wonderful visual symbol of the outcome we hope to advance even today. Vision helps move us beyond competition, even beyond cooperation, to a supraordinate purpose under which all can serve. Here is where there is ownership and unity that arises out of the style of the servant-leader. Foresight provides the lead of the leader, because, with confidence, he or she can then forge the way and take the lead when opportunity presents itself. Operating with foresight brings a certain sense of tranquillity, even amid the conflicting forces and momentary pressures, for now we are in a proactive stance and people's needs are being served. There is almost a note of celebration once you get to this place, and, indeed, celebration should take place. In renewal, I attempt to help churches have celebrations in order to slow the pace, affirm what has happened, and build spirit for the future.

Developing a Creative, Measurable Plan

If foresight helps us foresee the unforeseeable and is the central ethic, then, in my experience, foresight can lead to developing a creative, measurable plan. At first glance, this seems to be more than one could ask. Working as I do in renewal of churches, planning is one of the areas that is hard for faith communities to grasp. Through foresight, we help congregations shape an incremental, measurable three-year plan. This is a very artistic process. I use a triangle and have the church members put their vision on the top, the strengths on one lower angle, and the needs on the other angle. I put foresight at the center. Then we peer down the center of the triangle to see what kind of plan might unfold. This is definitely an art, never a science. Using foresight, we look at what incremental steps would build, one on another. Where would vision guide us? How can we use our strengths to meet the needs before us? How can we see things whole? This is a flexible plan, and once we begin, other things often happen unexpectedly. But I tell church leaders that unless we begin, nothing usually happens.

Church after church comments on how right it feels as they get into implementing their plan. They wonder why they did not begin this before. One church, Calvary Baptist, experienced striking results in the very impoverished town of Chester, Pennsylvania. Here was a church living in the shadow of great leaders, like Martin Luther King Jr., who served there during his days as a student. Now the church was in serious decline. Tommy Jackson, the pastor, took the course in church renewal and said that he wanted to take what he called the "lower road" of the servant. In his renewal plan, he began by dividing the city up into block zones and assigning a deacon to each zone. The deacon would respond to the needs of his zone and follow up on individuals who came from that zone. Soon a food cupboard and a homeless shelter emerged. The membership stabilized and Calvary began to grow. A homeless shelter was formed; a food distribution center was established. After such success, this pastor went on to a second three-year plan. Tommy Jackson began with a city-wide training on servant-leadership for his members, many of whom worked daily in this inner-city area. I learned that you don't get pastors together for a conference on servant-leadership for church renewal, ask them to tell their stories, and expect to get to lunch on time. This was our experience in a conference cosponsored by the Greenleaf Center, with many supporting sponsors from various denominations.

Foresight can then lead us to action. Robert Greenleaf tells how Thomas Jefferson got some great things done by building upon his vision. Greenleaf notes that Jefferson did this one action at a time. After the Declaration of Independence, Jefferson did not go on to play a part in the war. He went back to Virginia and stuck to his task: writing statutes that would embody the new principles of law that would govern the new nation. He worked tirelessly on these, went to Monticello to revive himself, and then returned to Williamsburg to get these statutes placed into law. Amazingly, as Greenleaf says, when the new nation was born, Jefferson was in France as Ambassador, but he had done his work. His statutes were in operation in Virginia. Robert Greenleaf's quote is priceless here. "Such are the wondrous ways in which leaders do their work—when they know who they are and resolve to be their own men and will accept making their way to their goal by one action at a time, with a lot of frustration along the way."

As we see in this case and as we find in the churches, the critical point is to implement a plan. Here foresight continues to play a role, because these concepts are being implemented on a daily basis. Each step accomplished presents another challenge. Foresight is not a "once done, forever" concept. We must continually use these principles to evaluate and to find the next steps of implementation. Leadership involves training, mentoring, encouraging, and guiding. It's all part of foresight, and foresight becomes an ongoing process. As new situations present themselves, the servant keeps referring to vision, strengths, and needs. Using discernment, we begin to see our next step. Leadership has to do with continually shaping and re-shaping plans and priorities.

In conclusion, foresight is the lead of the leader. Foresight is crucial in shaping organizations to be visioning, spirited, serving communities. Once its fruits begin to be realized, momentum builds. There is a lift that the leader begins to feel. There is a certain song in his or her heart. In my research, I have not found an explanation for why, in the Scriptures, the "suffering servant songs" are called "songs." But I believe that this song in the heart arises from the satisfaction one feels, knowing that when even the difficulties emerged, panic was not present. The leader served and then led, in the spirited way that Robert Greenleaf talks about. Foresight is like a gift that is received, cherished, and utilized. Foresight is the tool the leader uses to lead in that moment when opportunity affords itself and helps to shape a plan. Foresight is indeed the lead of the leader.

Tamyra L. Freeman is an independent consultant who supports organizational and community development initiatives as a special projects manager, team facilitator, and trainer. She was introduced to the work of Robert K. Greenleaf through a Greenleaf Center workshop in 1994, and has served as an adjunct facilitator for the Greenleaf Center. She is actively involved in the Creative Problem Solving (CPS) Initiative at the Blumberg Center/Indiana State University, a licensee of the Creative Solving Group—Buffalo (CPS-B).

Scott G. Isaksen and K. Brian Dorval are principals of the Creative Problem Solving Group—Buffalo. Their approach to Creative Problem Solving (CPS) includes helping people within organizations to better understand their creative talents, improve their climate for creativity, obtain increased clarity regarding the results they seek to obtain, and be more deliberate about their creative process.

In this essay, Freeman, Isaksen, and Dorval examine some of the productive practices that emerge from careful study of the linkages between creativity and servant-leadership. They use four different lenses to illuminate the concept of creativity: (1) creative persons; (2) the climate they are most likely to create in; (3) the processes they use to create; and (4) the nature of the products or results they produce. The authors offer their observations in the hope that readers will offer theirs, and, as Greenleaf would say, ". . . out of the dialogue all of us will be wiser."

18

SERVANT-LEADERSHIP AND CREATIVITY

Tamyra L. Freeman, Scott G. Isaksen,
and K. Brian Dorval

PRACTITIONERS OF SERVANT-LEADERSHIP must, by definition, be interested in creativity. This is perhaps a strong proposition, but one that we believe is reflected in the writings of Robert Greenleaf. He closes his seminal essay, *The Servant as Leader,* with these words, "Except as we venture to create, we cannot project ourselves beyond ourselves to serve and lead." Greenleaf seems to be suggesting an integral relationship between servant-leadership and creativity.

In our practice, we have come to believe that servant-leadership is a moral imperative for the creativity practitioner. We also believe that developing an understanding of creativity is essential to the servant-leader. Servant-leadership challenges many of the common everyday perceptions of leadership. Our approach to creativity is pushing the boundaries on people's common understanding of creativity. The concepts of servant-leadership and creativity are emerging in our work as fundamental. We believe they have tremendous potential to shape the practice and inquiry of today's leaders. This essay represents a first step in our exploration to better understand and articulate the relationship between the two concepts.

Our journey as authors has led us to examine some of the productive practices that emerge by carefully studying the linkages between creativity and servant-leadership. We offer our observations in the hope that you will offer yours, and, as Greenleaf would say, ". . . out of the dialogue all of us will be wiser."

Why must we create? Greenleaf provided a variety of answers to this question throughout his writings. For example, he said that "the leadership of trail blazers . . . is so situational that it rarely draws on known models. Rather, it seems to be a fresh creative response to here-and-now opportunities." We are all experiencing the effects of an accelerated pace of change, intensified competition, and increased complexity within our organizations. We often find it a challenge to respond at all, let alone freshly and creatively! We believe that the reason creativity is central to serving and leading is that there is no preexisting formula that tells us what to do or how to do it. *Servant-leaders must create their way into the answers.*

If you are interested in becoming more effective at serving and leading, we believe you will find it beneficial to learn more about creativity. Many have found it helpful to use four different lenses to illuminate the concept of creativity. When you use these lenses, you can view creative persons, the climate they are most likely to create in, the processes they use to create, and the nature of the products or results they produce. The best picture of creativity we can draw includes views from all four of these lenses.

Creative People

The popular view of creativity is that some people have it and others don't. Creativity is seen as something that is reserved for the chosen few. We find it more productive to think about creativity existing in every person at some level. After all, everyone solves problems and everyone makes decisions. Our explorations have focused on understanding the different preferences people have for how they use the creativity they possess to bring about change. Based on the research of Michael J. Kirton, we know that some people prefer revolutionary forms of creativity (new thinking, out of the box) and others prefer evolutionary forms of creativity (new and improved thinking inside the box).

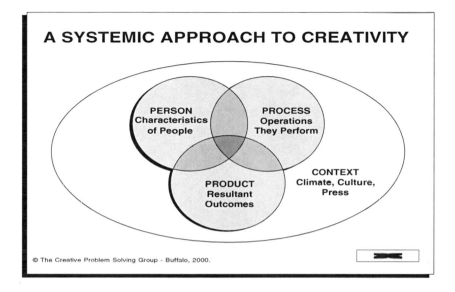

A SYSTEMIC APPROACH TO CREATIVITY

PERSON
Characteristics
of People

PROCESS
Operations
They Perform

PRODUCT
Resultant
Outcomes

CONTEXT
Climate, Culture,
Press

© The Creative Problem Solving Group - Buffalo, 2000.

Transforming people, organizations, and society as a whole requires both radical and incremental forms of creativity. As a result, organizations that exclude one type of creative talent are less
likely to have long-term success than those that take an inclusive
approach and value people's contributions along the full spectrum
of creativity. Rather than discounting those who are different,
people can learn to understand and appreciate those who have
different creativity styles and use the diversity present to strategic
advantage.

Greenleaf was also sensitive to this need to utilize the diversity of
talent available to the organization. In *The Institution as Servant,* he
offered the following insight:

> Highly developed operating and conceptual talents are not com-
> pletely exclusive. *Every* able leader-administrator has some of
> both, even though being exceptional probably in only one or two.
> Both of these talents, in balance and rightly placed, are required
> for sustained high-level performance in any large institution. By
> optimal balance between the two is meant a relationship in

which both conceptualizers and operators understand, respect, and depend on one another, and in which neither dominates the other.

You can become a more effective servant-leader by deliberately strengthening your appreciation and use of diverse creative talents. For example, we worked with an advertising agency to help the organization be more nimble—better able to respond to a changing environment. One key challenge the agency had was the barrier that existed between designers and account managers/finance people. The unproductive tension between them was reflected in the language they used to describe each other: "suits" versus "creatives." You can imagine who was who. By helping them to understand the unique creative talents *each* could contribute to the situation, they were better able to appreciate and use one another's strengths in responding to the changing environment.

Creative Climate

In our work, we separate the concepts of culture and climate. Culture is made up of the deeply held values, beliefs, and traditions in the organization. Climate is comprised of the perceptions people have about what life is really like in the organization. Climate refers to the patterns of behaviors that create the day-to-day reality. We have found that people are more likely to use their creativity when the environment around them supports them to do so. The field of creativity has made progress in understanding what types of climates support creative productivity.

When you establish a supportive climate for creativity and change, you have an environment in which people trust each other. People have freedom to acquire and share information, and different points of view are productively exchanged. There is positive emotional energy (challenge and involvement) in the environment, and people have time and support to consider new ways of doing things. Good-natured playfulness and humor are in great evidence. As Greenleaf indicated, "[T]here is clearly a climate favorable to creativity by individuals that the group, as a community, can provide."

There are obvious differences between favorable and unfavorable climates. For example, our colleague, Goran Ekvall, was asked to improve the idea/suggestion system in an automotive company. Upon visiting two plants, he noticed the system in one plant was working well while the system in the other plant was not. The key difference he observed between the two plants actually had nothing to do with the suggestion system itself; it had to do with the climate in each plant. The way he addressed the problem was to improve the working climate in the second plant.

What Ekvall found in the automotive plants, as well as through his decades of work on climate within other organizations, is that leadership behavior is the key to establishing a climate supportive of creativity. In most research, *leadership* has the greatest impact (it accounts for more than half the variance) on the creation of a climate for creativity and change. You can select the brightest people, train them in all sorts of creative-thinking tools and techniques, and work on the most exciting tasks, but if the leadership is off, these approaches simply do not work.

One of the challenges that we encounter frequently, when working with organizations to understand and change their climates, is the mistaken belief that only senior executives set climate. While we concur that high-ranking positional leaders have a unique responsibility to demonstrate patterns of behavior that support creative productivity, every person in the organization contributes to climate. In fact, our day-to-day reality may be much more affected by our colleagues and immediate supervisors than by individuals at the top of the organizational chart.

For those committed to servant-leadership, Greenleaf's words remind us of the importance of starting the change process with ourselves. "[T]he servant views any problem in the world as in here, inside himself [or herself], not out there. And if a flaw in the world is to be remedied, to the servant the process of change starts in here, in the servant, not out there." We believe that the practice of servant-leadership leads to a climate conducive to creativity. One of the most powerful things you can do as a servant-leader is to change your behavior first, before asking those around you to change theirs. For example, if you really want to create a climate that supports creativity, the next time someone approaches you with a new idea, try responding to the person by first identifying three things you like about the idea. Then, identify three concerns or limitations you have about the idea, but phrase your concerns as a question beginning with "How to . . .?" Then identify two or three things that are unique or different about the idea. This type of response to new thinking will do much to establish a climate supportive of people using their creativity.

Creative Process

The good news is that when you establish a climate conducive to creativity, more people will be likely to use theirs. The challenge that comes with more creativity, of course, is to focus or channel the group's energy in productive directions. Left alone, unbridled creativity can lead to unproductive chaos. This is why we have found it important to add structure to the creative process so that chaos and order can coexist.

What people often find surprising is that you can deliberately support the creative process. Rather than seeing it as involving only intuition, the creative process can be enhanced by paying attention to the explicit stages of thought that people naturally go through when being creative. As Greenleaf suggested, "One follows the steps of the creative process which requires that one stays with conscious analysis as far as it will carry him. . . ." one then withdraws and releases the analytical pressure, "if only for a moment, in full confidence that a resolving insight will come."

The challenge is to focus the creative processes of different people in ways that are valuable and useful to the organization. For years, creativity practitioners have been helping people be deliberate about their creativity. Much of this practice stems from Alex Osborn's original work with brainstorming and has typically focused on helping people generate new ways of thinking. Our broader perspective on creativity includes more than tools and techniques for generating. Any deliberate creative process must also involve analyzing, developing, refining, and prioritizing options.

We believe that developing knowledge about the creative process puts you in a better position to unleash and focus your creativity and the creativity of those around you. You can move beyond the idea that creativity only happens by accident, and you can help it to happen purposefully and mindfully. You can become deliberate about utilizing your foresight, intuition, and conceptualization as Greenleaf described it.

For example, we helped the senior management team of an international symphony be more mindful about its creative process. We worked with them to develop a vision for the future of their organization. At the time, they were overreliant on their endowment. They were at serious risk of financial ruin in five to 10 years if they didn't change. We used explicit and deliberate processes to help them create a new vision that included alternative sources of revenue. Within four years, these new sources of revenue were generating sufficient income to extinguish their ongoing dependency on the endowment.

Creative Products

When we think about creative products, the traditional association we make is with great works of art, famous plays or performances, or technological breakthroughs and inventions. However, many other results and outcomes deserve the label *creative*. You may believe that, in order for something to be creative, it must be new or unique. Ultimately, we believe it must also have some value or usefulness.

For those who work in organizations, *innovation* is the term that is often used to describe creative products. Innovation refers to the ability of an organization to turn ideas into products and services, and to successfully get them to the marketplace. A common measure of innovation is the percentage of revenue generated from products that are less than five years old. This introduces the idea that creative products are typically tangible, like an actual product that can be displayed and purchased.

As you pursue innovation, you may also want to consider the intangible resources that can have a profound impact on the innovative productivity of your organization. Greenleaf challenges us to do what "is reasonable and possible with available resources." Unfortunately, these intangible resources are not always understood, appreciated, or tapped.

The opportunity you have as a servant-leader is that you can deliberately mine untapped or unacknowledged intangible resources in a way that benefits your organization. For example, Ken McCluskey, of Manitoba, Canada, has demonstrated the power of drawing out the intangible. His implementation of initiatives like Lost Prizes, Second Chance, and Northern Lights has demonstrated that at-risk youth can reclaim their creative talents and become better contributors to society. These initiatives were all aimed at helping students move from low self-esteem, poor educational achievement, and criminal behavior toward more personal confidence, higher educational achievement, and productive social behaviors. One of the key factors in supporting these youths was helping them find and unleash their unique talents toward more productive ends for themselves and society.

As a servant-leader, you have an opportunity to help reclaim intangible resources, including people's talents, in order to increase your organization's capacity to innovate. Focusing on creative products such as a *relationship* with your customer, the *perceptions* customers have of your products, and the *attitudes* people have toward their work can all have a profound impact on the overall success of your organization.

What gets measured tends to get paid attention to. You can broaden your perception of the creative product, and the perceptions of those around you, to include both the tangible and intangible. One way to do this is: Put measures in place that focus on both. The classic measures for innovation can help target the tangible outcomes you wish to create. Measures of customer satisfaction, perceptions of your products, and attitudes of people at work can all help you better target your use of servant-leadership to tap the untapped intangible.

We believe that understanding creativity in the way we have outlined it here can help you to capitalize on diversity, establish a healthy climate for change, use deliberate processes to release creative talent, and, through all this, better target the range of new and valuable outcomes you want to create. The bigger and more important question then becomes: To what end?

Greenleaf's Moral Imperative

In the history of western civilization, much attention has focused on the bottom line. Many, if not most, of the measures we use to evaluate successful leadership and creative productivity in organizations identify such things as return on investment (ROI), return on capital employed (ROCE), time to market, and so on.

Greenleaf's work reminds those of us in the creativity field of the importance of focusing our attention on the *top* line. His best test of servant-leadership ". . . and difficult to administer is: Do those served grow as persons; do they, while being served, become healthier, wiser, freer, more autonomous, more likely themselves to become servants? And, what is the effect on the least privileged in society; will they benefit, or at least, not be further deprived?" This is an important and powerful target for our own accountability in our efforts to help people and organizations become successful. Success should not be identified using only measures such as shareholder value.

Seeing Things Whole

If you want to engage in servant-leadership to create both top- and bottom-line results, we believe you need to pay attention to the entire system of creativity. In a comprehensive survey of 476 organizations in seven countries, researchers at Pricewaterhouse-Coopers sought to determine the capabilities that account for an organization's ability to successfully produce new products and services. They identified three main capabilities. The more successful organizations embraced a more inclusive leadership approach, everyone was encouraged to use his or her creativity. They relied less on the formal hierarchy or senior leaders, which resulted in increased initiative throughout the organization. These organizations also took creating the right climate seriously. They legitimized the work of climate building and took steps to ensure that the conditions within their organizations supported personal and organizational effectiveness. Finally, the successful organizations developed and used deliberate processes to stimulate and nurture ideas. This resulted in significantly greater idea flow.

What we find most interesting about this research is that the organizations that were most productive and profitable worked harder on all three of these capabilities. The implication is clear: there is no single magic bullet. Helping organizations become distinctive means considering and working on the entire system. Developing a kind of leadership that serves, is inclusive, and encourages initiative; establishing patterns of behavior that result in the right kind of climate; and investing in deliberate processes and procedures are all important.

We believe Greenleaf's reminder about the top line is a vital message. It helps us remember the ultimate reason why we practice creativity and help others to unleash their creative talent. It is not just about ROI, new products and services, or inspiring visions—although these are important. It is, in Greenleaf's words, about helping people to avoid denying ". . . wholeness and creative fulfillment by failing to lead. . . ." It is about helping those led become wiser, freer, more autonomous, and more likely to serve others in a way that benefits society.

Ultimately, we believe it is important to focus attention on both the top and bottom lines. Integrating the two helps people unleash their creative spirit and the spirit of those around them. At the same time, this integration helps people to use their creativity to make a difference in organizations. When people are able to release their creativity, they use more of their gifts and talents. When people release their creativity, organizations are more successful. This is why we believe that the relationship between creativity and servant-leadership is so important. It helps us get away from the unproductive view that either people prosper or organizations prosper. Through servant-leadership, both can prosper at the same time.

Judy Wicks is founder and president of White Dog Enterprises, Inc., established in 1983, which owns and operates the White Dog Café and The Black Cat, a retail gift store that promotes the work of third-world people. The Café has received national recognition, including the *American Benefactor's* "America's 25 Most Generous Companies," in 1998; the *Condé Nast Traveler* list of top 50 American restaurants, in 1993; and *Inc.* magazine's best small companies to work for, in 1993. Wicks is coauthor of *The White Dog Café Cookbook: Multicultural Recipes and Tales of Adventure from Philadelphia's Revolutionary Restaurant.*

Judy Wicks weaves stories from her past to form a delightful tale of how she shapes her workplace and personal life to serve others: customers, employees, the community, and the world. Through conscious choices to live out servant-leadership principles, she shows us the spirit that prompts her to start out each day saying, "Good morning, beautiful business!"

Judy Wicks was a keynote speaker at the Greenleaf Center's 2000 annual international conference.

19

TABLE FOR SIX BILLION, PLEASE

Judy Wicks

BACK IN THE DAYS when I had a nonprofit publishing company and was also running a restaurant, I thought of those two activities as being totally unrelated. It was in the nonprofit work that I felt I was serving the world. In the restaurant I was serving people, but it was in a different way—it was only to make a living. I didn't see how these things could be combined. I think too often we are taught to leave our values at home when we go to work, so that we are forced to compartmentalize our lives and our values. Often, the golden rule we use at home to teach our children is overruled in the workplace by the rule of maximizing profit. At the White Dog Café, we call ourselves a full-service company. We don't just mean we have table service for our customers. Our whole mission is to serve fully in four different areas: (1) serving each other as fellow employees; (2) serving our community; (3) serving our natural environment; and (4) serving our customers.

Let me tell you how I got to where I am. In the small town where I grew up, north of Pittsburgh, my first role model in servant-leadership was my mother. She was the leader of the town's Girl Scout troop. My dad taught me how to play baseball, because I was the oldest child and he was a baseball fan. When I got into fifth grade, I couldn't wait until spring because I knew we were going to have softball practice, and I was a pretty good ball player. On the first nice spring morning, the gym teacher said, "We're going to play softball today." I leaped out of my chair ready to go. And he said, "Okay, all the guys go down there to the field. Girls, go over there and practice cheerleading." I just couldn't believe this; I didn't know enough to object. Nowadays he'd be sued, but back then I just went along with it. I refused to cheerlead; instead, I stood behind the backstop and watched the guys play.

Being left out like that did something to me. I bought into the idea that girls were second class. Other messages in our society—the year was 1957—were saying the same thing—girls weren't as good—and that made me think less of other girls and of myself. So I really learned what discrimination does to people: how destructive it is, how it makes you look down on yourself for being in a certain group, whether it's a religious minority, a racial minority, or a sexual preference minority. It took me a long time to get over that. But the other thing I realized was: The whole group loses out when you leave people out of the game. I was a really good baseball player, and the team would have been better if I had been allowed to play.

I learned another important lesson when I became a VISTA (volunteer in service to America) after graduating from college in 1969. I was living in an Eskimo village in Alaska, which was an incredible experience for me. One day, a woman knocked on my house and said, "Come on, come on!" I put on my parka and went out. All the women in the village were carrying buckets and moving quickly toward another woman's house, and they said, "Seal party, seal party!" And I wondered, "What's a seal party?" Well, in this village there was a tradition. When a man caught his first seal of the season, after a long hard winter, his wife invited all the families over to her house, and she divided all the seal meat up and distributed it evenly to the families in the village. And after the meat, blubber, and fur were distributed to these buckets, the woman would hand out other things she had accumulated over the year—buttons and ribbons and fabrics and so on. Then she threw bubble gum and root beer barrel candies up into the air, and we all caught them in our skirts; that was my favorite part. The tradition demonstrated the Eskimo way of life, which is to share. They didn't believe in accumulating wealth, accumulating more than they needed. And when they got more than they needed, they redistributed it to others in the village. As a young person, this was incredibly surprising to me when I compared it to our society in the "lower 49" states. I realized how different we were from the Eskimos. If you admire something that an Eskimo has, if you say to an Eskimo woman, "I really like your necklace," she will take it right off and give it to you. The Eskimos don't believe in envy; they don't even understand what it means. So I thought about how our economic system is actually based on envy. Through advertising, we get people to be envious of each other. We say that if you buy this lipstick you'll be sexier than your girlfriend, or if you buy this car you'll be more powerful than the other guys. We actually try to create envy. We reward people who are greedy; and we admire the most those who hoard the most. What a difference it was for me to experience the Eskimo culture.

Those two experiences, on the baseball field and in the Eskimo village, really helped formulate a different philosophy for me, a different way to see. I started to understand that true economic sustainability is not based on hoarding, but on sharing, and not taking more than we need; not on excluding, but on giving everyone the opportunity to contribute. Taking good care of human and natural resources produces long-term economic sustainability. That is what I base my business philosophy on.

To resume the story of my business career, let's go back to that baseball field. When I was standing behind that backstop, realizing I was never going to get to play baseball, I did a 1950s kind of thing—I decided I would marry the best baseball player! I chose him that day when I was ten years old. He was a good hitter *and* a good pitcher, which is very unusual. I went back to my classroom, got out my tablet, crossed off "Judy Wicks" and wrote in "Mrs. Richard Baseball-Player, Mrs. Richard Baseball-Player" all over my tablet. And when we graduated from college, that's who I married. We went off to VISTA together, and eventually came back to our small town. We were both mavericks, and couldn't imagine being employed by anyone, so we decided to start our own business. We decided to open a store because we thought that was very simple—you

just buy something at one price and sell it at a higher price! We
started The Free People's Store in Philadelphia, because we really
liked the community there. We wanted it to be a nonprofit store because we hated capitalism and business, and we felt that was what
was behind the Vietnam War and other problems. We actually had
a bin in the store filled with things for free, so if you didn't have any
money, you could still come to the store and leave with something.
(That store grew into a national chain called Urban Outfitters,
which my ex-husband still runs.) About a year and a half after we
started the store, it was doing well, but I began to wonder whatever
happened to Judy Wicks, that little girl whose name I crossed off my
tablet. I had to seek my own path, so I decided to leave the business
and the husband. I got into the car, and, half a block away, went
through a red light and got into an accident. No one was hurt but
the car was pretty badly banged up. As I stood on the sidewalk, a
man came along and said, "May I help you get home?" And I said,
"I'm not going home. My bags are packed, I've just left my husband,
and I need to keep going. So now I have to find a job 'cause I've
wrecked the car. I have no home, I have no business, and I need a
job." And he said, "I work at a restaurant and I think they need a
waitress." I said, "I'll take it," and that's how I got into the restaurant business—by accident!

I started at this restaurant as a waitress, became the general manager, eventually became a partner in the business, and ended up
being there for 13 years. I was doing my nonprofit work at the same
time I was working at the business. I was really becoming disgrun-
tled by what I saw as wasting my time in the restaurant business
when my true love was the nonprofit work. I was sitting at the bar
one night and an elderly man was sitting there. I told him, "I think
I want to get out of this business. It's just about money and that's
not of interest to me." He said, "Oh my dear, it's not really about
money. When a coin passes from one hand to another, it's not the
coin that counts—it's the warmth of the hand." Then I started to
see the business differently: it was about relationships, about people. Money didn't have to be the most important thing.

About this time, a group of Salvadoran refugees was demonstrating about U.S. involvement in El Salvador. They had marched

from Boston and were en route to Washington, D.C., and they were staying in a church near the restaurant where I was working. I wanted to do something for them, so I invited them to come to breakfast at the restaurant. The Salvadoran refugees came wearing cowboy hats and sandals. I got a friend to cook bacon and eggs for them, and I was their waitress. When they left, I had tears in my eyes as I watched them go off on their journey. My partner in the business didn't think that this kind of activity was appropriate for the image of the restaurant, and eventually I was forced out of the business. So much for expressing your values through your work! So I thought, "I'll just start another restaurant down the street in the first floor of my house." And that's just what I did.

I started the White Dog Café in 1983 as a coffee and muffin take-out shop. In the Eskimo village, I had learned to make soup and bread. I figured as long as you have soup and bread you don't need anything else, so that's what I made at the White Dog Café. We went from muffins and coffee to soup and bread, which I made up-stairs at my house and took downstairs. And my kids—I had a two-year-old and a four-year-old at the time—were just kind of hanging on my skirts while I was trying to make the soup and bread and take it downstairs and sell it. We advanced to hot food. We had a charcoal grill in the backyard and the waiters would go down into the basement, out the back, pick up the food from the chef, and take it upstairs. The dishwasher was right in the dining room where the customers would pass their dishes to him. If you had to go the bathroom, you went upstairs to our house. On your way to the bathroom, you waved to my kids who were sitting on the couch watching TV. At the end of the night, the last waiter would deposit the money under my pillow. That was how we began. We now employ 100 people and gross close to $5 million.

I realized my life was very integrated when I was living above the business. It's an old-fashioned kind of family business, like the family farm, the tailor shop, or the family store. There was something very integrating and holistic about living above the shop; I very much believe in that concept. During the industrial revolution, when factories started up, families were separated. The parents went off to work and the kids went off to school. That created a whole division in our society, and it separated our values. The kids in school are separate from the work world and separate from home life, and business isn't connected to the community in the same way as the family businesses.

Nowadays, an annual "Take Your Daughter to Work Day" is sponsored by the Ms Foundation. I think that's a good way of overcoming the gap separating schools and work and home. When I worked my first restaurant job, I took my daughter to work with me three days after she was born. I had her up in the office in the daytime, and at night I'd put her in a little basket on the piano. I went back to home after the first day of work when I had her with me, and I actually got in bed and then thought, "I'm missing something. Oh my gosh! I left the baby at the restaurant!" So I went tearing downstairs and opened the door and there she was, sleeping soundly on the piano. And I realized, for me it's not a problem of bringing my daughter to work; it's a problem of remembering to bring her home again!

I only have one location; I also really believe in that. Even though having a chain of restaurants is supposed to be a mark of success in our business world, I believe that you really lose something when you have a chain: your relationships with the people, with customers, with employees, with the farmers who grow your food. Those things are really important to me, so I've always wanted to keep just the one location. I'm a "Small is beautiful" person. Part of the beauty of staying small is having those relationships and being able to experience an interconnectedness with each other and with nature. I see this interconnectedness as something spiritual, and if we make people aware of it, we can go a long way to solving most of our problems.

Years ago, I was driving down the street and stopped at a red light right in front of a high school as students were leaving. It appeared that most of the students were African American. I realized that this was the school my own kids would go to if I weren't sending them to a private Quaker school. And yet I didn't know these kids—the kids who went to the community school in my own neighborhood. All I knew about these kids had come from TV or magazines about black urban youth. I had a driving need to know these kids. I called the principal and asked if any students in the school were interested in going into the restaurant business; if there were, I wanted to start a mentoring program at the White Dog Café. This was about ten years ago. We picked six tenth-graders. They spent two days in the kitchen, two days in the dining room, a day in the office, and a day in our retail store. We hired some of these kids into jobs when they got to be seniors in school; one of our line cooks is from one of the first mentoring groups. At the end of the school year, we have an event that has become a reunion for kids from earlier mentoring groups. It's an outdoor dinner and dance we call the "Hip Hop." The kids put on the event with the help of our staff; they pick the DJ and have urban music. At one of these events, I was watching as kids came in who had been in past groups. One young man came in with his girlfriend. We give a $1,000 scholarship to one of the kids who is going on to college. He had been the recipient of our first scholarship. He was now a sophomore in college. As he was coming across the dance floor, I felt tears well up in my eyes. I thought to myself, "You finally know who those kids were that you saw coming out of that high school. They're our children." I now have a commitment to serving all children as though they're our own.

One night, I had this dream: I walked into a restaurant and, instead of asking for a table for two or a table for four, I said, "A table for six billion, please." I want a table for everybody in the world. I have this vision of everyone in the world sitting at one big table where there's enough to eat for all, and everyone has a seat at the table politically and economically. Everyone has enough to eat, everyone can share, and everyone can be served. So I started an international program and called it "Table for Six Billion, Please." I believe in building international community, so I started a sister restaurant program where I would establish relationships with restaurants in countries where there was misunderstanding toward the United States: Cuba, Vietnam, Nicaragua, and the Soviet Union. I would bring my customers out to dinner in those countries. We nicknamed it our "Eating with the Enemy" program. We show that it's through communication and dialogue that we achieve world peace, rather than through military or economic domination. The other thing we do is learn from other countries by visiting schools, farms, and hospitals. We also have a local sister restaurant program. We form sister relationships with minority-owned restaurants in Philadelphia, and advertise them in our newsletter, which goes out to 20,000 people. For example, we would invite people to an evening in the *barrio*, beginning with an art opening at a Puerto Rican cultural center, then out to dinner at our Puerto Rican sister restaurant, and then dancing at a Latino dance club. The first time I did this, a big article in the Philadelphia *Inquirer* told about the "Bad Lands"—the area where our sister restaurant was located. The newspaper had a map of the worst drug trafficking areas in the whole city, and there was a black dot on the corner where the sister restaurant was located. I thought, "Is anybody going to go on this lovely little excursion to the Bad Lands?" So we had a program at the White Dog called "The Good People of the Bad Lands," which featured community leaders who came in and talked about the positive things that were going on in those communities. This is one of the ways I use good food to lure innocent customers into social activism!

During a Greenleaf Center conference, I went to a breakout session given by Julie Cowie on persuasion, one of the characteristics of servant-leadership. She talked about "gracious invitation," and I realized that's what I do. I give a gracious invitation that you can't resist—there's going to be food and wine and dancing, and it's all linked to learning to celebrate diversity and learning about issues that face our society. We have a whole series of "Table Talks"—dinners combined with a speaker on issues of public concern such as growing economic inequality, our inflated military budget, campaign finance reform, and the failed war on drugs. Storytelling—real stories by real people—is combined with a meal. It's another way that we demonstrate our interconnectedness.

I want to talk a little bit more about how we serve in our four different areas. I already talked about how we serve our community, but we also serve each other as fellow employees. We do many things to create an atmosphere of trust and respect and open dialogue. We have consideration for families, for people who have children as well as elderly parents. If someone has a sick child, they either can stay home or they can bring the child to work. I brought my kids to work during the breast-feeding years. I encourage other women who are in the office to bring their kids. We've had four different babies in the office at different times. If someone has an elderly parent, we say, "Go home, go home if you need to." We have an annual "Anniversary Howl" where we "howl" our accomplishments of the previous year. Typically, in the restaurant business, many of our employees have other interests outside of the restaurant—they're painters, musicians, actors, and students. It really used to frustrate me that they had all these other interests, until I realized: Why not celebrate those interests too? So, at "The Howl," we celebrate not only what we accomplished as a company but also the individuals who work there and what they've accomplished outside of work. People bring in their paintings and their photographs and we have a wine-and-cheese opening. Anyone who had a baby during the year is asked to bring in pictures; if some people do nonprofit work, they do a little display on that. In this way, we recognize and appreciate and honor things that people do outside of work. I give a "State of the Dog" address and do a big chart showing how much money came in, how we spent our money, how much profit was made, where the profit went (we give 10 percent of profits to nonprofit activities). We also give the "Silver Bone Award" (little sterling silver bones) to people who have been there for five years, and sterling silver logo earrings or cufflinks to people who are celebrating 10-year anniversaries. At another time, we have the "Old Dogs Dinner" for people who have been at the Café for three years or more. The new people serve the old people at the "Old Dogs Dinner," which starts out with cocktails at my house. We have a lot of fun.

One of the things that drew my attention recently was the concept of the living wage. The *living wage* is the amount of money it takes to actually live on, as opposed to the minimum wage, which, at $5.15 an hour, is not enough to live on. That's why we have working poor in this country. It used to be that the minimum wage and the living wage were about the same, which would make sense, but now there's a huge gap between what it takes to live on and what the minimum wage is. In the restaurant business, people are often paid only the minimum wage. We never paid anyone only

$5.15 an hour, but we did have people on the payroll at $6.00 and $7.00 an hour.

When I heard about the living wage, I thought it was a really nice idea, but it wouldn't apply to the restaurant business because of the industry's small profit margin. If I tried to pay $8.00 an hour to dishwashers and bus boys and prep cooks—my entry-level people—I'd go broke, I thought. But I kept thinking about it and thinking about it. I thought about Greenleaf's idea that the good society is where the less able and the more able serve each other. It's easy to think of ways that the less able can serve the more able. It's easy to picture the less able washing our dishes or mopping our floors or cooking our food for us. But how can the more able serve the less able? And I realized that what I needed to do more than anything else was to make sure that my people made a living wage. I made a commitment that, within one year, everybody would be moved up to at least $8.00 an hour. I didn't want us to do this all of a sudden because we wanted people to earn it, but we wanted them to know they had the opportunity. I met with the dishwashers and told them what I wanted to do, and what they had to do to earn it—things like show up on time, take initiative, and so on. Within one year, we had everybody up to $8.00 an hour or more. It was one of those leap-of-faith things when I realized it was the right thing to do. I didn't know exactly what would happen. I wondered, "If I pay the dishwashers $8.00 an hour, what about the people who are cooks now who make $8.00 an hour? What are they going to think? Are they going to want $10.00 or $12.00 an hour? Am I opening a can of worms here?" But that's not what happened at all. People were glad that I paid the dishwashers more. They understood what I was doing, they went along with it, and it really worked out. We're more profitable now that we're paying the living wage than we were before.

One of the most exciting things about it was that people who are being paid the $8.00 an hour are now contributing to our workplace giving program. They may have just $.50 a week taken out of their paycheck, but then the Café matches it, and eventually a $50 contribution goes to a charitable organization. There are six different organizations that they can choose to donate to. We have a dishwasher who is now a philanthropist. We also have a 401(k) where we have matching funds. My goal is the growth of all people in our organization: providing meaningful work whether someone is a dishwasher or a cook or a manager, and providing opportunities to learn and grow even if someone stays a dishwasher. I recently took one of our dishwashers to Cuba on a program where we pay half the expenses.

Another way we serve is through serving the earth. We now get our energy from a nonprofit energy company, so 44 percent of our electricity comes from windmills. We heard about a carbon offset program (you measure your carbon emissions, and then offset them by planting trees), so we're now doing that. We started a reforestation project in one of the countries that we travel to as part of our sister restaurant program. The coffee that we serve at the White Dog comes from an indigenous cooperative in Chiapas, Mexico, and we're now working on helping them export honey. We buy all our vegetables in season from Pennsylvania organic family farmers, because we feel that family farms are so important—they're stewards of the earth.

Another thing that I resisted for a while was the whole idea of humane farming. We had already switched to free-range chickens because I had heard about factory farms for chickens. Then I started hearing about the inhumane way that pigs and cows were treated. Although I'm basically a vegetarian, I don't object to eating meat as long as the farm animals have a good quality of life. So when I first started hearing about hog factories, I got really upset about the cruelty, but I tried not to think about it. I felt like I was part of it because I was in the restaurant business, and I didn't want to go out of business. Finally, it became another one of those leap-of-faith things. I decided I didn't want to be in the restaurant business if it involved the torture of animals. I said to the chef, "Take pork off the menu. Take off the bacon, take off the pork chops, take off the ham, take it all off the menu until we can find a way to buy pork that has been raised in a humane way." We started this journey with pigs and then with cows. At first, we had to buy a whole pig or cow. We'd have a whole carcass on the floor of the kitchen, with the chef trying to figure out how to use all these different parts. Now, whenever I say I have a new idea, they always say, "Oh, no." At this point, all the meat products we serve at the White Dog come from humane farms, and now we've started to teach our competitors how to do the same thing—how to buy from family farms, to help reestablish those distribution systems that have been lost in the past.

I've talked a little about our giving 10 percent of profits to non-profit organizations. I got an award once for being a philanthropist. But I thought, "Gee, I don't give enough money away to be a phil-anthropist, so I don't know what to really say when I get this award." So I looked up "philanthropist" in the dictionary and it said, "the inclination to increase the well-being of mankind." And I thought, "Hey, I do that—maybe this really isn't just about money." And then I started thinking about philanthropy and about how we think philanthropy is what we do at the end of our life or what we do at the end of the year, rather than what we do during the year, how we actually live our lives. Around that time, I was at an event for young professionals where a few leaders in the com-munity were giving advice on volunteerism and philanthropy. The man who spoke before me was a city council person, a conserva-tive politician. And he said to the young people, "I'm going to give you the same advice that my father gave to me and that is that you can't do good until you do well." Then I went next and said just the opposite. He felt you had to do well, you had to become rich, be-fore you could start to give back. I suddenly realized that separat-ing doing good from making a profit is what has caused all the problems in the world. You know the kind of problems that Dee Hock talked about earlier in this conference—the environmental devastation, the social devastation—it's been caused by separating profit from goodness. There's no reason why we can't combine those two things. And if we do combine those two things, if we make our money in a way that benefits mankind, then we can solve the same problems that we created by separating the two. I think this is a really important idea. I was talking to a woman who worked for the foundation of a large corporation and she said, "I feel so bad because no matter how much I give away from the foun-dation, I can never overcome the destruction this corporation causes to the environment and to people from the way that they made the money in the first place." So I think we have to change the way that we make our money, not just focus on charity at the last minute, when we give away the crumbs we don't need at the end of our lives or the end of the year.

Let me tell you about how the Café got its name. When I first moved into my house about 30 years ago, there was a knock on my door around midnight, and I went down to answer it. A woman was standing there. She asked, "Is this the house of the great Madame Blavatsky?" And I said, "There's no Madame here. I live here and my name is Judy." She said, "No, no, no, the great Madame Blavatsky lived here in 1875. This is 3420 Sansom Street, isn't it?" I said, "Yes, but I've never heard of her." And she asked, "Well, can I come in and see where she once lived?" And I said, "Well, okay," and so she came in and went whirling around my house. "Oh, this is where her bedroom was, and this is where her parlor was," and so on and so on. And then she was off in a taxi and I thought she was just some kook.

About a year later, I was on the bus in Philadelphia when I looked out the window and saw a sign in the window of a building that said, "Who was Madame Blavatsky?" I yelled, "Stop the bus—I'm getting off. That's the lady!" So I got off and went into the building. It was the United Lodge of the Theosophists, and I started learning about Madame Blavatsky, who was the cofounder of the Theosophical Society. Basically, she believed in uniting the world through universal truths and felt that all religions were related. When people asked her what religion she belonged to, she said, "I belong to all of them." I thought she was a pretty cool lady and when I started the restaurant years later, I decided to name it after her.

I got a collection of letters that she wrote at the time she lived there, and found a letter that she wrote to a friend, talking about how she had fallen and injured her leg. Her leg had become infected and the doctors advised that it be amputated. She said to her friend that she wouldn't have the amputation, that she wouldn't let her leg go to the promised land before her and have it written on her tombstone, "Gone to meet her leg." So she shooed off the doctors and cured herself by having a white dog sleep on her leg. And that's where I got the name the White Dog Café.

She wrote some incredible, complicated books, but there's one little passage that I really love. "Let thy soul lend its ear to every cry of pain, like as the lotus bares its heart to drink the morning sun. Let not the fierce sun dry one tear of pain before thyself has wiped it from the sufferer's eye. But let each burning human tear drop on thy heart and there remain nor ever brush it off until the pain that caused it is removed." That's why I called my restaurant the White Dog Café, after Madame Blavatsky.

In the morning, when I open my closet door, I have a sign in there that says, "Good morning, beautiful business." It's a reminder to me of just how beautiful business can be when it is used to serve others. My business is a way that I express my love for other people. It's the way that I increase my capacity to care, and increase the capacity to care for my employees and my customers. It's really, in a sense, my ministry. And in the morning I think about how beautiful business could be. Michael Jones talked about the exchange of gifts that was the old way of doing business; I think it can still be like that. When we cook the best possible meal, and someone produces the best possible computer, and someone else plays the piano, or sings the song, this is an exchange of our gifts. Why can't that be the way our economy is? Why can't we create a new global economy different from the one protested in Seattle—the one that's dominated by the large multinationals? Why can't we have a global economy that's based on relationships like the one between the White Dog Café and the coffee growers in Chiapas—an economy that respects people and respects the natural environment? I envision an interconnected economic system that's based on love, and respect, and care, and service that mirrors the spiritual interconnectedness of all living things. What would that be like? Then we would really have a table for six billion! Can you envision that table with everyone in the world around it? And if that were to finally happen, perhaps we would join hands and offer this grace:

> Mother of our earth, heavenly father, universal spirit who dwells in each of us, forgive us for the harm we have done to our planet and the plants and animals who live here with us. Forgive us for the harm we have caused each other. Thank you for

giving us the courage to put aside our fears of not having
enough for ourselves so that we could make room for every one
of us around this table of great abundance and nourishment.
Thank you for the creativity it has taken to find ways for each
of us to participate in the making of this great feast so that we
can each join in the satisfaction of our work well done. Bless
this food that we now eat with the greatest joy, knowing that
you are present in the pleasure of every bite and the love we see
all around us in each and every smiling face. Amen.

PART FOUR

SERVANT-LEADERSHIP FOR THE WORLD

Joseph Jaworski is the founder of the American Leadership Forum and a co-founder of Generon, a Boston-based consulting firm. Generon's work brings together scenario-based strategy formation and generative leadership development to help corporate and civic leaders not just adapt to circumstances but create life affirming futures. He is the author of *Synchronicity: The Inner Path of Leadership,* a best-seller on a number of leadership book lists.

In this essay, Joseph Jaworski relates some of his personal experiences of *Synchronicity* and shares what he has learned as a result of his study of this phenomenon. Over the last three years, Jaworski and his colleagues who teach at the MIT Sloan School of Management have been engaged in an intensive research project focusing on the human capacity to sense what is going to emerge before it manifests. Jaworski and his colleagues conducted over 100 dialogue interviews with eminent thinkers, scientists, and practitioners in the field of knowledge creation, leadership, creativity, and high performance. As leaders, we can learn to sense and bring forth emergent futures by strengthening the servant-leadership attributes of awareness, presence, and being which play a major part in the process Jaworski describes.

Joseph Jaworski was a keynote speaker at the Greenleaf Center's 1999 annual international conference.

20

SYNCHRONICITY AND
SERVANT-LEADERSHIP

Joseph Jaworski

THE SUBTLEST DOMAIN OF LEADERSHIP—but perhaps the most vital—is recognizing and strengthening our innate capacity to sense and bring forth emergent futures.

This capacity sounds special, but it is not the attribute of a special few. We all have it, even though we have developed it to a greater or lesser extent. I've discovered that the experience of this capacity is characterized by six essential elements, which I can best describe by telling some stories. But I should add that this exploration is still very much a work in progress.

1. *High energy.* This is the feeling that you get when you walk into the locker room of a championship team or a high-performing organization. You can actually feel the energy. It's palpable.

2. *Coherence.* Sometimes, people are so closely connected that they seem almost able to complete one another's sentences. This kind of coherence can occur in a small group or even in a company as a whole.

3. *Deep sense of satisfaction.* In the midst of this phenomenon, there is a sense of discovery and satisfaction—a sense of being outside everyday reality.

4. *Altered time/space conditions.* Athletes and others report that in the midst of these experiences, there is sometimes an altered sense of time or space. Most people report that time seems to slow down under these circumstances.

5. *Distributed leadership.* One of the most important elements of this phenomenon is that a lot of self-organization occurs; people are not being told what to do, they are just acting in sync with one another. One person acts as leader and then, in a seamless transition, leadership passes to another person.

6. *Highly significant results.* The results of these experiences are highly significant. In addition, they seem to be produced as if by "magic." In one sense, everybody is working extremely hard; but in another, the work seems almost effortless.

Artists refer to this sort of phenomenon as the "economy of means." With just the slightest nudge, at a particular point and time, all sorts of unbelievable occurrences take place. People come together or show up at just at the right time. I believe that in this particular domain the highest forms of creativity actually take place.

The Swiss psychologist Carl Jung referred to this phenomenon as *synchronicity*—those perfect moments when things come together in an almost unbelievable way, and events that you could hardly predict seem to guide you along your way.

I've been studying synchronicity for a good part of my adult life, largely as a result of powerful experiences. The earliest of these experiences occurred when I was a freshman attending Baylor University in Waco. One of the largest tornadoes ever to hit Texas passed through Waco late on a March afternoon. I was sitting in my dorm during a huge thunderstorm, when all of a sudden there was a terribly frightening noise that sounded like a thousand freight trains coming. Then stillness. I walked outside and saw that even the rain had quit. I kept walking and then discovered that the post office, one block away, had been cut in two. Half of it was just gone. I walked another half block and there was a baseball park that had been blown away. I was one of the first ones on the scene where the real devastation had taken place. Five hundred people died in an instant as a result of that tornado.

But what happened after that—this phenomenon that I'm talking about—seemed to me to be even more remarkable. Over the next three days, people completely self-organized. They seemed to know exactly what to do, at exactly the right time. And every one of these conditions—the high energy, the coherence, the altered space and time conditions, the distributed leadership, and the rest—was present. It was almost unbelievable to experience.

After college, when I started trying lawsuits, I again experienced this synchronicity. Some of these experiences occurred in the trial preparation stage, when I would talk to witnesses, and others happened in the courtroom when I was actually arguing to a jury, or when I was talking to a witness. This experience would seem to be present not just to the witnesses with whom I was speaking and to me, but also to everyone in the courtroom.

Synchronicity seems to happen a lot in athletic endeavors. Bill Russell, the former great center for the Boston Celtics, describes this phenomenon in *Second Wind:*

> Every so often a Celtic game would heat up so that it became more than a physical or even a mental game. It would be magical. That feeling is very difficult to describe and I certainly never talked about it when I was playing. But when it happened, I could feel my play rise to a new level. It would last anywhere from five minutes to a whole quarter or more. It would surround not only me and the other Celtics but also the players on the other team and even the referee. At that special level, all sorts of odd things happened. The game would be in a white heat of competition and yet somehow I wouldn't feel competitive. Which is a miracle in itself. I'd be putting out the maximum effort, coughing up parts of my lungs as we ran, and yet I never felt the pain. The game would move so quickly that every fake, every cut and pass would be surprising, and yet nothing would surprise me. It

was almost as if we were playing in slow motion. During those spells I could almost sense how the next play would develop and where the next shot would be taken. My premonitions would constantly be correct. And I always felt then that I not only knew all the Celtics by heart, but also all of the opposing players, and they knew me. It happened many times in my career when I felt moved or joyful, but these were the moments that I had chills pulsing up and down my spine.

Russell's words describe precisely the phenomenon that I'm talking about. After years of these experiences, I began a quest to determine what they were all about and how to access this experience of synchronicity. Along the way, I have had a number of guides who have helped me to understand more about it.

I met my principal guide in 1980—David Bohm, the architect of quantum theory. Einstein said that Bohm was the person who taught him everything he knew about quantum theory. At the time, I was in charge of our law office in London, but I had these stirrings in me to do something about leadership in America. In 1980, I had decided to leave my law firm. One Sunday morning, during the period when I was winding down my law practice, I came back from a run and picked up the Sunday *Times*. I looked down at the headline on the inside of the paper and there was an article about David Bohm that contained the words "wholeness and the implicate order," which referred to the theory Bohm was advancing in his recently published book.

I got on the phone immediately, and when I found him, he agreed to see me the next day. That meeting with him was a very clear turning point in my life because, for the first time, I began to understand this phenomenon of synchronicity. Bohm explained it to me in terms of field theory and the "general fielding of mankind." I asked him what he meant by the "general fielding of mankind," and he said, "We are connected through and operate within living fields of thought and perception."

He described more to me, telling me about fields and field theory, which I knew nothing about. He said, "Fields are forces of unseen connection that are influenced by our intentions, and by our ways of being." And he added, "These influences are nonlocal."

When I asked him what he meant by "nonlocal," he talked about "Bell's Theorem," which he called the most profound discovery in the history of science. In 1964, the Irish physicist Jay S. Bell, a student of Bohm's, discovered that when two subatomic particles are paired and spinning in a bubble chamber, if you separate them and then change the spin on one particle, the spin on the other simultaneously changes, *no matter what the distance is between the two.* They could be a continent apart. It's not that one sends a signal to the other—they just change instantaneously. Bohm explained that in a particular field, time–space conditions are not relevant. And when you act in one part of the whole, there are nonlocal results far away.

When I walked away that day, my mind was reeling, and I was seeing the world in a completely different way. What Bohm was saying to me is that *there is separation in the world without separateness.* I knew I had been in the presence of real greatness, and that it was going to take a lifetime to unpack and understand all of what Bohm had told me. But what happened next was even more astounding to me, and that is that I began experiencing this phenomenon of synchronicity on a sustained basis. Over the next eighteen months, doors began opening for me and helping hands began showing up in ways that were absolutely magical.

Within three days of my meeting with Bohm, I was walking down the street and happened to notice a *US News and World Report* with the headline "R_x for Leadership in America." I picked it up and read an article in it by Tom Cronin, who was a presidential scholar living in Colorado. He was espousing many of the concepts that I was thinking about. I flew to Colorado to meet him, and he told me, "The next person you need to talk to is John Gardner." I said, "I couldn't even get in John Gardner's door. He doesn't know me, though I've read everything he's written." He said, "I was his aide when he was in the White House. I'll introduce you." He picked up the phone, and two days later I was in John Gardner's office.

Over the next few months, this kind of thing happened again and again. Gardner led me to Harlan Cleveland, who led me to

Rosabeth Kantor, who led me to Warren Bennis, who led me to James MacGregor Burns. By the end of 18 months, I had 17 world-class people trying to help me figure out what to do about leadership in America.

Seventy-five years ago, the great philosopher Martin Buber wrote about this phenomenon: "What is to come will come when we decide what we are able to will." Buber distinguished between two types of wills. He said that we must surrender our unfree will, which is controlled by things and instincts, in favor of our grand will, which he defined as our destined being. Buber said, "In doing this we begin to listen to what is emerging in the world, to the course of being in the world, not in order to be supported by it, but in order to bring it to reality as it desires." This is the absolute key.

My colleagues and I believe that the most powerful doorway into the territory of phenomena such as synchronicity is to ponder and understand, and then to deeply internalize the concept of this "grand will," or "grand intention." We've mapped a five-stage process to help us access synchronicity intentionally.

> *The first stage of accessing synchronicity is to observe, observe, observe.* This kind of observation requires you to empty yourself of your habitual preoccupations in order to gain a sense of wonder. You've got to be open and accessible—so open, in fact, that you become one with the world instead of being apart from it.

> *The second stage is to form the intention.* This kind of intention has to do with Buber's concept of surrendering to the "grand will." It requires you to understand so much about yourself that you know what your calling in life is, why you are here. Greenleaf states it beautifully when he talks about being lost enough to find yourself.

> *The third stage is to retreat in order to let the inner knowing emerge.* Once you are open and can really see what's going on in the world and understand your Self, the next step is to retreat to allow the inner knowing to emerge. In retreat, you must listen with all of your heart.

The fourth stage is to broadcast your intention. As David Bohm said, we all exist in living fields of thought and perception. When the intention of a person or an organization is strong enough, a kind of radiating field is produced. In other words, the intention is "broadcast," and people begin showing up and convening in ways that are difficult to imagine. But given what Bohm taught me about nonlocal influences and separation without separateness, perhaps this phenomenon is not all that surprising.

Once people begin convening, you can act in the instant to bring forth the new. It's not that you make up a business plan at this point or suddenly find the capacity or control to do what you want to do. It's that you bring forth the new in the form that *it* desires. The dynamic is similar to what happens in the old stories of the Chinese master artists who would go and sit by a landscape for weeks at a time, appearing to do nothing. And then, in an instant, they would begin to paint their masterpiece and be finished in another 15 or 20 minutes.

My way of understanding all of this is deeply aligned with the fundamental beliefs of servant-leadership. Robert Greenleaf said that the search for servant-leadership is a quest for wholeness and that the real insights are beyond the range of verbal communication. In my search for an understanding of synchronicity, I've come by another route to the same understanding. It is possible to see others as being a part of you. There does exist separation without separateness.

Dr. Rubye Braye is the president of JIL Group and a former vice president of an information technology firm in northern Virginia. She devotes much of her time to the study of leadership and eCommerce in profit and not-for-profit institutions. Now a lieutenant colonel, USA Retired, she served 21 years and held numerous leadership positions, including the command of a military ocean terminal—the first woman to successfully do so. Prior to her military career, Dr. Braye worked as a news reporter, radio program commentator, and organizational development consultant. Dr. Braye works with the Greenleaf Center as an adjunct facilitator, offering servant-leadership program development, education, training, and consultation services.

Rubye Braye quotes General Peter Schoomaker, commander in chief of the U.S. Special Operations Command, who said that the conventional wisdom regarding military leadership—strict command-and-control procedures, and a rigid, top-down hierarchical organization—is an outmoded, inaccurate, and dangerous model for leadership—and for followership. Schoomaker adds, "To win in the future, everybody's got to know how to be a leader." In this essay, Rubye Braye examines the state of military leadership in the United States and recommends servant-leadership as an ideal model for effective military leadership. She looks at servant-leadership characteristics from a systems perspective, discussing the application of these characteristics relative to self, relationships, and tasks/resources.

21

SERVANT-LEADERSHIP: LEADING IN TODAY'S MILITARY

Rubye Howard Braye, LTC (R), PhD

Those who know do not say. Those who say do not know.

—Unknown

MANY YEARS AGO, Sheldon Kopp said, "If you meet the Buddha on the road, kill him." Then and now, the message is that no one really has the answers. That certainly appears to be true for leadership: There are no quick and easy answers to becoming an effective leader or leading effectively. Those who seem to do it the best do not spend a lot of time talking about it. However, there are characteristics that afford individuals an opportunity to manifest the most powerful force in the universe—love—toward self, others, and all that one touches. These individuals are the true leaders. All of us have a list of them, for they exist in most institutions, including the military. The evidence is compelling.

Presently, dissatisfied young officers are leaving the services, especially the Army, in droves. This nationwide problem has created grave concern among the service leadership and has become the topic of much discussion. In an April 2000, *Washington Post* article, Thomas E. Ricks reported that the Army Chief of Staff, General Eric K. Shinseki, commissioned a survey of 760 Army officers at the Command and General Staff College at Fort Leavenworth, Kansas. The purpose of this survey was to understand why so many captains, in particular, were bailing out after five to 10 years in the military. The results were startling and revealed that many had scathing criticism of the Army's current leadership. Some of the reasons for leaving included lack of trust, loyalty, lack of straight talk in briefings, credibility, decreasing benefits, and less-than-meaningful work. While it was unclear how the leadership had gotten off course—from the perspective of those surveyed—it was clear that it would take a new approach to get the service leadership redirected. It appeared that the problem was not so much with those surveyed, but rather with those leading them.

Because soldiers are expected to make the supreme sacrifice—give their lives, if necessary, in defense of the nation and all that we stand for—it has become clear that today's soldiers are not as willing to blindly follow leaders without question. More and more, they have concerns about their leaders at every level. The soldiers and the leaders both know that they need to be prepared to use a different model for self-preservation. They all need to serve in a different manner that is still consistent with time-honored traditions of duty, honor, and country.

According to General Peter Schoomaker, commander in chief of the U.S. Special Operations Command, for years, officers and noncommissioned officers received the conventional wisdom. They were told that "military units are most likely to succeed in the field when they follow strict command-and-control procedures—when they operate within a rigid, top-down hierarchical organization. Officers at the top of the military pyramid issue orders, and the grunts on the ground swiftly and unquestioningly obey and execute those orders." This is "an outmoded, inaccurate, and dangerous model for leadership—and for followership," says Schoomaker, in "Operation—Leadership," published in *Fast Company* (September 1999). He adds, "To win in the future, everybody's got to know how to be a leader."

If everyone needs to know how to be a leader and how to lead, what needs to change? After months of pondering the issue, it occurred to me that many leaders at the top have forgotten what it was like to be a junior soldier. Many would be hard-pressed to remember how angry they felt at unfair treatment from those who just did not care about them or their work, and from those without heartfelt love and care for their charges. We called these officers the stargazers; they were so bent on promotion that they would do anything.

Some of them still exist. They seem to find it difficult to hear the needs of the soldiers, and even more difficult to respond. Many leaders seem focused on self and survival; it is tough for them to focus on others in real and meaningful ways. Other leaders seem to be going through the motions of caring, but they lack a deep involvement. They are simply working to complete the years required for retirement or transition. Those who think and behave otherwise rarely survive. The soldiers know this. Rather than wait to get kicked out, they are leaving. They see the truth and are leaving leaders who have failed them. It's not only in the Army that this is happening; the situation is quite similar in the other services.

This failure was clearly articulated by a Marine with 28 years of service, Colonel Wayne Shaw, who retired recently from Quantico. In this portion of his retirement address, he describes leadership in his early days of service and now:

> They were men of great character without preaching, men of courage without ragging, men of humor without rancor. They were men who believed in me and I in them. They encouraged me without being condescending. We were part of a team and they cared little for promotions, political correctness or who your father was. They were well-educated renaissance men who were equally at home in the White House or visiting a sick Marine's child in a trailer park. They could talk to a barmaid or a baroness with equal ease and make each feel like a lady. They didn't much tolerate excuses or liars or those with too much ambition for promotion.

Shaw did not stop there. He reminded us that these leaders stayed close to the Marines; they were courageous and trustworthy. In fact, according to Shaw, "You could trust them with your life, your wife or your wallet. Some of these great leaders were not my superiors—some were my Marines."

Today, we need more leaders of this genre—male and female—at all levels, particularly at the senior levels of government and military leadership. According to Shaw, it is a tragedy to have senior defense officials and generals make public statements about things they themselves don't believe. Worse is when they know that every service member knows the statement is a lie. Most are just out of touch with our society and their charges. Unfortunately, many generals would be hard-pressed to answer Shaw's questions like: How much does a PFC make per month? Who is your Congressman and who are your two Senators? When did you last trust your subordinates enough to take ten days' leave?

The Chairman of the Joint Chiefs of Staff, General Henry H. Shelton, recently testified that he didn't know we had a readiness problem or pay problems. This reveals a remarkable level of isolation, when we know that service members are leaving not just to seek civilian opportunities, but to get away from intolerable conditions.

If the Army is to thrive, not just survive, the leadership problems creating the situation must change. One cannot *do* better unless one can *be* better. One cannot be better unless one cares enough. Those needing to change must have open, teachable spirits. Age is immaterial.

To counter the problematic thinking and behavior, servant-leadership is a viable model. It has the potential to facilitate self-development, assist individuals in identifying what they believe, and encourage individuals to take appropriate action. Servant-leadership is considered a model, but it can more accurately be described as a philosophy, for it helps individuals address questions that start with "Why?" For example: Why is it essential that I have an inner awareness? Why is it critical that I listen to others? Why must I be a good steward?

Answers to these questions, and others, serve to inform leaders. However, it takes more. The leaders need to be empowered and mobilized at every level to change the outmoded wisdom. To get engaged, leaders must be encouraged to move in a new direction. Knowledge and understanding alone will not promote change. It takes a level of sensory awareness that leaves every nerve ending alive with the moment. It also takes vigilant awareness with an acute ability to hear the concerns, feel the pain, and see the ever increasing difficulties in the lives of those who are served.

In the early 1970s, Robert K. Greenleaf articulated an old concept and framed it in new language. He described leadership in a new way and outlined a test to be able to identify those who lead in this way. He spoke of service in the context of leaders and followers with foundation principles and values. He further supported this service concept with characteristics and the use of servant-leadership in society. In *The Servant as Leader,* Greenleaf explained servant-leadership as follows:

> The servant-leader is servant first. . . . It begins with the natural feeling that one wants to serve, to serve first. Then conscious choice brings one to aspire to lead. . . . The difference manifests itself in the care taken by the servant—first to make sure that other people's highest priority needs are being served.

> The best test, and difficult to administer, is: Do those served grow as persons; do they, while being served, become healthier, wiser, freer, more autonomous, more likely themselves to become servants? And, what is the effect on the least privileged in society; will they benefit or, at least, not be further deprived?

It is unlikely that Greenleaf, a Quaker, had the military in mind when he wrote this philosophy and test. However, the test and characteristics are just as relevant for the services as they are for leaders in other institutions in society. A quick review of 10 characteristics of servant-leadership confirms this. In reviewing them, keep asking yourself: What leader has no need of these characteristics, if there is a desire to live a purposeful, effective life as a leader?

Self	*Relationships*	*Tasks/Resources*
Awareness	Listening	Stewardship
Foresight	Empathy	
Conceptualization	Healing	
	Persuasion	
	Commitment to growth of others	
	Building community	

The concept of servant-leadership has three major components: self, relationships, and tasks/resources. To help learners begin to lead as servant-leaders from a systems perspective, it is important to be aware of the application of these characteristics relative to self, others, tasks/resources, and the situation.

Leadership starts with self. Each of us is called to leadership. Years ago, Morris Massey shared a concept that still rings true: Who you are now is a result of where you were when. There is no changing the past, but we are not frozen in time. The past is history, the future is a mystery, be here right now. Living in the now, experiencing the now, starts with an inner life—awareness, foresight, and conceptualization. The captains who are leaving the Army are saying the leaders are either leading from a place that used to exist or may exist. The glory of the past and their fears of the future immobilize them. Being in the now allows awareness to drive what we experience, how we experience it, and how we live from the inner to the outer life. This includes work.

Outer life offers reasons to change from the inside out. This is a key concept in that many people pursue change based on external circumstances and factors, which are often temporary and ineffective. Conversely, insight opens the door to change. This is possible because of awareness. Awareness creates a framework within which one can begin to really be in touch with reality. From that position, one can identify *love* versus *fear*. Here, one continually asks of the senses: What do I really hear? What do I really see? How do I really feel? These answers help form a basis for truth and trust. Many times, what we really experience through our awareness is quite different from the stereotypes we have been taught to see or taught to fear. Rarely does the stereotype match the reality. When awareness provides truth, different actions often follow. This is what soldiers are asking leaders to do today. Stop. Really experience. Really see. Really hear. Experience with the whole being. Then, really act with courage and conviction.

Perceptions afford a glimpse into the future, which we often call "foresight." When we are able to see what the future will afford, it is possible to frame what we see in a way that others can see, too. This is conceptualization. It comes from awareness and serves as a basis for foresight. Without these two characteristics at work, it is difficult, if not impossible, to conceptualize how ideas, information, and knowledge can be shared. Authentic poets, artists, and political candidates do this all of the time. Military leaders can and must do this better. It is no wonder young officers and junior soldiers don't believe their leaders.

Leadership is also based on relationships where people are always considered more important than things. This is a foundation principle. When we make this distinction, decisions are simpler because life—all human life—has a prioritized value. There are times when it is important to view leadership as shared power. Leaders join others as allies and partners to achieve common objectives. Aligning with colleagues requires listening, empathy, healing, persuasion, commitment, and building a sense of community. Because the military includes families, leaders must often be acutely aware of the needs of spouses and children. Service members do not exist in a vacuum, separate from their families. Like the military, families are also systems or units; leaders with families serve as leaders in these units, as well. Thus, on and off duty, there is a scope of responsibility that extends beyond work where the foundation principles remain the same. Military leaders must not only have but also use the characteristics of servant-leadership in all roles—at work, home, community, school, and the like. This makes leadership real and authentic—no personal life and professional life. One simply has a life.

When in charge, one who is aware is actively listening—with empathy, healing, persuasion, commitment—and building a sense of community. From this inner place, one can decide and act.

The last characteristic is stewardship. Military leadership also demands the husbanding of resources: supplies, equipment, weaponry, billets, vehicles, land, and the like. This is true whether the resources are personally owned, or are owned by the military, the community, or another country. In this context, husbanding is stewardship. Stewardship does not just occur—it is a conscious act to care and to conserve, balanced with appropriate use. It requires that leaders remember that actions in one part of the world have repercussions in other parts of the world because the planet is a system, delicately balanced.

One must be always consciously aware that the practice of stewardship is also the deliberate husbanding of resources—from local to global—especially from an environmental perspective. This includes a perspective that considers the long view. In some instances, the military has permanently contaminated areas, rendering them uninhabitable for humans, flora, and fauna. They become wastelands. Leaders can make and have made a case for these atrocities over the years, but the consequences far outweigh the benefits in most instances. Therefore, the questions that leaders must ask themselves are many. They start with: "Could the same results be possible without using the weapon that will create an untenable condition forever?" Frequently, the answer is "Yes." This use of awareness, foresight, and conceptualization can open the way for other options worthy of consideration.

Make no mistake, this is work. Opening oneself to deeper, broader awareness requires sensitivity that many shun, choosing numbness instead. As evidence, consider the immediate gratification sought by those who overeat, overspend, overwork, speed, consume, and race through life. In the lives of many, there is little time to search for and find truth.

There is a dark side in all of us; sometimes it is revealed as insecurity, natural chaos, fear, denial, and fear that the universe is essentially hostile and that people are out to get us, says Parker Palmer in *Insights on Leadership*. This shadow that is not benign is often revealed in a crisis; we learn what we are made of. At that point, the hardest thing we have to do is embrace the shadow, says Jung. This means we must be aware and understand this as an entity. The knowledge alone does not result in change. True awareness helps us act differently to alter the outcome.

It is worth noting that prejudice is part of the hidden side, be it gender, race, nationality, or age prejudice. Regardless, it must be addressed. Again, awareness is often the first step, and inclusion is usually the response. According to Isabel Lopez, "There is room at the table for all" (*Insights on Leadership,* 1998).

While it is possible for leaders who are service members to continue to lead poorly and be subject to poor leadership, service members at all levels can point fingers and continue to search for answers outside of self. In fact, scapegoats are easy to find. Ask any old-timer. For years, the Army has surveyed soldiers like they were the problem, when, in reality, lack of awareness and lack of courageous action have created and perpetuated the unacceptable conditions. Now is the acceptable time to change. Perhaps it would make more sense to have the leaders surveyed with questions that address their care, concern, and actions regarding those they lead. Many would be disappointed in themselves and then, perhaps, finally be open to the awareness and other characteristics needed to confidently and courageously serve as leaders.

Dee Hock is the founder and chief executive officer emeritus of VISA U.S.A. and VISA International. VISA is owned by 22,000 member banks, which both compete with each other for 750 million customers and must cooperate by honoring one another's $1.75 trillion in transactions annually across borders and currencies. Dee Hock is the author of *Birth of the Chaordic Age,* which is the story behind the "chaordic" structure of VISA International. In 1991, he became one of 30 living Laureates of the Business Hall of Fame, and in 1992, he was recognized as one of eight individuals who most changed the way people live in the past quarter century.

In this essay, Dee Hock paints a picture of the possibilities—the realities—not just of the future, but of our immediate present. Hock is a practical visionary; he says that the most effective, humane, and successful organization in the future will be "chaordic," complex, self-organizing, and adaptive. And the most effective, humane, and successful leaders for these organizations will be servant-leaders.

Dee Hock was a keynote speaker at the Greenleaf Center's 2000 annual international conference.

22

LEADERSHIP AND THE CHAORDIC AGE

Dee Hock

IT IS DIFFICULT TO THINK or talk seriously about organizations or management these days without running across what many leading scientists believe will be the principal science of the next century: the understanding of complex, self-organizing, adaptive systems. It's usually referred to by the word *complexity,* a word that seemed to me much too vague to describe these systemic structures. After puzzling through some dictionaries looking for a different, more useful word, I decided it was simpler to construct one. Because these kinds of organizations are thought to emerge and thrive in a very narrow band on the edge of chaos, with just enough order to give them pattern, I borrowed the first syllable from "chaos" and the first syllable from "order," and "chaord" emerged. By *chaord,* I mean any self-organizing and governing, adaptive, nonlinear, complex organism, organization, or system exhibiting behavior characteristics of both order and chaos. Another way to think of it is as an entity in which behavior exhibits observable patterns and probabilities not governed or explained by the behavior of its parts. My favorite way of looking at it is characterized by the fundamental organizing principles of nature and evolution. So, very quickly, you can find yourself in that definition as a complex organism blending chaos and order, not explained by your constituent parts, and obviously in accordance with the organizing principles of nature.

Let me confess at once that my consuming interest has never been business, banking, or credit cards, but rather the organizational patterns of nature and evolution, and how they compare with the organizational patterns of our societal institutions, and what that purports for our future. My purpose is to help diagnose that tornado of technological change that's literally blowing apart all our societal organizations—to say nothing of the biosphere—and the effect it's going to have on us as human beings and on our need to learn and adapt. That passion began very early; I was born in a small mountain community to laboring parents. As a child, I was deeply in love with nature; with school and church came bitter confinement and crushing boredom, along with a sharply rising awareness of the chasm between how institutions professed to function and how they actually do; between what they say they're going to do *for* people, and what they actually do *to* them. I was aware of this chasm throughout high school and two years at a small college. I had my first management job at the age of 20. This awareness, combined with a somewhat rebellious nature, led to what can only be described as 16 years of guerrilla warfare between the naïve young lamb who irrevocably committed unorthodox ideas of organization and management, and three command-and-control, centralized, industrialized corporations. I'm not going to bore you with details, because it's an old, old story. Each time the lamb was determined to change the companies, the companies were determined to corral the lamb, and with the same inevitable result: just another hunk of unemployed mutton, bruised and bleeding on the sidewalk.

Those 16 years turned preoccupation into an obsession with institutions and the people who lead them. Thirty years ago, this led to three questions that have since dominated my life. They were important then. They are critical today.

1. Why (I asked time and time again) are organizations everywhere, whether political, commercial, or social, increasingly unable to manage their affairs?

2. Why are people everywhere increasingly in conflict with and alienated from the organizations of which they are a part?

3. Why are society and the biosphere increasingly in disarray?

I believe it's apparent that we're in the midst of a global epidemic of institutional failure. I don't mean failure only in the sense of collapse, like the Soviet Union or corporate bankruptcy, but the much more common and pernicious form: Institutions increasingly unable to achieve the purpose for which they were created, yet continually expanding as they devour resources, demean the human spirit, and destroy the biosphere: schools that can't teach; corporations that can't cooperate or compete, only consolidate; welfare systems in which no one fares well; unhealthy healthcare systems; communities in which people can't communicate; police that can't enforce the law; judicial systems increasingly without justice; governments that can't govern; and economies that can't economize.

I believe that the answers to those three questions have much to do with compression of time and events. Some of you can remember the days when a check used to take a couple of weeks to find its way through the banking system. We called it "float," and knew what to do with it. It can be thought of as an early form of interest-free venture capital. Today, we're all aware of the incredible speed with which money moves globally and the profound effect it has upon us. But we ignore much more important reductions of float. Consider information float. It took centuries for information about the smelting of an ore to cross one continent and bring about the Iron Age. But when a man stepped on the moon, it was known and seen in every part of the globe in 1.4 seconds—and that's hopelessly slow by today's standards. Think about technological float. It took centuries for one of the first bits of technology—the wheel—to attain universal acceptance.

Today, countless devices utilizing microchips sweep around the earth like the light of the sun into instant universal use. And think about cultural float. Throughout history, it took centuries for the habits of one culture to materially affect another. Now, anything that becomes popular in one country can sweep through others in a matter of months. Think about space float. In just a little more than a single, very long lifetime, we went from the speed of a horse to interstellar travel. People and material now move in minutes where they used to move in months. Information travels in fractions of fractions of a second. And all of them go to places where they never could have been moved before. You can even consider life float. It took roughly two and a half billion years for the nonnucleated cell to become a nucleated cell. Every progressive leap to a more complex life form took half the time it took for the proceeding one. And now, with the emergence of biotechnology and genetic engineering, the creation of new species may literally collapse to a matter of months or years. You can take this endless compression and think of it as the disappearance of time or of change flow—time between what was and what's going to be, between the past and the future. Today, the truth is that the past is ever less predictive; the future is ever less predictable; and the present scarcely exists at all. We see accelerating change everywhere—with, I think, one extraordinary exception: There has been no loss of institutional float.

Although their size and power have increased enormously, there's been no truly new idea of organizing human relationships since the concepts of university, nation-state, and corporation emerged. And the newest of those concepts is more than three centuries old. Although they had a great many illustrious ancestors, it was primarily Newtonian science and Cartesian philosophy that fathered those organizational concepts, and the Industrial Age that mothered them, giving rise to the machine metaphor. The machine metaphor declared that the universe and everything in it, whether physical, biological, or social, could only be understood as clocklike mechanisms composed of separable parts acting on one another with precise, linear laws of cause and effect. That metaphor has dominated thinking in the whole of Western society—and, increasingly, in the rest of the world—to an extent I don't think any of us fully realizes. We've since tried to structure society in accordance with that belief, thinking that with ever more scientific knowledge, ever more specialization, ever more technology, ever more law and regulation, ever more hierarchical command-and-control, ever more efficiency, we could learn to engineer organizations within which we can pull levers at one place to get precise results at another, and know with absolute certainty which levers to pull to get which results. For more than three centuries, we've been engineering those organizations and pulling the levers. Never mind that people had to behave like cogs and wheels in the process, and that rarely, over time, have we ever gotten the predicted result. What we've eventually gotten is painfully apparent: obscene—and that's the only word I can use—obscene maldistribution of wealth and power, collapsing societies, and a crumbling biosphere.

To understand fully why that's happening, I think, requires a deeper diagnosis. I ask you to explore with me, for a few moments, a single capacity: the capacity to receive, utilize, store, transform, and transmit information. I call it "CRUSTTI" for short. I don't mean information from the misconception of information as data, but from Gregory Bateson's brilliant reflection that information is "a difference that makes a difference." If you can't differentiate something—or if when you do, it doesn't make any difference to you—it's not information. It's just noise. Keep in mind two other characteristics of information that are very important. First, it's essentially unbounded. It cannot be contained. And second, information propagates when it's transmitted; that is, when it is shared, it is not lost to the source but is gained by the recipient. And when one bit of information impregnates another bit of information, it gives birth to new information. It's very biological.

It's apparent that the earliest examples of single-cell life possessed capacity to receive, store, utilize, transform, and transmit information. And in fact, that capacity preceded the cell, for to do that is precisely the function and definition of DNA. That capacity even preceded DNA, because when the ultimate physicist examines the ultimate particle of matter, matter changes its behavior and becomes a wave. When it does, the physicists change their behavior as well. Both are engaged in a strange quantum dance. Clearly, they're exchanging a difference that makes a difference. They're exchanging information. In ways we don't begin to understand, information transcends particles, creates communication between them, and binds them into more complex structures such as the nucleus of the atom.

The fascinating thing about all this is that the greater the capacity to receive, store, utilize, transform, and transmit information, the more diverse and complex the entity. This holds true through the entire rising chain of life from particle to the neutrino, to the nucleus, from atom to amino acid, to protein, to molecule, to cell, to organ, and eventually to organism. Another way to think of it is, from bacteria to bees to bats to birds to buffalo and right on through to baseball players. But you see, evolution didn't stop there. In time, it transcended the boundaries of organisms and led to communication between them, binding them into even more complex systems. Whether it's the dance of the bees, the pheromone of ants, the sonar of bats, the song of birds, or the language of humans, once that capacity escaped the organism, communities of organisms—flocks, herds, tribes, hives—instantly came into being.

Let's follow this single thought with respect to our species because it's very important. With accelerating speed, we've transcended boundary after boundary of diversity and complexity. With language, information escaped the boundary of a single mind and became shared; immediately, tribes developed, for its time an enormous increase in organizational diversity and complexity of pure species. With written language came expansions to that which could be manually recorded, stored, and transported; another great leap in societal diversity and complexity immediately followed. With mathematics, the first global language, came another leap in societal diversity and complexity. Leap followed leap, and each was exponentially greater in size and less in time. With the printing press came expansion of CRUSTTI to that which could be mechanically recorded and transported. With the telegraph came electronic alphanumeric capacity. With the telephone, phonic capacity. With television, visual capacity. Now, multimedia capacity. Each one was instantly followed by a huge increase in societal diversity and complexity—that is, vast changes in the way we live, work, and play.

And then, all of a sudden, something extraordinary happened: with the revolution in micro-electronic technology, in a little more than three decades, we have on the order of a-thousand-times-better algorithms, 500-thousand-times more computing power per individual, and 500-million-times more mobility of information.

The entire collective memory of the species—that is, all known and recorded information—is soon going to be a couple of keystrokes away. We don't yet begin to understand the technological significance of such an increase in capacity to receive, utilize, store, transform, and transmit information, let alone the societal diversity and complexity it has unleashed or the changes in institutional concepts and leadership it demands. And yet, that's really nothing. Around the corner are other revolutions of immensely greater significance, such as bio- and nano-technology. Simply stated, nano-technology is the engineering of self-replicating computers and assembly machines so tiny they can stack the basic building blocks of nature—atoms—as though they were bricks. The science has already been discovered. All that remains to be done is the building of assemblers at the atomic scale, and molecular biologists have already pioneered their creation by borrowing the structure of cells. Billions of dollars are pouring into this field, and the finest minds I can find believe (and I agree with them) that within three decades we'll be constructing organs, organisms, products, and services from the atom up. The capacity to receive, utilize, store, transform, and transmit information will be hundreds, perhaps thousands, of times greater than we now experience. The message is pretty simple: Fasten your seatbelts. The turbulence has scarcely begun. And we're going to manage that society with seventeenth-century notions of organization and management? Not a chance of a snowball in that proverbial hot place!

Unless evolution has radically changed its ways, we face an explosion of societal diversity and complexity hundreds, perhaps thousands, of times greater than we now experience or can yet imagine. And that demands certain things. It's really not complicated. The equation is: Increase in informational capacity equals exponential increase in societal diversity and complexity, which equals exponential change in institutions and leadership. And we're simply not keeping up. It's no wonder our society's coming apart. It's the last part of that equation we're abysmally slow to understand. Let me illustrate this with a little bit of history. In 1958, the Bank of America issued 60,000 credit cards to the residents of Fresno, California. After years of losses, the credit card business finally became profitable, and they blanketed the state with cards. Five California banks banded together to launch MasterCard. Other large banks issued proprietary cards and offered franchises. Action and reaction exploded. The banks dropped tens of millions of unsolicited cards on an unsuspecting public with little attention to qualifications, while television, in some markets, was screaming such blather as "The card you won't go berserk with." That was a challenge the public accepted with enormous enthusiasm. In no time, this infant industry was in chaos. In 1968, as the vice president of a modest bank in Seattle, franchised off Bank America, I became involved in the formation of a complex of licensee committees to look into this mess.

It turned out to be much worse than anyone had imagined—far beyond any possibility of correction by the existing organizational structure. It became necessary to right the service—to try to reconceive, in the most fundamental sense, the concepts of bank, money, and credit card. Several conclusions slowly emerged. First, money had become nothing but alphanumeric data recorded on valueless paper and metal. It was going to become alphanumeric information in the form of arranged electrons and photons that would move around the world at the speed of light, by infinite paths, throughout the entire electromagnetic spectrum and at minuscule cost. "Credit card" was the wrong concept: It had to be reconceived as a device for the exchange of monetary value in the form of arranged electronic particles. Demand for that exchange would be lifelong, global, 24 hours a day, seven days a week, at the customers' discretion, wherever they happened to be, which nobody could possibly know. Our perceptions started to change—embedded in this desperate situation was an incredible opportunity. Any organization that could globally guarantee and transfer monetary information, in the form of arranged electrons and photons, would have a market—every exchange of value in the world. It beggared the imagination. However, embedded in that opportunity was an even deeper problem. No bank could do it. No stock corporation could do it. No nation-state could do it. In fact, no form of organization then existent that we could discover could do it. It was going to require some kind of global community organization that could link together, in wholly new ways, an unimaginably diverse complex of financial institutions, consumers, merchants, government entities, and so on. It was really beyond the power of reason to imagine what such an organization would look like, let alone how it could be engineered.

It seemed to me, however, that evolution routinely created, with apparent ease, much more complex chaords—rainforests, marine systems, bodies, brains. So I asked three other ordinary people to join me in addressing a single question based on a single assumption: If anything imaginable was possible, if there were no constraints whatsoever, what would be the nature—not the structure, but the nature—based on biological principles, of an ideal organization to create the world's premier system for the exchange of value? We isolated ourselves in a remote hotel, fought with each other night and day, and could agree on nothing. We were in the old Newtonian mechanistic way of thinking: What do we want to do? How are we going to organize it? Who's going to be in charge of it? Finally, in utter frustration, someone muttered, "I'm beginning to wonder if I know what an organization really is." We decided to explore that question, asking what would be the principles, the institutional genetic code, that would allow the kind of institution needed to organize itself, just as the human body does. Slowly, painfully, a dozen or so principles emerged. I want to share a few of them with you.

They came first in the form of questions, which is the way most change really comes about. "What if," we said, "it were self-organizing, with all participants having the right to self-organize at any time, for any reason, at any scale, with irrevocable rights of participation and governance at any greater scale? What if power and function were distributed, with no power vested in or function performed by any part that could reasonably be exercised or performed by any peripheral or local part? What if governance was distributed, with no individual or institution or combination of either or both, particularly management, able to dominate deliberations or control decisions at any scale? And what if it could harmoniously blend competition and cooperation, with all parts free to compete in unique and independent ways, yet able to yield self-interest and cooperate when necessary to the inseparable good of the whole. Isn't that precisely what every cell in your body does every second of every day? And what if it were people-centric rather than management-centric, with reliance on all employees for their own development, training, and learning; working freely with all others for that purpose, and thus releasing the human spirit and human ingenuity?"

In the beginning, none of us, myself included, thought that such an organization could ever be brought into being, but, in June 1970, we proved ourselves wrong. After two years of intense effort, the organization that later became VISA was brought into being. To make a single important point later, I want to tell you just a few things about it. In the legal sense, it's a non-stock-for-profit membership corporation. In the broader sense, it's a reverse holding-company because the institutions that create its products are simultaneously its owners, its members, its customers, its subjects, and its superiors. It can't be bought, raided, traded, or sold, because ownership is in the form of irrevocable rights of participation. There's no stock. It swiftly transcended language, currency, customs, and cultures. It now successfully connects a bewildering variety of more than 20,000 institutions, 14 million merchants, a billion consumers, and countless other parties in 240 countries and territories. Its participants/owners/members simultaneously and seamlessly engage in fierce competition, while at the same time engaging in the most intense cooperation in elements essential to the health of the whole. Competition and cooperation are not opposites. They amplify each other when held in proper balance. There are multiple boards of directors within a single legal entity, none of which is inferior or superior because each has jurisdiction over certain areas or activities. No part knows the whole, the whole doesn't know all the parts, and none has any need to. The entirety, like all chaordic organizations, including body, brain, and biosphere, is largely self-regulating. When I left VISA, a staff of fewer than 500 people on four continents were operating on less than ½ of 1 percent of the revenue of the members. They coordinated the entire system as it skyrocketed past $100 billion in a trajectory to the present annual volume of $1,700 billion. Those people had no equity. They were not recruited from business schools. They could never become wealthy for their services. Yet, without any consultants, those people selected the VISA name and completed the largest trademark conversion in commercial history in one-third the anticipated time. They built the archetype of the present communication systems in 90 days, for less than $30,000. Those systems have now evolved to clear more electronic transactions in a week than the entire Federal Reserve System does in a year, and at a cost of less than a penny apiece.

I tell you these few things because I want to make two points. First: The most abundant, least expensive, most underutilized, and constantly abused resources in the world are the human spirit and human ingenuity. The source of that abuse is the mechanistic-dominated, Industrial Age concepts of organization and the management practices they spawn. Second: Given the right chaordic circumstances, from nothing but dreams, determination, and the liberty to try, quite ordinary people consistently do extraordinary things. I believed then and believe today that we were creating an archetype of institutions for the next century. However, it is not a model to emulate for it is fundamentally flawed and has regressed to some degree over the years. It is something to study and improve upon. I believe the power for these concepts is immensely greater than even the success of VISA would indicate.

Let's bring this home to the question of servant-leadership. In the kind of organization that I described, the old concepts of management were simply irrelevant. We had to think about leadership and management in a totally different way. Over the years, I've had countless groups of people together to discuss management. Asked to describe the three most important responsibilities of any manager, the replies would be extremely diverse and different. However, they would have one thing in common: they were always downward-looking. They had something to do with hiring, motivating, training, organizing, and directing subordinates. This is totally wrong.

I believe the first responsibility of the manager is to manage self, one's own integrity, knowledge, wisdom, ethics, temperament, words, deeds. It's a never-ending, incredibly difficult, and often shunned task. It's so much easier to tell someone else what to do. Yet, without proper management of self, no one is fit for authority, no matter how much he or she acquires. In fact, the more managers acquire, the more dangerous and destructive they become. Management of self should have half our time and the best of our ability. And in doing so, the ethical, moral, and spiritual elements are inescapable. You have to deal with them.

The second responsibility of any manager is to manage those who have higher authority: bosses, supervisors, directors, regulators. Without their consent, support, and trust, how can we follow convictions, exercise judgment, use our creative ability, or create the conditions by which other people can do the same? Shouldn't that have at least a quarter of our time and energy?

The third responsibility is to manage peers: those who have no authority over us and over whom we have no authority. They can make our life a heaven or a hell. And by peers, I mean the entire environment—competitors, customers, associates—all those over whom you have no authority and who have none over you. Shouldn't that have at least a fifth of our time?

The fourth responsibility becomes obvious. If you've attended to self, superior, and peers, there's nothing left except those over whom you have authority. The common response is that all one's time and energy will be consumed managing self, superiors, and peers, leaving little, if any, time for subordinates. Precisely. You only need to select good people and enable them to understand and practice the concept. If those over whom you have authority manage themselves, their peers, and you superbly, what do you have to do except see that they are amply recognized and rewarded, and get out of the way? And why should that take more than 5 percent of your time?

The question always emerges, "Yes, but how do we manage superiors and peers?" You don't have any power over them so the answer is equally obvious. You can't. But can you influence them? Motivate them? Disturb them? Excite them? Persuade them? Set them an example? Arouse them? Forgive them? Well, of course you can. There is absolutely no set of rules and regulations so rigorous, no organization so hierarchical, no bosses so abusive that they can prevent you from behaving this way, short of killing you. They can make it more difficult, but they can't stop it. It's entirely up to you. Eventually, the word will emerge. Can you *lead* them? This is the essential difference between management and leadership. It's not complicated. Educed behavior is the essence of leadership. Compelled behavior is the essence of tyranny. Where behavior is compelled, even by innocuous rules and regulation, there is tyranny, however petty. And where behavior is educed, there is leadership, however modest. A true leader neither needs nor uses power. The mechanistic way of looking at leader and follower as being distinct and different is equally flawed and misleading. In every moment in life, we both lead and follow. There's never a time when our knowledge, judgment, or wisdom is not more useful than that of another. And there is no moment in time when the wisdom of that other is not in some way more useful than ours. There is no moment in time when our words and deeds are not influencing everyone around us and when theirs are not influencing us.

The truth is, everyone is a born leader. Who of you reading this will deny that from the moment of birth you were leading yourself to crawl, stand, walk, talk, and all that followed? You may have had help, but you were leading yourself. And who will deny that, from the moment of birth you were leading parents, siblings, and friends? Watch the baby cry and the parents jump. We were leaders from the moment of birth, until we were compelled to go to school to be managed and to learn how to manage. It's really true leadership, leadership by everyone, chaordic leadership—in, up, around, and down—this world so badly needs. And mechanistic, industrial-age, dominator management is what it so sadly gets.

I believe we're in an unprecedented moment in time. The capacity to receive, store, utilize, transform, and transmit information has completely escaped the boundaries of all existing forms of organization: nation, state, cities, governments, churches, families. It's transcending and enfolding them into new, much more complex, and diverse systems, the shape of which we dimly perceive. The truth is that today we don't know where a business begins or ends. We don't know what the distinction is among supplier, manufacturer, distributor, retailer, consumer, or banker, or even whether those old concepts are useful in thinking about such distinctions. We don't know where the nation-state begins or ends, or what the true distinctions are among education, work, play, religion, and culture.

We grow desperate trying to make the new social realities conform to the old notions of organization and leadership. In all of recorded history, that has never worked, and it's not going to work this time either. We don't have an environmental problem, or a healthcare problem, or a welfare problem, or an economic problem, or a crime problem, or a political problem, or an educational problem. They're all symptoms, not the disease. At bottom, we have an institution-and-leadership problem. Until we diagnose it and treat it properly, all those other symptoms will grow increasingly worse. And if we don't change our consciousness, if we don't reconceive our ideas of organizations and management, where is it going to leave us? It's going to leave us locked inside the seventeenth-century separatist concepts of linear, mechanistic, dominator organizations within which, in millions of logical, rational, isolated, ever increasing acts, we pour into the biosphere billions of tons of man-made toxic substances that it cannot recycle; punch massive holes in the ozone layer; foul our fresh water; pile up countless tons of virulent poisons with a half-life of 24,000 years; force 85 percent of the earth's people to exist on 15 percent of the resources; push two out of six people into abysmal poverty; turn vast areas of the planet into desert; and commit countless other disconnected acts with virtually no understanding of how they are cumulative atrocities, or how they are combining to affect the planet, our lives, and the lives of our grandchildren.

We're at that very point in time, in my judgment, when a 400-year-old age is rattling on its deathbed, and another is struggling to be born—a shifting of consciousness, culture, science, society, institutions, incomprehensibly greater and swifter than the world has ever experienced. The great unanswered question of the age is whether we're going to get there through massive institutional failure, enormous social and environmental carnage, and regression into ever more dictatorial pyramids of power that will inevitably collapse, causing even more carnage, before new concepts emerge.

Or have we at long, long last evolved to the point of sufficient intelligence and will to create the conditions by which these chaordic organizations and leadership can come into being? Are our institutions and people capable of their own continuous learning and transformation in order to harmoniously coevolve with all other institutions, with all people, and with all other living things, to the highest potential of each and all?

I simply don't know the answer to that question. But this I do know with certainty: It's far too late, and things are far too bad for pessimism. We might as well get a smile on our face and get on with it. If we caused the problems, we can cause the solution—if we have the will and the courage, and if we care enough. In times like these, it's no failure to fall short of realizing all that we might dream. The failure is to fall short of dreaming all that we might realize.

Scott W. Webster is assistant director of the Center for Public Leadership at the John F. Kennedy School of Government, Harvard University. He is a former James A. Finnegan Foundation Fellow, Pew Charitable Trusts Teaching Fellow, and Fellow of the Society for Values in Higher Education. Most recently, he is coauthor, with James MacGregor Burns, et al., of *Dead Center: Clinton–Gore Leadership and the Perils of Moderation.*

One of the highest forms of servant-leadership is the desire to serve in the public interest. In this richly anecdotal and historically based essay, Scott Webster examines the push-and-pull of public life, servant-leadership, and the American temperament in politics.

23

SERVANT-LEADERSHIP, PUBLIC LEADERSHIP: WRESTLING WITH AN AMERICAN PARADOX

Scott W. Webster

PRESENT WHEN THE FIRST box of moon rocks was to be opened on live television in July 1969, the well-known Harvard geologist Clifford Frondell could barely contain his anticipation. As the box's contents finally came into plain view, in a delicious if decidedly unscientific lapse, Frondell blurted, "Holy shit! It looks like a bunch of burnt potatoes!"

One wonders if a similarly quixotic statement—a mix of raw emotion, unabashed glee, and perhaps a twinge of disappointment—might be expected if ever the souls of James Madison and Thomas Jefferson could bend time to peer at twenty-first-century America. Would they be amazed that the Constitution of their day still lives and breathes? Or aghast, for instance, that so few of their latter-day countrymen are farmers, a pursuit once believed the lifeblood of democracy?

The quality of persons in public life and in positions to exercise leadership in the public interest matters greatly. So it was two hundred and twenty-five years ago and so it is today. Yet conventional wisdom holds that no generation of Americans has matched the Founders' for sheer ingenuity, public-spiritedness, and, well, downright usefulness. After all, men from Madison and Jefferson to George Washington to John Marshall to Alexander Hamilton to Benjamin Franklin devised the rules by which we still govern ourselves.

Though they had fathered—in both scale and expressed purpose—a system of self-government unique in the annals of human history, the Founders were hardly a bunch of Pollyannas. "When planning for posterity," Thomas Paine cautioned his contemporaries in 1776, "we ought to remember that virtue is not hereditary." And they did remember. To wit, principles and provisions like checks and balances; federalism; biennial, quadrennial, and sexennial elections; and impeachment found their way into the new constitution.

Paine's admonition was nine-tenths human psychology and one-tenth hubris. The policies of Britain's King George III in the 1760s and 1770s had illustrated the tyranny that one individual could exert over others. Paine's feverish determination to rally colonists to defeat such tyranny necessarily bred a conviction that his fealty to representative government and to the principles of public leadership was rare among men in his own generation, and perhaps in succeeding ones, too. The constitution that governed the new nation needed to weather the machinations of those who would usurp governmental power to advance purely private ends.

But Paine's words have lingered in—perhaps even poisoned—the American imagination far longer than even he may have believed prudent. Most Americans admire the Founding Fathers, yet regard subsequent and particularly contemporary public figures as Lilliputian by comparison. *Individuals* from Abraham Lincoln to Frederick Douglass to Susan B. Anthony to Franklin D. Roosevelt to John F. Kennedy have of course entered the pantheon of venerable public leaders, but *as a generation* a special fondness is reserved for the first one. Its members are a breed apart.

Americans' affection for the Founding Fathers is to be expected. In the Declaration of Independence, the Constitution, and the Bill of Rights, the Founders articulated principles that remain sacrosanct and have rightly been subsequently seized upon by those groups of Americans originally excluded from self-government. The Founders quite literally charted a new course for human history—away from authoritarian regimes to more democratic ones. As against the backdrop of the late eighteenth century, and indeed, as against all of human history, the revolutionary nature of this change in *Weltanschauung*—and in the attendant social order—is nearly impossible to convey to present-day Americans. Moreover, though not faultless, Madison, Jefferson, and others demonstrated that men could subordinate their private ambitions to the greater public good. They thus understood the key principle of what in today's parlance is labeled "servant-leadership." Suffering under years of British colonial rule, the Founders wanted to exercise leadership in service to the principles of liberty and equality that had eluded them for so long.

As history marches on, the American Revolution casts a longer, not a shorter, shadow. Its fundamental gains are enjoyed not only by Americans, but, increasingly, by citizens in democracies worldwide. Yet, in the United States, the Revolution's legacy is not entirely sanguine. By dint of their own struggle against authority and their own efforts to curb it, the Founders—Tom Paine among them—made Americans wary even of those who presumably toil for the public good.

These, then, are the contradictory legacies of the American Revolution generation: the merit of public leadership and the perceived ubiquitous shortcomings of public leaders. It is a peculiarly American paradox.

Republicanism

One of the greatest acts of George Washington's career as a military officer came not on a field of battle but in a house of government. Two days before Christmas 1783, he stood before the Continental Congress and resigned his commission as commander-in-chief of all American forces. The Treaty of Paris, officially ending the American Revolution and recognizing American independence, had been signed nearly four months earlier, but Washington's move rivaled even the war's outcome for sheer unexpectedness. Observers were stunned. Here was a victorious general electing to go not the way of Englishman Oliver Cromwell, but rather of the Roman, Cincinnatus Lucius Quinctius. Cromwell sought to convert military prowess into political power; Cincinnatus—and Washington—eschewed such spoils, surely theirs for the taking, in favor of private life.

The significance of Washington's example was lost neither on his own countrymen nor on a watchful world. With one gesture, he signaled that public affairs would indeed be conducted differently in post-Revolutionary America—that the fight just waged really did represent a new order of things. Public leaders would serve the public interest, not their own.

Washington's sudden retirement also resonated because it gave material form to the concept of *republicanism*. This term referred to a social and political order characterized by independent and property-holding persons, whose status owed primarily to their own merit rather than merely to those whom they knew or married. Individuals in a republic were citizens, not subjects, and they were willing to sacrifice private gain (witness Washington) for the *res publica,* or good of the whole community.[1] Put differently, a republic was everything that a monarchy—under which American colonists, and even all of human civilization for two millennia had existed—was not.

For insights and inspiration on the topic of republicanism, the Founders turned not only to European philosophers like Machiavelli, Milton, and Harrington, but also to the Romans, and specifically to the great era of the Roman Republic. Cicero, Virgil, Tacitus, and Plutarch wrote approving histories of the likes of Cincinnatus and Publius Valerius, the latter of whom helped overthrow Rome's last king. Small wonder, then, that Publius became the collective pen name of Alexander Hamilton, John Jay, and James Madison as they wrote essays—85 in all, and now referred to as *The Federalist Papers*—appearing in newspapers throughout the country in defense of the Constitution. In 1787, as Constitutional Convention delegates

---

[1] Eric Foner and John A. Garraty, eds., *The Reader's Companion to American History* (Boston: Houghton Mifflin Company, 1991), pp. 930–931.

toiled in Philadelphia's summer heat, a woman asked Benjamin Franklin what sort of government was being assembled. "A republic," he famously replied, "if you can keep it."[2]

Franklin's wit barely concealed the Founders' disquiet. Among the learned, republics were adjudged rare and short-lived. Their dependence on equality and on a virtuous citizenry made them so. Unlike monarchies, power and authority in republics flowed from the bottom up, not from the top down. Consequently, the quality of public leaders proved difficult to manage and then sustain. Republics employed fewer of the typical monarchical devices—for example patronage, hereditary privilege—for fomenting allegiance and cohesion. Relationships among citizens were more horizontal and less vertical. Moreover, republics presumably endured only in small, homogeneous contexts, such as eighteenth-century Holland. Experiments with republican rule in large, heterogeneous venues— eighteenth-century England, for instance—dissolved into chaos and military dictatorship.[3]

The American experiment, of course, did not dissolve. Fresh from the spoils of Saratoga and Yorktown, Americans basked in the sort of republic that Franklin had promised his Philadelphia interlocutor. As historian Gordon S. Wood notes, "The character of republicanism—integrity, virtue, and disinterestedness—[was placed] at the center of public life. . . . No generation in American history has ever been so self-conscious about the moral and social values necessary for public leadership."[4]

Democracy

As the eighteenth century gave way to the nineteenth, America became a noticeably different place. A population that stood at four

---

[2] Franklin, as cited in Richard Brookhiser, *Alexander Hamilton, American* (New York: Touchstone, 1999), p. 67.

[3] Eric Foner and John A. Garraty, eds., *The Reader's Companion to American History* (Boston: Houghton Mifflin Company, 1991), pp. 930–931.

[4] Gordon S. Wood, *The Radicalism of the American Revolution* (New York: Vintage, 1991), pp. 103, 197.

million in 1790 had more than doubled to 10 million in 1820. Only one person in 30 lived in a city (defined as a community of 8,000 or more) in 1790; in 1820, one in 20 did. And by 1830, more than a quarter of all Americans lived west of the Mississippi River.[5] Still more changes and challenges—industrialization, slavery, states' rights, imperialism—loomed on the horizon in the nineteenth century alone. In the face of these transformations, the nature of public leadership remained no more stagnant than any other phenomenon.

Increasingly, democratic values supplanted republican ones. Much of what we associate today with American politicking—including strident campaigning, the emergence of parties, and the unabashed promotion of private interests in legislation—had canvassed the landscape by the mid-nineteenth century. Perhaps most damaging to republicanism, in the wake of Andrew Jackson's presidency, fewer and fewer persons seeking public office made pretensions to being disinterested or above the fray. The prospect of actively pursuing an elected position, regarded as too crass in Washington's day, had become commonplace to the succeeding political generation.

Fortunately, the battle between democracy and republicanism was—and remains—something other than a zero-sum game. Rather than one notion replacing the other entirely, a synthesis emerged. The two constructs are simply different gradations on the same scale. Republican principles, for instance, are still central to the American character: temperance with respect to wealth; fervent belief in equality; preoccupation with corruption; and disdain of dependency. And though members of the Founding generation dismissed democracy as mob rule, American history has rendered a kinder verdict. Even Jefferson conceded, in his old age, while watching classical republicanism morph into liberal democracy, that "the public good is best promoted by the exertion of each individual seeking his own good in his own way."[6]

---

[5] Alan Brinkley, *The Unfinished Nation: A Concise History of the American People* (New York: McGraw-Hill, 1993), pp. 218–219.
[6] Jefferson, as quoted in Gordon S. Wood, *The Radicalism of the American Revolution* (New York: Vintage, 1991), p. 296.

The $64,000 question, of course, is: Did these democratic convulsions affect public leadership? Moreover, given the unique factors present in the cauldron that was the American Revolution, are comparisons between modern-day public leaders and the Founders actually reasonable and fair?

The answers are, respectively, Yes and No. Yes, democracy's growth indelibly colored the nature of public leadership. No, evaluating the efforts of all post-eighteenth-century public leaders against the likes of Jefferson and Madison is not entirely evenhanded; it smacks of a stacked deck.

Democracy opened the floodgates to public leadership in America. The United States was the first country in the history of the world to grant the right of self-government to common men. Indeed, in a remarkable turnabout, commonness and being "of the people" became virtues where once they were vices. Men who in previous eras and in other societies would have no legitimate claim to elective office pronounced themselves candidates for public office from cities to rural townships and all parts in between. As compared to the Founders, these men were "humbler in antecedents and cheekier in their sensibilities."[7]

The competition proved intense. Rather than being *above* the fray, political aspirants occasionally *were* the fray. An 1833 ruckus between Virginia politicians Thomas Walker Gilmer and William Cabell Rives erupted in Charlottesville when Gilmer objected to Rives's opposition to nullification and saw fit to convey his point of view by trying to pull Rives's nose. Rives then allegedly bit Gilmer's thumb and treated him to a horsewhipping.[8] Certainly not the stuff of Washington and Jefferson!

But then Washington and Jefferson were no angels, either. They, too, lived just this side of heaven. As with many men, public or not, corrupt temptations occasionally swirled about them and their contemporaries. But their colossal struggle for liberty

---

[7] Michael J. Birkner, "Was There A Second Great Generation? Some Reflections on Early Political Leadership," *Virginia Cavalcade* (Autumn 1990), p. 62.

[8] *Id.*, p. 62.

directed their energies into positive channels and ultimately suppressed base instincts like greed or jealousy with an intensity that few other generations of public leaders have known.[9] Acknowledgment of this fact is too frequently missing from accounts that praise the Founders and chide succeeding generations as pale by comparison.

Missing too is an appreciation of the republican context in which the Founders operated, as against the democratic milieu that predominated soon after Washington and Jefferson had left the public stage. Though the Founders exercised leadership in the public interest, they themselves were a cut above the public—better educated, wealthier, more cosmopolitan. And their community of peers was relatively finite, with the rules of play being generally agreed to. It was, historian Michael J. Birkner calculates, "a cozy climate in which to conduct political business, a climate that gave politicians a greater leverage to do the statesmanlike thing."[10]

The coziness, though, proved ephemeral. "There is a substantial difference between a republic, in which a working aristocracy can act generally without fear of popular rebuke on the one hand, and an active democracy, where average people presume to tell their public servants how to vote and, in many instances, run for office themselves."[11]

Emphasis was everything. In a republic, public leaders serve ideas and ideals. In a democracy, public leaders more directly serve the people.

Contradiction

But what happens when the people don't believe they are being served? What happens when those who are presumably being led instead disavow their leaders and hold them in contempt?

---

[9] *Id.*, p. 54.
[10] *Id.*, p. 59.
[11] *Id.*, p. 60.

Such questions are enormously important, if complex. In fumbling for a response, one's mind might summon images of the American Revolution, for it was precisely such disaffection and estrangement that precipitated the colonists' break with England. Or one might also turn to today's newspapers, filled as they are with gloomy stories about waning interest in public affairs.[12]

The different historical frames of reference are instructive. Epochs separated by two centuries are nonetheless linked by a central concern over the relationship between leadership and service. *Plus ça change, plus c'est la même chose* (the more things change, the more they stay the same).

Americans' faith in public leaders has never been constant, but their faith in the principles of public leadership has.[13] A minor linguistic distinction, but an important one. It is the difference, as Lincoln might have said, between a horse's chestnut and a chestnut horse. Or, in Twain's formulation, between the lightning bug and the lightning. Which is to say there's a world of difference.

Though voter turnout and trust in government levels have ebbed and flowed over time, far less skittish are Americans' attitudes toward basic republican and democratic values.[14] For instance, a virtual consensus is to be found on the matter of whether democracy is the best form of government, whether public officials should be selected by majority vote, whether the minority's right to criticize the majority should be protected, and whether citizens should have equal means at their disposal to influence public policy. These ideas have endured in the United States; indeed, they have gained currency worldwide.

So what, then, of the contradiction? How can Americans embrace the message with one breath, but kick the messenger with the next?

---

[12] Alan Brinkley, "What's Wrong With American Political Leadership?" *Wilson Quarterly* (Spring 1994), pp. 47–54.

[13] Joseph I. Lieberman, *In Praise of Public Life* (New York: Simon & Schuster, 2000).

[14] Robert D. Putnam, *Bowling Alone: The Collapse and Revival of American Community* (New York: Simon & Schuster, 2000).

Part of the explanation lies in our own past. The fundamental contradiction has existed for most of America's lifetime. Lord James Bryce observed, in *The American Commonwealth,* that the American system of government is based on the theology of John Calvin and the philosophy of Thomas Hobbes. The Constitution, he wrote in 1888, "is the work of men who believed in original sin, and were resolved to leave open for transgressors no door which they could possibly shut."[15] Public virtue and republicanism had their place in the emerging America, but safeguards against the vicissitudes of human nature also needed to be erected. From the beginning, Americans hedged their bets and sought to reconcile two points of view.

Part of the answer is also to be found in our culture. Without overstating the point, dyads of tension have peppered Americans' lives: east versus west, north versus south, rural versus urban, rich versus poor, educated versus uneducated, materialism versus spirituality, community versus individual. The public leader versus public leadership dynamic is of this same ilk.

It is also worth recognizing that there are contradictions, and then there are *contradictions*. And thankfully, this particular tension between reverence for public leadership and wariness of public leaders is only of the first variety. It is less a debilitating ambivalence than a restorative one. For it mixes devotion to large principles with a guarded faith in elected representatives to uphold those principles. As such, it eschews the unhealthy effects of deifying a particular generation by attaching them too closely with the *sine qua non* of public leadership.

A group of friends in ancient Rome lambasted one of their own for divorcing his wife. "Was she not beautiful?" they implored. "Fruitful? Chaste?" Unnerved, the Roman removed his shoe and held it up, barking, "Is this not new? Is it not well-made? Yet not one of you can tell me where it pinches me!"[16]

---

[15] James Bryce, *The American Commonwealth,* Vol. I (London: Macmillan & Co., 1888), p. 299.

[16] Stimson Bullitt, *To Be A Politician* (1959; reprint, Seattle: Willows Press, 1994), p. 110.

Servant-leadership and public leadership properly pinch Americans. Like republicanism and democracy, they boast rich historical antecedents and are inextricably linked to each other. Indeed, the instinct to serve in the public interest is the highest manifestation of republican and democratic principles.

Yes, Virginia, there is such a thing as public leadership. And, steeped in a long tradition of service both to people and to ideas, it thrives in America.

John P. Schuster began his management consulting practice in 1981. He is currently a principal in The Schuster–Kane Alliance and Director of Rockhurst University's Center for Leadership. He has been a management columnist, and is a published writer and an accomplished speaker. He was a contributing author to *Insights on Leadership: Service, Stewardship, Spirit, and Servant-Leadership;* author of *Hum-Drum to Hot-Diggity: Creating Everyday Greatness in the World of Work;* and coauthor of *The Power of Open-Book Management.*

John Schuster takes us on the roller-coaster ride that is the new economy—love it or hate it, it's here to stay. How will the new economy shape our businesses, our relationships with our neighbors, our relationships with our fellow human beings in other countries, our perceptions of value and of money? Schuster illuminates the bright side and the dark side of the new economy and finds hope for us in the prospect of growing servant-leadership throughout the world.

24

SERVANT-LEADERSHIP AND
THE NEW ECONOMY

John P. Schuster

Civilization is a race between education and catastrophe.

—H.G. Wells

MR. WELLS HAS NEVER been more right than now—the opening decade of the twenty-first century.

Servant-leadership, in its many forms, is the force for education that can stem the catastrophe. And just what is the catastrophe? The catastrophe is the dark side of the New Economy. The New Economy has its sunny side, there is no doubt. But unless we educate ourselves and choose individual and community well-being over economic gain as the primary measure of progress in the New Economy, Antiquated Economy, or any other Economy, we are toast. It is not just a matter of getting several hundred million more of us on the Internet in the next five years, as some cyber-utopians would have us believe. The catastrophe won't be averted because we all gain the benefits of hyper bandwidth and wireless solutions. There are other deeper issues at play.

And why is servant-leadership the answer/antidote? Several reasons, one of which is its inclusiveness. But most of all because *servant-leadership is a kind of organizing principle for the human spirit, a kind of DNA for the soul.* And to avert the catastrophe, in addition to ample bandwidth and RAM, we will need mind, heart, and soul.

Before you dismiss me, because of the catastrophe part, as a neo-luddite, anti-technology, anti-free market, tree-hugging, grain-burger-ingesting wimp, let me tell you what I do. I assist enterprises and communities that engage and become players in the New Economy. Along with a dedicated group of colleagues, I facilitate strategy and teach business literacy so everyone can participate in the wealth generation process. I train trainers, along with my colleagues, on how to understand and create new business models.

I teach financial ratios to employees who want to contribute but never could quite figure out what in the world the people with the MBAs were talking about when they would make decisions based on risk-adjusted capital. We help the incentive pay systems that are supposed to align the interests of shareholders with the interests of employees—but which most often don't because only the executives understand what is at stake. We help these systems come alive for employees and mid-managers so the leaders of the organization actually reward employees for increasing profits.

On the personal side, I belong to a country club, have a nice home in the suburbs of Kansas City, trade stocks on-line if the market is going up (if it's going down, I haven't figured out what to do yet). My retirement is sitting in mutual funds, so I want and need the economy to perform well, long into the future. I have two mutual fund companies for clients.

Given this background, you won't be surprised that I did not demonstrate in Seattle in the fall of 1999 to stop the workings of the World Trade Organization. But I think I might start showing up at the protests, because lots of the architects for the New Economy, in Internet speak, don't get it. They don't get servant-leadership either.

That said, I throw stones out of my glass house only through the most open of windows.

As you are reading this, a 13-year-old somewhere in Bangkok is leaning up against a traffic light on a congested corner across from a Buddha shrine, hanging out with his friends, and lighting up a cigarette because I have money sitting somewhere in a mutual fund for my hard-earned retirement. That money is following one of the rules of investing, which is to always go to the place of greatest return. Money is like water that way—it always flows downhill to make more money. And in this instance, as a portion of my savings (I don't have all my retirement money in social investment funds) flows to a tobacco company marketing in the Eastern Hemisphere, my happy retirement is based in part on this 13-year-old and his friends consuming a lifetime of tobacco products.

That is my glass house. It looks a lot like yours. We all participate in this New Economy and most of its community/ecosystem-endangering dynamics. Reading books on servant-leadership, going to a conference on consciousness and ethics in business, doesn't take away the darker aspects of the New Economy that we have created and participate in.

Living out servant-leadership principles, however, can shed some light on the darkness. So let's look a little deeper at the issues. We'll start by describing the New Economy, the good, the beautiful, the diabolic. Then we will look at why servant-leadership can save us from the diabolic. We will spend more time on the New Economy part, since this book and others have been devoted to the many powerful facets of servant-leadership. You will be able to connect the dots in your own mind. But the New Economy is an unknown beast and deserves some analysis.

What We Need to Know about the New Economy

The New Economy is here. Business magazines like *Fast Company* are creating a mythology of the New Economy as it is happening, aggrandizing the Internet and free agency and the new business models that emerge to disrupt the old ways of doing things. Traditional and conservative magazines like *The Economist* held out for a long time and would talk about the "New Economy" only in quotation marks, seeing it as a pop-culture phrase that had nothing to do with economics. But even the conservative Brits are giving in to the widespread use of the term now and are willing to concede that some economic dynamics have changed.

What Is New about the New Economy?

Lots, really, but here are a few things worth considering.

Value Migration

Value migration—the term for shifts in the value of companies—is happening more rapidly than ever before. As I was writing this article, Eli Lilly lost $38 billion of value in one day when its case for prolonging the patent on Prozac was lost. That is value migration. The shift to technology stocks and away from smokestack industries is value migration. So is the shift from one part of a traditional value chain to another. Look at the air travel value chain—a traditional one. What effects are globalization and the Internet having on this chain, and where is value migrating?

Only the nimble travel agents will be able to capture value and not be skilled over (disintermediated is the formal term) in this chain. Value migrates to the Internet ticketing service. Boeing and Airbus engage in a gargantuan global battle as they go after value in the airline manufacturing industry.

With gajillions of dollars of capital, venture capital firms aplenty, the pervasiveness of the Internet, and entrepreneurs everywhere all converging into a global economy, there is a vast amount of value

---

Air Travel: The Value Chain

Vendor's Vendor⟶ Vendor⟶ Company⟶ Customer⟶Customer's Customer

Parts Suppliers⟶ Boeing Airlines⟶ Airline⟶Travel Agent⟶ People Flying

shifting every day. Free markets have done this for a few centuries. What is new? The scale and scope and speed. (Read Adrian Slywotsky's *Value Migration,* 1996, Harvard Business School Press, for more on this aspect of the New Economy.) This is why I and about 100 million other businesspeople are excited about the New Economy. What chaos and fun and opportunity are emerging in our time. Whee!!!

The Internet

We all know this one—the fastest adopted technology of all time. If you are a cyber-utopian, your motto is something like: "I surf, therefore I am." Where some see freedom and everyone gaining a voice, however, others see invasions of privacy and one more medium about to be tainted with our moral failings. Regardless, this is a huge part of the new economy and has created the tycoons of our time. Larry Ellison and Bill Gates are the Vanderbilts and Rockefellers of our age. Value migration to Amazon.com and others could not have happened without this new invention.

Two other new features that the Internet brings to the New Economy are: network effects and unit cost.

Network Effects

Networks are huge multipliers of value. Your fax machine wasn't worth much until millions of others bought their fax machines— then you were part of a vast network. The network, be it on a Microsoft platform or some other standard, multiplies so fast that the value of who is first to market with a new standard is almost incalculable. That's why little companies in Palo Alto with a few millions line of code end up being worth more than Bethlehem Steel.

Unit Cost

Much of the management world, for the past century, has focused on controlling unit cost, whether it involves a box of cereal or a ton of steel or a Nike running shoe. This effort will never go away, but an information product has a distinguishing economic intrinsic feature—once created, there is almost no cost to reproduce. This turns old profit formulas on their head as Microsoft realizes margins of 30 percent, at least for a while

Globalizing

The village is here. The cold war ends, trade barriers lessen, and free enterprise is the only system left. A global economy of $40-plus trillion blossoms in the years after the fall of the Soviet Union. And now capital and goods and the language of balance sheets and profits dominate the world. What we used to dominate in the West is now a global game. When I was in Kuala Lumpur, Malaysia, last year, I could have been in Orlando. And this is a country that fights against being westernized.

What Isn't So New about the New Economy?

Capital drives growth. The venture capital put into the new companies is how we innovate economically. Capital built the industrial sector and it is building the New Economy. Wal-Mart's huge capital reserves allow it to expand globally and threaten Europe's retailers.

Growth is still the only real measure on the national agenda. Growth is what economists live and breathe. Now it is our national cultural obsession. As Peter Block says, he doesn't have to ask himself how he feels anymore, because when he gets up in the morning, someone is telling him how the NASDAQ is doing. We have renewed the measures of growth, stock price over profits, NASDAQ over dividends, the number of IPOs and the amount of venture capital. But growth is the measure.

We are still using natural resources as our base for the economy. As far as we can tell, no one has yet found synthetic substitutes for clean air and water and rich topsoil. So the New Economy may be digital-based, but the strip malls of the world and 500 million vehicles on the planet (up from 50 million in 1950) still impact air and water and land use. And we take natural habitat for human use and kill species at accelerating rates. [My old high school and college chum, Dave Quammen, has written the definitive book on species loss: *The Song of the Dodo* (Scribner, 1996). It is a beautiful, sad, and alarming read.]

Greed still lines up alongside human creativity in our form of free markets. Capitalism, as we know it in America in the New Economy, and which is being exported to the world as fast as possible, is a robust set of methods for encouraging and rewarding innovation. Many of its features deserve to be imitated. Unfortunately, in its current form, it also rewards greed for those less advanced in their humanity, and the greedy side of us does not take into account important social costs. The global capital flow feature of the New Economy—remember the 13-year-old in Bangkok?—intensifies the nasty side effects of a system that overrewards the producers while putting the unwanted side effects, like low-paying jobs replacing jobs that could support a family, into communities and ecosystems.

The New Economy: The End Game of Capitalism

The New Economy had to become what it is. It was forced into being. It is an economic necessity. It is the logical end and the new beginning of a series of developments that changes how we think and live.

Why is it an economic necessity? Because large numbers of humans got smarter and smarter about capitalism and its wealth-generating effects. The junk-bond raiders showed us how to spin out undervalued assets in the 1980s, and how to increase cash flows and share prices. In the 1990s, millions of business thinkers, seasoned executives, or wet-behind-the-ears MBAs hovering around the world's business schools, watching Jack Welch and Bill Gates (and, for a long time, Warren Buffett) and their European and Asian counterparts, created the ways to capture value with new business models. Then the Internet hit and the IPO machine took off, and McKinsey and the big-boy consultants provided the formulas to generate more cash from fewer assets.

This is what created the New Economy as capitalism's end game. More of us figured out the rules. The end game is wealth, and the phrase "wealth generation" started tripping off the lips of millions of Americans whose parents would be embarrassed at the thought of being wealthy. That had been for the bluebloods. Now it was for everybody.

Mutual funds grew like mushrooms and made it possible to be "the millionaire next door." Baby boomers with more cash than they thought they'd ever have started retiring in their early 50s because they had enough income for a lifetime.

Dividends Out, Stock Appreciation In

In the meantime, the beat goes on. The MBAs of the world have the formula to keep on growing. They don't worry anymore about dividends (rewards for a company that performed well in the past). They focus solely on future cash flows from investments, and stock prices goes up, and down, based on the likelihood of that happening. In the New Economy, the stock market is where you place your bets on cash flow.

As you read this, millions of business minds are thinking of the next way to find more customers who will spend more cash on products produced from as few assets as possible. It is a beautiful, huge, endlessly creative game. Let's hope that just as many alert minds are thinking about ways to produce well-being, and harnessing the wealth-producing features of economics to the good of families, communities, and individuals. My guess is that, in this last group, a sizable portion of them have read some very thought-provoking, decades-old essays by a gentleman named Greenleaf.

The Good and Beautiful about the New Economy

The New Economy is driving out old inefficiencies in the value chains. It is tearing up some of the good-old-boy networks that locked in profits for certain segments of an industry without really adding value. It is creating value, lowering prices, and increasing choices, with new business models and more effective means of delivering goods and services.

More of us are capitalists. By getting stock in our pension plans and through other means, many of us now relate to the economy not just through wages but through equity. Winston Churchill said: "The problem with socialism is that so many people share in its misery and the problem with capitalism is that too few people share in its rewards." The commoditizing of mutual funds and Internet trading are helping people join the party.

The New Economy is an entrepreneur's dream. We are in an intensely creative time. Venture capital is available, and we are generating an endless stream of ideas to build new business models and ventures.

Those with something to say have more voice. The free access on the Internet provides a platform. Motley Fool, the financial advisers, is a great example. Who are these guys? Where'd they come from?

One futurist glows about the Internet as new mindspace:

> The Net world is a second universe, a kingdom in our midst, with sights and sounds, landscapes and knowledge-scapes, markets and amusements, romances and resources—many of which have never before been seen on earth. It burgeons forth, this Village of villages, gaining each hour more and more inhabitants, who live and move and have their being in a world which is nowhere and everywhere.—Jean Houston, "cyber consciousness," *Yes!, a journal of Positive Futures,* August 6, 2000.

What's Diabolical About the New Economy?

The gap between the haves *and the* have-nots *is getting bigger.* Now is a crummy time to be a wage slave. Wage-dependent people are missing the party created by the markets in the New Economy. The rich are getting richer faster because they have capital and their returns are bigger than those with little or no capital. Good news here: There are lots more people with stock—about like 50 percent of the U.S. households. Bad news here: it is not nearly enough—the gap is getting wider. For instance, in New York, the highest-income

5 percent of families gained nearly $109,000 between the late 1970s and the late 1990s; the lowest-income 20 percent lost $2,900 per family ("State Income Inequality Continues to Grow in Most States in the 1990s Despite Economic Growth and Tight Labor Markets," Economic Policy Institute and the Center on Budget and Priorities, Washington, D.C., January 18, 2000 report).

We are feeling good about our economy, but it's like looking at a beautiful sunset over a weedy field—don't look too close. Selective perception and the media help us look at those who have the bucks and the means of making them, not those on the outside of the party looking in. There is no question that the "haves" are good people—I am a "have" and I hang around with a lot of others who have more. We just don't see our glass house very well much of the time, and we don't worry about the 13-year-old in Bangkok with a cigarette in his mouth.

The numbers are great for millions, but not at all great for other millions and, if we include the whole planet, billions more. Capitalism has always had this gap-increasing feature, but it has intensified recently. The wealth transfer mechanisms that used to dampen this effect, like tax policy, have been engineered to have less impact than at mid-twentieth century, as we have put our faith in capitalism. [Read Jeff Gates, *Democracy at Risk: Rescuing Main Street from Wall Street* (Perseus Books, April, 2000), or Dave Korten, *The Post-Corporate World* (Berrett-Koehler Publishers, 1998).]

Capitalism is mean-spirited and exclusive. People are not mean-spirited as a whole, but the part of us that is, often gets channeled into the business world. Our economy is for the rugged and the strong—those who possess our cultural strengths of individualism, competing, and boot-strapping. But its strength has become a weakness through overemphasis. I know businesspeople who kick butt all day long at work, then go to philanthropic meetings to do good. Philanthropy, for all its goodness, is not the answer. From a systemic point of view, in fact, the increases in philanthropic money are more and better band-aids for an economy and a society that exclude, marginalize, and leave victims.

It masks itself. For every Motley Fool, or some other hip new venture in the New Economy, there are a hundred working parents somewhere who want to get home to their kids but have too much e-mail to answer. Our media brings us important streams of data on growth and new jobs, but it masks the fuller picture of the New Economy when we focus on growth and technology, and not on well-being.

It feeds on itself. Margaret Thatcher-ites created an acronym, TINA—*there is no a*lternative. This was their way of saying the free market as we know it is a force that cannot be denied or stopped. They were right—there is power and inevitability in the social force of markets. But markets as we know them are governed by rules that could be changed to make them more accessible and benign. We could stop some of the worst abuses of power in the markets if we wanted to. Environmental Impact Statements are just one example of what is possible to create a dialogue that includes quality of life, not just quantity of returns.

As it is, TINA sounds like an ominous warning to indigenous people around the world who cannot stop the developments that will replace their way of life, to people who like wetlands in their swampy, messy form because the fish and fowl live there. They'd rather go fishing than have the swamp drained so it can become a mall, no matter how great the food court is.

Those with capital naturally feed the system with more capital for more growth. At its worst, the economy is like a cancer, a burgeoning growth of cells feeding on itself with no regard for the host organism.

It chews up people, without trying. The comic strip *Dilbert* is about the gnawing that takes place within the system. There is no comic strip for those on the outside. Look at our workweek—an increase of 200 hours per year [Juliet Schor, *The Overworked American* (New York, Basic Books, 1992)]. We have passed the Japanese in the amount of time devoted to work in the average household.

We are faster in the New Economy, but are we better? George Carlin captures the chewing at us in the paradox for which he is known:

> We have wider freeways, but narrower viewpoints . . .
> We spend more, but have less: we buy more, but enjoy less.
> We have more conveniences, but less time. . . .

As capital now works, it destroys good and essential things as it grows itself. As Wal-Mart competes with the Europeans, it will also threaten the fabric of community life and small family-owned shops. In America, we valued rising share value and lower prices over small towns with equity in the family businesses that made up town squares. These shops couldn't stand up to competition from big capital. I'd welcome work at Wal-Mart as a consultant. A lot of good "haves" work there. But we must not forget the price we paid for having Wal-Mart in our portfolios. It did not come free.

It chews up the environment. Not for this article. But the richer we get, the poorer our natural stock.

Servant-Leadership: Antidote to the Dark Side of the New Economy

This beautiful, diabolical beast called the New Economy is our creation. We live with it because we created it, and we are pushing it along as fast as we can in our go-for-it style. And we are beautiful—and capable of being diabolic.

Fortunately for us, moral development happens alongside technological and economic development. With notable regressions everywhere, we nevertheless move ahead to abolish slavery, child labor, genocide, and the crimes against humanity. Servant-leadership is a core example of the moral development that we need in large doses, with the New Economy barreling along with such power.

Some futurists predict that H. G. Wells is right and that we are in for a catastrophe. If you live in the sub-Sahara and experience what AIDS is doing to the social fabric, the catastrophe is already here. Or they posit that only after a catastrophic failing on a large order that affects the haves will we rally our energies or change our ways of thinking and being. Maybe. The good news is that there is so much positive happening in the world to expand the brighter sides of the New Economy and shorten its shadow. Communities and individuals everywhere are taking matters into their own hands—partnering with government and business and nonprofits to make a difference. H. G. Wells may be right the other way too—education may beat out catastrophe.

Here are three examples of hopeful developments that may stop the darker side from expanding:

1. *The charter school development* (there are nearly 20 now in my hometown of Kansas City) is just one aspect of the education system's righting itself, dispensing with bureaucracy, and using tax monies for community-based education that will teach thinking and social skills within a community-/family-friendly context. Charter schools can bring many of the elements of service and servant-leadership into reality.

2. On the technology side, *the development of fuel cells* may take us to a hydrogen-based economy, not a carbon-based one, and we will stop pouring the bad stuff into the air. The gifts of nature that we preserve for future generations are acts of wisdom at the heart of servant-leadership.

3. *Growing interest in servant-leadership* is evidenced by the number of Greenleaf books sold every year and by the increased participation of businesspeople at servant-leadership conferences and other programs. Spirituality and service in business have become permanent discussion topics.

The healing power of servant-leadership is severalfold:

○ It provides new measuring sticks of human effectiveness; service is raised above acquisition as a means of becoming fully human.

○ It is wholistic; it takes into account the great human questions of meaning and purpose.

○ It is biased for people. Leaders get their power by showing service to their followers and to society, not just by creating a new economic enterprise.

○ It is community-oriented. The idea of drawing your legitimacy as a leader because you are serving your followers is the creation of community.

○ It emphasizes well-being over material riches.

○ It is inclusive because anyone can work for the good. It is a leadership model based on greatness of spirit. This is what Martin Luther King Jr. meant when he said that "anyone can be great, because anyone can serve."

○ It generates connections and healing, and it goes against the cultural wounds of separateness and winning through competing over others.

In his writings, Robert Greenleaf was sending out an invitation to us all, to anyone who took the time to read and ponder. His invitation was to think and act at a higher level. He surveyed the cultural landscape and saw that a new kind of thoughtscape and human beingness was necessary to address the ills of the society we all experienced. So he posed the questions and made some bold assertions about leaders and power. The power of sustained leadership, he said, comes from the capacity to align our lives in the service of others.

The challenges he saw in the mid-twentieth century are even greater today. There are more of us on the planet; we are moving faster, are more closely connected, and are bumping into each other in all kinds of endeavors. The personal invitation he sent out then is the same today, only more important and urgent, more resounding in its consequences.

The New Economy also invites us. It is a seething, pulsating mass of markets and human imagination and new developments that surround our thinking and doing. The New Economy is an invitation to dive into a globalized, networked, free market culture, to consume and create, to live and learn and love, to buy products from halfway around the world, and do our garage sale through eBay. *The economic invitation from the markets and technology of the New Economy doesn't look or feel like the moral invitation of Robert Greenleaf. We must have the imagination to see them together and answer them with a life of meaning and service in the world.*

The New Economy won't go away. But it can be changed by how each of us designs our life. We can bring out the best of the New Economy by who we choose to be.

The New Economy is built on the foundation of our socioeconomic culture—its strengths and wounds, its elegance and brutishness. It won't add meaning and heart or anything lasting unless we will it to do so. *It is not out there ready to happen to us. It is inside of us, ready to be imagined and created.* The principles of well-being and life-enhancement that are at the root of servant-leadership are the salvation of the New Economy in its present less-evolved forms. Let's hope we find a way to take the medicine and start the healing we desperately need.

Let us learn to serve.

Dr. Margaret Wheatley is president of The Berkana Institute, and a principal of Kellner-Rogers & Wheatley, Inc. She is a fellow of the World Business Academy and an adviser to the Fetzer Fellows Program of the Fetzer Institute. Formerly, she was associate professor of Management at the Marriott School of Management, Brigham Young University, and Cambridge College. She is the author of the best-selling book *Leadership and the New Science* and coauthor, with Myron Kellner-Rogers, of *A Simpler Way*. Dr. Wheatley has worked with a wide variety of Fortune 500 clients, educational institutions, not-for-profit, and health care organizations to achieve organizational coherence in the midst of chaotic environments.

In this essay, Margaret Wheatley talks about the real work of the servant-leader, which she says is "to really see other people and to bring them together, to trust people more than they trust themselves." She shares her ideas on time, on individualism, on organizational structure and meaning, on human creativity, and on seeking individual wholeness and healing.

Margaret Wheatley was a keynote speaker at the Greenleaf Center's 1995 and 1999 annual international conferences.

25

THE WORK OF THE SERVANT-LEADER

Margaret Wheatley

IT'S WONDERFUL TO SEE all of you here. I spoke here in 1995 and it was to a smaller group of earnest seekers who were trying to figure out this thing called servant-leadership. To see more than double the number of people here makes me feel very grateful to you for coming. I want to say that as I travel around the world and as I get to talk to just about every variety of organization that I can imagine, I feel compelled to tell you that the world needs you. Not only that, the world is waiting for you.

I want to offer you some of the thoughts I'm having about how natural servant-leadership is. And I hope that in giving you my thoughts, you leave here with a stronger belief that you represent the future. Without you, this future will not happen. I hope that with my words I give you more courage, more clarity, and a greater sense that this is a worldwide movement you're engaged in and not just some strange idea that happens to appeal to you. This really is a movement in the direction of being able to create a future that we all want. I feel a strong imperative: I feel the peril of this moment, that if we don't learn how to come together differently—in our organizations, in our communities, in our families—if we don't learn how to come together differently, then we are doomed.

One of the strange things going on in western culture is that we have become, I believe, victims of many different beliefs. I'm only going to talk about two of them today. The first is the belief that we can ignore time: the belief that we can negotiate with time, that we have in fact forgotten about things like natural rhythms, about cycles, about change, as part of the natural process. Instead, we believe that it's a straight trajectory into the future, and we can go as fast as we please. Of course this moves us away from nature, from rhythm, from a sense of place, and we are really struggling with this. I believe that our current effort to try to ignore time and growth and stages and cycles is truly driving us crazy.

Laurens Van Der Post, the great South African writer-photographer-philosopher, said that things had gotten so serious in the world that he really feared for us. Someone asked him, "Well, what would you recommend, Sir Laurens? What would you recommend that we do?" He said, "I would declare a year of silence." And Pablo Neruda said the same thing, but for this purpose. He said, "Perhaps a huge silence might interrupt this sadness of never understanding ourselves, and with threatening ourselves with death."

Now since I'm a practical person, I imagine that the advice you're going to take from what I've said so far is to go back to your organizations and tell everyone to shut up. That is not what I'm saying. I want us to comprehend the fact that as we go faster and faster on this great trajectory toward the future, it is only making us sad and crazy. It is time for us, as leaders, to realize that we cannot create the future we want by increasing the speed of change, by increasing the hurriedness and the franticness. At some point, it's up to us to say, "We must take time to think. We must take time to reflect." I think one of the most courageous acts a servant-leader can do right now is to attempt to slow things down, so that people can think about what they're doing. It's a revolutionary act to reflect these days. It's not in our job description. Luckily, it's in our species description.

What frustrates me so much is understanding the great gift of human consciousness and the ability to notice and to reflect and to learn, and then to see how we are pretending it is not our gift to the planet. Instead of celebrating and honoring and trying to raise up this capacity for self-awareness and reflection, we simply say we're too busy.

Servant-leadership is quite natural. I want to tell you a story I heard on NPR recently, when there were so many terrible hurricanes. A geologist was being interviewed. He was a beach geologist, so his field of study was beaches and sand and the like. And at the time he was being interviewed, there was a large hurricane pounding the Outer Banks off the Carolinas. He was being interviewed about what hurricanes do to beaches. We all know what hurricanes do to beaches and beach houses and such. We feel they're very destructive, right? They destroy homes and take down power lines and take away sand, and whole beaches disappear in a hurricane. This is what got my attention: The geologist said, "You know, I can't wait to get out on those beaches again once these storms have passed. And I hope to get out there in the next 24 hours." And the interviewer said, "What do you expect to find out there?" and I was listening, and I thought he was going to talk about all the destruction he was going to find. What he said really surprised me. He said, "I expect to find a new beach."

Wouldn't it be wonderful if we could be in the same relationship with life as that beach geologist, where we would look for newness rather than predictability, where we would look to see what just happened rather than agonize that what we wanted didn't happen? So much of our focus right now is against newness and against surprise. These are elements of life that are inescapable. When you look at anything in the living world, all you see is newness and creation. The scripture that says, "Behold, I make all things new," feels to me like a biological statement these days. It's constant newness. But as a leader, as someone who is trying to help an organization move to the future, you have to ask yourself: "What is my position toward newness, toward creativity?" Often, we are surprised by newness in a way that makes it impossible for us to welcome it. We actually see newness as an affront to our plans. We see other people's creativity as an affront to our leadership, and this is very dangerous if we're trying to be a servant-leader, because we are trying to encourage life. Part of the job description of a servant-leader, for me, is that we have to be the ones who welcome newness; who look to be surprised rather than are fearful of surprise; who look for difference rather than try to ask people to conform and to move into all those small boxes on our organizational charts. And this is something we each need to contemplate. What is our relationship to surprise and to newness? What is our relationship to creation?

The other big stumbling block is not just our attitude toward time and our resistance to newness. It's this strange belief that we exist as individuals separated from one another. This is the dominant belief, I believe, in Western society. In Africa, in any communal or indigenous society, we see the other end of the spectrum, which is a belief only in community. But somewhere in there, there's got to be a new balance. I believe it's up to us to discover how we use our individual creativity as a gift to the whole, and how we move away from this belief in our separate existences that Einstein called an "optical delusion." I look at this group, here, and I can see 1,200 separate individuals, or I can look out at you and try and re-see, try and remember that we are all connected. According to Tibetan Buddhism, the root of all suffering comes from our belief that we are not connected. The source of suffering is the belief that we are independent actors. In the West, we created this great mythos that you and I exist as individuals and that the purpose of life is to grow into who we are for ourselves and not for others. I was rereading a little bit of Robert Greenleaf's work, and I was very struck by his understanding that servant-leadership starts as a feeling, a desire to serve others, that then becomes a commitment to move that desire into practice, to actually take on the great courageous task of serving others. But it starts first with a desire, with a feeling. This is very similar in Hinduism and in Buddhism to the notion of the *bodhisattva,* which was just recently defined to me as "One whose heart leaps out at human suffering and desires to help alleviate it." One's heart leaps out. And of course, this is the real step to becoming a servant leader. One's heart leaps and then we have no choice but to find the courage to keep our hearts open. Not to be so overwhelmed by insult or failure or pain or suffering that we close up our hearts and walk back and say, "No. No. No. That's too much. I can't deal with this now."

One of the great struggles right now is that, daily, something occurs that requires our heart to leap out and to try and connect with human suffering, whether it's in Littleton, Colorado, or Kosovo, or the Sudan, or Nigeria, or Rwanda. There are many opportunities for our hearts to leap out, but I'm personally finding that being asked so often to extend my compassion around the world makes me very tired and quite overwhelmed. And therefore, I'm more in touch with what was also described to me clearly in Greenleaf's writing: it takes enormous courage to serve other people. It takes enormous courage to keep our hearts open and to believe that we are big enough to hold that much suffering.

You have not signed up for an easy responsibility, but I also don't think you signed yourself up to feel overwhelmed. You signed up to explore servant-leadership because your heart leapt out at some moment experienced by your community or by a fellow human being. The great gift that is given to us is that we have hearts that were willing to open; and now the truly courageous act is to figure out how on earth to keep them open because the world only confronts us with more suffering, not with less.

Eudora Welty, an American Southern writer, had a wonderful description of her work. She said, "My continuing passion is to part a curtain—that invisible veil of indifference that falls between us and that blinds us to each other's presence, each other's wonder, each other's human plight." Parting this veil of indifference is what you are about. To part this curtain, to move it back and to say in any organization, in any setting, "There is more here. There is more capability. There is more talent. There is more creativity. There is more humaneness here in these people than others have seen."

In this great myth of individualism, we have created a culture of people who are often selfish, who are often self-serving, who are often greedy, who are often indifferent to each other's presence, wonder, or human plight. But it feels imperative for me to say that the people we are faced with now, with their negative behaviors of cynicism, anger, withdrawal, and paralysis—which are worldwide in my experience—those negative behaviors are not who we are.

And it is not those negative behaviors that made your heart leap out. Whenever your heart leapt out, and you knew you needed to serve, that is a moment to recall, because at that moment you knew the truth about human nature. You knew who we are. And the motivation to be a servant-leader is always, in my experience, from the recognition of who we really are. Beyond the cynicism, beyond the dependency, beyond the paralysis, beyond workers and colleagues and communities who don't know how to talk to each other any-more—beyond all of that, you knew at some point that in every human being, there is enormous capacity. And you wanted to help bring that capacity forth.

It's interesting that I'm putting this in the past tense, isn't it? I'm struck by that right now. I'm trying to recall you to the moment when things were most clear, but obviously I'm assuming that they aren't as clear now. And it is my experience that as we set out on this journey to be a servant-leader in this future that is unknown, there are so many pitfalls. There are so many black holes along the way that you can forget, "Why in God's name did I ever take this on?" For me, the work is always to recall the clarity I had that led me into anything. That clarity is always a profoundly spiritual mo-ment of the recognition of the truth of something. In this case, I believe that the clarity that was spiritual, the truth that you recog-nized, was that human beings are not by nature selfish, greedy, angry, or cynical. You must have seen the truth of us to be sitting here today. Even if you are not feeling the truth of who we are as a species right now, I'm asking you to recall that moment so you can bring it forward into today. This is who I think we are as a species.

I think one of the great gifts of humanity to the planet (which, unfortunately, we're not demonstrating very clearly), the great gift of who we are to the planet, is not only that we are self-reflective, not only that we have consciousness. Those are big, but it's not all. We are, by nature, a species that seeks intimacy. There's a new book by a biologist who says the reason you and I even developed language was because we wanted to be together. This is Humberto R. Maturana that I'm quoting now: "The great impulse in human evolution was a desire to be together." That's what led us to fig-ure out how to talk, how to speak, how to communicate. And then the other great desire is that we have a need to make meaning of things. We're constantly looking, constantly seeking to understand "Why?" We have this great impulse for meaning, this great desire and need to be together, and we have this great gift of conscious-ness. Each of those desires is available through servant-leadership and has been denied through every repressive, controlling form of leadership. In the command-and-control type of leadership—the "I'll tell you what to do" approach—an enormous dishonoring is involved. People feel this dishonoring. In response to being dishonored through command-and-control leadership by being put into a box, by being told what to do—in response to all of that, people become what we have now. People become angry. People become cynical. People become depressed. People become paralyzed. We created those bad behaviors because we didn't recognize who we were.

So much of our lives right now leads us away from each other. With the focus on individualism, the focus on careers, the focus on self-servingness, the inability to simply sit on a porch—I'm going to sound real old-fashioned here—but to sit together, to notice each other's wonder, each other's presence, each other's human plight—we don't have time for each other any more. And I believe that it is this focus that we don't have time, this belief that we don't have time, this belief that we don't need each other, this belief that we can make it on our own, that there really is such a thing as an individual: I believe this is what is killing us. There is a wonderful song from Nigeria that I will not sing because I can't remember the melody, but the lyric is about individualism. The lyric goes, "Oh, to be an individual is a very bad thing. Ah! To be an individual is a very bad thing. Oh, God! Oh, God! Please, God, don't make me an individual."

I believe that Greenleaf knew so much, was accessing so much of what I would call "eternal wisdom" when he said the criterion of successful servant-leadership is that those that we serve are healthier and wiser and freer and more autonomous, and perhaps they even loved our leadership so much that they want to serve others also. I believe that Greenleaf and many great spiritual teachers were simply signaling to us that we are naturally a species that wants to be together, that needs to be free, that needs to be autonomous, and that needs and will naturally tend toward its own health.

All of life, *all* of life is life-affirming. All of life seeks its own health. It doesn't need us to do it, and I believe more and more that people in organizations don't need us to make them healthy.

People need us as leaders to trust that their healthfulness is in them already. People need us as leaders to figure out the processes by which people can reconnect with each other. If you believe that health is already there, then your task as a leader becomes figuring out how to evoke it. If you believe that pathology is the only thing that's there, then you move into a very directive form of leadership where you're trying to fix people or give them the benefit of your wisdom. Chuang Tzu said—and I think this is a great definition of a servant-leadership that just happens to be 2,400 years old—he said, "It is more a matter of believing the good than of seeing it as the fruit of our efforts." This is something for you to consider. To what extent in the exercise of your own leadership are you trying to evoke, elicit, bring forth the good that you know is there? That's the great gift. That's the gift that Jesus certainly gave to us, that Mohammed gave to us, that great spiritual leaders give to us: the belief that we are innately good and that we can be responsible for our own healing.

So much of what we do in organizations is completely counter to what I just defined as good leadership. So much of what we have defined as effective leadership in organizations is finding the program, the right training manual, the right technique, and forcing people to conform. We don't think we're forcing them, but we are. It is such a dishonoring of people that what I notice everywhere is people respond to it for the major insult that it is. "So you're telling me I have to be different? You're telling me I'm not smart enough to have created this myself? You're telling me I have to do this?" Greenleaf talked about people feeling freer and autonomous. These are natural conditions. We need to feel free, to choose, to decide, to participate. We need you as leaders out there believing that there is good in us and it's your task to figure out how to bring it forth. People are so battered and bruised, and people feel so badly about themselves, and people feel tired and so stressed, that sometimes it's terrifying to realize the emotional and physical distress we're in as a culture right now. I now define a leader as one who has more faith in people than they do in themselves. You need to have more faith in people's capacity than they do in themselves, because people have lost their way—people have lost their sense of themselves.

A great Tibetan teacher, Trungpa Rinpoche, said that "it is a dark time when people don't know who they are, and therefore lack courage." If we think that we are this depressed, stressed, paralyzed group of people, how on earth could we have the courage to change the world? Where would we find courage if we believed that we are such a bad group of people? You as the leader must remember what you saw, the goodness that you saw in people that called you to be a servant. If you can remember that, now is the time to raise up that vision of our goodness in your community and in your families, with your colleagues, with your employees. You are the one who must hold the vision of other people's goodness for them until they re-discover it. This should sound familiar. We always knew that great teachers were those who saw more in us than we saw in our young selves, and I'm just saying that now the need for that is even stronger because people are so battered and bruised these days.

While I've been really impressed by Greenleaf's spiritual depth, I think the thing I was most impressed with recently was his talk about how spirit emanates from within. And for those of us lead-ing organizations now, or trying to be leaders in organizations, when we don't know what the destination is, the real work is to lead from within, but not just from within you. Not just from your own spirit. I realized that when an organization has a spirit—and I'm not talking about spirituality in work—when an organization knows its spirit, it can lead itself from within just as we can lead ourselves from within as servant-leaders. So then we are in the ques-tion: What is the source of organizational spirit? What is it that gives an organization of 40,000 people, or one individual, its spirit? Because it is from that center place, that centering place of spiritual richness and energy, that an organization can navigate any future, just as, at an individual level, we can only navigate the chaos be-cause we know who we are.

There's a wonderful description of the former president of the Fetzer Institute, Robert Lehman. Somebody described his leader-ship in this way: "He doesn't know where we're going, but he knows how to get us there." That is a great description of leadership in these times. For me, the "how to get us there" is to make sure that, as an organization, we have strong awareness, strong consciousness of self. Who are we? What are we trying to do? The need is to develop not a clear map that we navigate from, not a strategic plan, not a new organizational chart. The real work is to return to the center from where our spirit emanates, and, in organizations, that means things like purpose and vision and mission. But we have trivialized those terms. I want the imagery to be similar to how we feel about our own spiritual centers. I want it to feel that essential to our lives. It's not about writing the right vision statement. It's not about putting up a beautiful piece about our mission. It's about how can we be in conversation to evoke this rich place of spirit? How can we as an organization or community be together in conversations about why we're doing this work? How can we come together to dwell in the rich territory of meaning-making?

One of my learnings in the past few years is that the desire to serve others is a natural impulse, and that any time people in an organization are given the chance to dwell in this deep center of meaning, they always reach out. They don't move in, they reach out. They embrace more of the world. I believe the natural direction of life is out. Love is extending, not contracting. So the natural flow in our relationships is toward each other. We've really, in this culture, forced people to contract, to be fearful of one another. If the natural direction is out—to embrace, to open, to bring in more—here are a few examples of that. And you can think about this in your own experience, especially if you're in a for-profit institution where we might think this impulse doesn't exist. But I'm finding, even in the strangest industries, that when people are given the chance to write a mission statement, to talk about the purpose of their work, they've taken the world.

Here's my most recent favorite story. I have lots of them; I'll tell you two. One is that at one point I said to a group of people, "You know, even if you make dog food, you want it to mean something for humanity." And there was someone who made dog food in the room at the time. (Of course, I didn't know that until he came up.) But he confirmed what I was saying. In one of their plants, they had asked employees to write their own mission statement, and it began with "Pets contribute to human health." Do you see? They took their work immediately out into the world to give it meaning.

Much more recently, I learned of Hewlett Packard's Research and Development Division's work with 800 employees, to reformulate and reorganize themselves around a stirring sense of purpose. Their new sense of purpose was to be: "We will be the best R&D facility in the world." That's a good American kind of "We're number one." They did a superb, very participative process, spending a few years to collect people's stories and find out what was the meaning of working at Hewlett Packard in research and development for 800 people and feeding that back to everybody. They did a lot of very creative things. But in the second year, a woman stood up in one meeting and said, "I'm sorry. I just don't get charged up by becoming the best research facility in the world. But I could get a lot of energy if we were striving to become the best research facility *for* the world." Now, some people might have thought, "Well, isn't that cute," or "Just like a woman." But here's what happened next. Her words went to another employee's heart, and he was a graphic designer for Hewlett Packard. So he went back to his shop and he created, just for himself, a poster that captured being the best R&D facility for the world. And in this poster is the original founding garage (you know, every computer company started in a garage!), and Hewlett and Packard are standing outside the garage looking in at their new baby, their new creation. But what's inside the garage is not a computer. What's inside the garage is the planet. And it's just luminous. Now, they received over 50,000 requests for that poster. This so resonated it didn't matter about class, race, gender. This resonated because we, as human beings, have a desire to serve.

And this is an impulse I simply encourage you to trust. You are not the only ones who are trying to act from a sense of spirit that is emanating from within. Most people in your community or your organization want their work to be grounded from the same sense of call, from the same ground of energy, which is purpose, spirit, service. These are natural to human beings. You can trust that. It may take you a few months to discover it in certain people because we are very bruised, but you can trust that what called you is an impulse that is also calling people in every form of organization. It is what calls us together as a species.

There's one other thing that I want to say. I've just recently discovered something from looking up some very ancient teachings and
from examining my own experience. It's why I love Eudora Welty's
little description so much. What I'm starting to notice is that in the
midst of suffering, in the midst of terrifying circumstances, in the
midst of modern organization, when we actually find one other,
when we see one other, when we notice our shared humanity—each
other's wonder, each other's presence, each other's plight—when we
actually see each other, the experience is always one of joy. The circumstances don't seem to matter. This is the most hopeful realization
I've had recently. The circumstances don't matter. The suffering isn't
what's critical. It's that the suffering might bring us to see one another. And in the moment when we see one other, we have a profoundly human experience which is the experience of joyous
recognition. Now, what I have found hopeful about this—and I really hope I keep believing this—what I have found hopeful about this
is that it has changed what I'm looking for in my work. I'm not looking to end the ills of the world. I am not believing that by anything
I do, I can eliminate human suffering. I am not believing even that
it's going to get better. But I realize that if I'm on the search to really find and see human beings, that I will have the experience of a
lifetime, that I will feel blessed, independent of the circumstances. I
will have seen you and in seeing you, I will see the Sacred. I'm going
to see the Divine and that is always an experience that is joyful. Now,
if that is true, that the source that sustains us—our sustenance—is
finding each other, then this is where, as leaders, we really need to
rethink what we're doing. It could take us from focusing on activities to fix things to focusing on processes that bring us together. Your
real work would be—I think it already is for many of you—to figure
out how to bring people together and to trust that they will find their
own healing. But the work is first to find each other.

There are many patterns, many beliefs, out there about leadership, about people, about motivation, about human development.
The essential truth I'm discovering right now is that when we are
together, more becomes possible. When we are together, joy is
available. In the midst of a world that is insane, that will continue
to surprise us with new outrages . . . in the midst of that future, the

gift is each other. We have lived with a belief system that has not told us that. We have lived with a belief that has said, "We're in it for ourselves. It's a dog-eat-dog world out there. Only the strong survive and you can't trust anybody." That's the belief that's operating in most organizations if you scratch the surface. The belief that called you to be a servant-leader, I believe, is the belief of who we are as a species. We have need for each other. We have a desire for each other, and, more and more, I believe that if *the real work is to stay together,* then we are not only the best resource to move into this future—we are the *only* resource.

In Greenleaf's later work on religious leaders, he changed the description of the consequences of servant-leadership. He gave up the word *autonomous* and talked about *feeling at peace.* That's very significant to me. It's not only that we're trying to encourage people's autonomy, but when we work as servants to others, we actually will feel more at peace. Anything that's peaceful for me signals that that's our natural state. I think Greenleaf was really describing something that I have also found strongly in my work: As we come together, we are able to experience joy, and even beyond joy, we are able to experience peace. We need to learn how to be together: that is the essential work of the servant-leader.

AFTERWORD:
A REMEMBRANCE OF
ROBERT K. GREENLEAF

Larry C. Spears

*The following remembrance of Robert K. Greenleaf (1904–1990)
first appeared in The Greenleaf Center's newsletter* The Servant-
Leader *(Winter, 1990–1991) shortly after Robert Greenleaf's death
on September 29, 1990. It is a recounting of my one-and-only meeting with Robert Greenleaf, which occurred shortly after I began my
service as CEO of The Greenleaf Center, and just nine days before
Greenleaf's death.*

*At the time, the future of servant-leadership, and of The Green-
leaf Center, seemed not nearly as strong as they are today. Awareness of Greenleaf's writings was mostly word-of-mouth, and there
were a few who had doubts as to the continuation of The Greenleaf Center after his passing. I was aware of Robert Greenleaf's concern as to his legacy and sought to share with him, in his final days,
my own vision and insights into what I believed was a brighter future still to come for the organization that carried his name. I felt
in my bones that servant-leadership was about to blossom all over
the world as a result of the many seeds that he had sown in the preceding 20 years, and I shared that belief with him. In addition to
trying to reassure him about the future, I brought with me to that
meeting many remembrances of the past, in the form of letters
from dozens of people who had shared with me in those first
months of my tenure just how great an influence servant-leadership*

and Robert Greenleaf had been to them. Bob Greenleaf's son, New-comb Greenleaf, has commented that he believes that following our meeting on September 20, 1990, Robert Greenleaf was able to let go of his final concerns for the future of servant-leadership and The Greenleaf Center, and to meet his death with a greater sense of peacefulness. I like to believe that was the case. And I know for a fact that I was changed by our one meeting together.

Over the years, The Greenleaf Center has had requests for reprints of this column. We thought it appropriate to close this book with a brief reminiscence about the final days of the man behind the movement.

—The Editors

SOME MONTHS AGO WHEN I knew I would be in Philadelphia for a meeting of the Board of Managers of *Friends Journal,* I wrote to Bob Greenleaf to ask if I might visit him. There was no way of knowing then that our visit on September 20 would occur only a week before his death on September 29.

The sequence of those two events has caused me to do a great deal of reflection. I shall forever cherish my one and only meeting with Robert Greenleaf. It also led me to think about all the people who have known Bob over the years and would have treasured a last visit with him. I thought I would write about my experience in the hope that his many friends might also, in a way, share in a last visit with him.

Immediately prior to visiting with Bob at Crosslands, the Quaker retirement community where he lived, I spent a half hour talking with the social worker who frequently read to him. She told me a bit about his recent life there; how his weakening condition and several strokes had caused him great frustration; how he loved listening to classical music; and a bit about his personality traits. She mentioned that he was one of the most unassuming people she had ever met, and she recounted a story that seemed illustrative of his extremely modest nature: Bob Greenleaf had supposedly once been asked by a new resident at Crosslands what kind of work he had done in the past. Greenleaf, who had retired as Director of

Management Research at AT&T, and who then went on to become a noted author, lecturer, and consultant to corporations, universities, and foundations, had simply responded, "I worked in an office."

Walking into Bob's room, I found him sitting in his wheelchair and facing the window. He turned his head and smiled, and said hello to me. I sat down in a nearby chair and introduced myself. As I did, I noticed on the windowsill several pictures, including a picture of my two sons, which I had sent to him along with a birth announcement about our younger son's arrival this past summer. Matthew had been born on the same date as Bob's birthday—July 14. I picked up the picture and turned it toward him. He smiled and said, "Nice children."

Robert Greenleaf had been concerned in past years about the continuation of both the servant-leader concept and the Greenleaf Center. In a letter from the mid-1980s he wrote, "My major concern for the Greenleaf Center is for its future. I may be hanging up my sword any day now, and I would like to feel the work I have done to encourage building greater integrity into our many institutions will be continued and enlarged in new directions." It seemed important to me to share with him some of the many positive things that occurred at the Center in 1990—and to convey my own sense of the ongoing revitalization of the Robert K. Greenleaf Center.

Bob had not seen the Center's new office in Indianapolis; however, we visually walked around it through a series of photographs. I described the area and building where we are located, and showed him the half-dozen literature cabinets filled with hundreds of copies of his books, essays, and videotapes. He was clearly moved by this visualization of our office, and he stared for a long time at a picture of a lithograph created by his late wife, Esther, which hangs on the Greenleaf Center's wall.

Greenleaf carefully examined xerox copies of ten display advertisements that had recently been placed within a variety of national magazines. As he heard about the significance of this project—and particularly when he was told that his work and ideas would be reaching over a half-million readers through these publications—he chuckled and said, "Good work." I read to Bob the laudatory quotes about his work—from a half-dozen people—which are contained in a new information brochure. A look of amazement swept across his face. It seemed likely to me that he had either forgotten these expressions of appreciation from others; or, perhaps he had simply not ever had them all read to him at one time. We sat quietly for some moments and he said, "I don't know what to say."

There was, of course, nothing that he needed to say. It was I who had come to do the saying on behalf of many of us—to remind him of the legacy that he has left each of us—and to thank him for his life's work. I told him of the many expressions of gratitude for his writings, and I expressed appreciation for my own opportunity to serve the Greenleaf Center. He listened as I also told him of the hundreds of people whom I have met who have been profoundly influenced by the servant-leader concept; and I said to him that I believed that his ideas were likely to become increasingly influential in the coming years. He stared intently for a few moments, and then audibly sighed.

Our single meeting was of great importance to me. It has also been suggested that it may have been of considerable importance to Bob Greenleaf as well, providing him with a reminder of his positive influence, and of the many lives that he touched during his 86 years—as well as communicating the increasing vibrancy of the Center which he founded in 1964 as the Center for Applied Ethics. I like to think that we both benefited from our meeting that week before he died.

I stood up and took Bob's hand in mine, and thanked him for our time together. He stared thoughtfully at me and said, "Thank you for coming, Larry." As I walked out of his room I turned around for one final look. Bob had picked up the Greenleaf Center's newsletter and was slowly turning the page.

ACKNOWLEDGMENTS

WE ARE PARTICULARLY INDEBTED to the staff and board of The Greenleaf Center, past and present. Through them, we have grown in our own understanding and practice of servant-leadership. We also wish to thank three foundations—Lilly Endowment, the W. K. Kellogg Foundation, and the William Penn Foundation—for their support of The Greenleaf Center. Thanks, too, to the tens of thousands of members, customers, program participants, donors, and other supporters of The Greenleaf Center.

Larry Spears would like to offer his special thanks to his family, friends, and colleagues around the world who have enriched his life—especially, his wife, Beth Lafferty; his sons, James and Matthew Spears; and his mother, Bertha Spears. Special thanks also go to Michele Lawrence for her good spirit, hard work, and personal encouragement over the years and around this book.

Michele Lawrence would like to offer her special thanks to her husband, Joe Lawrence, and her daughter, Alexandra Lawrence, for their unfailing patience, kindness, and encouragement during this project, and just for being great people. She would also like to thank her mother and father, Tracy and A. L. Richmond, and her parents-in-law, Betty and Dr. Joe Lawrence. Thank you also to the living lab of servant-leadership, the Greenleaf Center staff, in particular Larry Spears, who was willing to share the responsibility and joy of putting this book together. And thank you, Kelly Tobe, for hiring me all those years ago!

Finally, we would like to express our deepest appreciation for the many servant-leaders working within countless organizations around the world. Your efforts in growing servant-leadership point the way to the future of humankind.

ABOUT THE EDITORS AND
THE GREENLEAF CENTER FOR
SERVANT-LEADERSHIP

Larry C. Spears is a writer, editor, and chief executive officer of The Greenleaf Center for Servant-Leadership. He is the editor of five previous books: *The Power of Servant-Leadership,* 1998; *Insights on Leadership,* 1998; *On Becoming a Servant-Leader* (with Don Frick), 1996; *Seeker and Servant* (with Anne Fraker), 1996; and *Reflections on Leadership,* 1995. His essays are also included in the books: *Cutting Edge: Leadership 2000,* 2000; *Stone Soup for the Soul,* 1998; and *Leadership in a New Era,* 1994. He is Series Editor for the *Voices of Servant-Leadership Essay Series* (published by The Greenleaf Center); and he is the founder and Senior Editor of The Greenleaf Center's quarterly newsletter, *The Servant-Leader.* Spears has also published over 300 articles, essays, and book reviews.

Spears was named chief executive officer of the Greenleaf Center for Servant-Leadership in 1990. Under his leadership The Greenleaf Center has grown dramatically in size and influence. Larry Spears shares several experiences in common with Robert Greenleaf: In addition to their mutual interests in servant-leadership and writing, both men grew up in Indiana and migrated to major cities after college (Greenleaf to New York City, Spears to Philadelphia); they were deeply influenced by their experiences within The Religious Society of Friends (Quakers); and they share(d) an abiding interest in how things get done within organizations.

A frequent traveler, Spears has spoken on servant-leadership to groups in North America, Europe, Australia, and Asia. He is a longtime member of the Association of Fundraising Professionals and has written many successful grant proposals. He is a Fellow of the World Business Academy. His personal interests include spending time with his family, science fiction, and vacations in his beloved Cape May, New Jersey.

Michele Lawrence has been with The Greenleaf Center since 1993, working in various programmatic capacities. She currently directs the annual international conference; acts as editor of The Greenleaf Center's quarterly newsletter, *The Servant-Leader;* is involved in design and marketing of the Center's Catalog of Resources; and performs the functions of chief operating officer. She was the original webmaster of the Center's Internet Web site, bringing it online in May of 1996.

Her personal interests include spending time with her family, reading (especially the Aubrey-Maturin novels of Patrick O'Brian, for the life and leadership lessons), and periodically escaping to a rented cottage on the coast of Maine.

The Greenleaf Center for Servant-Leadership, headquartered in Indianapolis, Indiana, is an international nonprofit educational organization that seeks to encourage the understanding and practice of servant-leadership. It has offices in Australia/New Zealand, Canada, Europe, Korea, the Philippines, Singapore, South Africa, and the United Kingdom. The Center's mission is to improve the caring and quality of all institutions through servant-leadership.

The Greenleaf Center's programs and resources include the worldwide sale of books, essays, and videotapes on servant-leadership; an annual International Conference on Servant-Leadership held each June in Indianapolis; a variety of workshops, institutes, retreats, and speakers; a membership program; consultative services; and other activities around servant-leadership.

Servant-leadership is being practiced today by many individuals and organizations. For more information about servant-leadership and The Greenleaf Center, contact:

The Greenleaf Center for Servant-Leadership
921 East 86th Street, Suite 200
Indianapolis, IN 46240
Phone (317) 259-1241; Fax (317) 259-0560
E-mail: greenleaf@iquest.net
Web site: www.greenleaf.org

PERMISSIONS AND COPYRIGHTS

The Foreword is an original essay created for this collection by Ken Blanchard. Copyright © 2001 Ken Blanchard. Printed with permission of the author.

The Introduction, "Tracing the Past, Present, and Future of Servant-Leadership," is adapted from *Insights on Leadership*. Copyright © 1998 Larry C. Spears. Printed with permission of the author.

Chapter 1, "Essentials of Servant-Leadership," is an excerpt from the essay *The Servant as Leader* by Robert K. Greenleaf, copyright © 1991 by The Greenleaf Center. Printed with permission of The Greenleaf Center.

Chapter 2, "Servant-Leadership and Community Leadership in the Twenty-First Century," is an original essay created for this collection by Stephen R. Covey from a keynote address he gave during The Greenleaf Center's 1999 Conference. Copyright © 1999 Franklin Covey Co., *www.franklincovey.com*. Franklin Covey trademarks are used throughout. Article and trademarks are used herein under license. All rights reserved. Printed with permission of Franklin Covey Co.

Chapter 3, "Servant-Leadership and the Imaginative Life," is an original essay created for this collection by Michael Jones. Copyright © 2001 Michael Jones. Printed with permission of the author. *www.pianoscapes.com*

Chapter 4, "Leadership as Partnership," originally appeared as an article by Russ S. Moxley in Volume 19, Number 3, 1999, of *Leadership in Action*, published by Jossey Bass. Copyright © 1999

Jossey Bass. Reprinted with minor modifications with the permission of the publisher.

Chapter 5, "Teaching Servant-Leadership," is an original essay created for this collection by Hamilton Beazley and Julie Beggs. Copyright © 2001 Hamilton Beazley and Julie Beggs. Printed with permission of the authors.

Chapter 6, "Fannie Lou Hamer, Servant of the People," is adapted from *Servants of the People: The 1960s Legacy of African American Leadership*, by Lea E. Williams, St. Martin's Press, New York. Copyright © 1996 Lea E. Williams. Printed with permission of the author and St. Martin's Press, LLC.

Chapter 7, "Servant-Leadership: Three Things Necessary," is an original essay created for this collection by Max DePree. Copyright © 2001 Max DePree. Printed with permission of the author.

Chapter 8, "Become a Tomorrow Leader," is adapted from *Old Dogs, New Tricks*, by Warren Bennis, Executive Excellence Publishing, Provo, Utah. Copyright © 1999 Warren Bennis. Printed with permission of the author.

Chapter 9, "Servant-Leadership and Rewiring the Corporate Brain," is adapted from *Rewiring the Corporate Brain* by Danah Zohar, Berrett-Koehler Publishers, Inc., San Francisco, California. Copyright © 1997 Danah Zohar. Reprinted with permission of the author and the publisher. All rights reserved. *www.bkconnection.com*

Chapter 10, "Servant-Leadership and the Best Companies to Work For in America," is an original essay created for this collection by Nancy Larner Ruschman. Copyright © 2001 Nancy Larner Ruschman. Printed with permission of the author.

Chapter 11, "From Hero-as-Leader to Servant-as-Leader," is adapted from an article by Ann McGee-Cooper and Duane Trammell in *The Systems Thinker*, Volume 10, Number 2, April 1999, published by Pegasus Communications, Inc. Copyright © 1999 Pegasus Communications, Inc. Reprinted with permission of the publisher. *www.pegasuscom.com*

Chapter 12, "The Business Case for Servant-Leadership," is an original essay created for this collection by James D. Showkeir. Copyright © 2001 James D. Showkeir. Printed with permission of the author.

Chapter 13, "On the Right Side of History," originally appeared as *Booklet 1* in the *Voices of Servant-Leadership Series,* published by The Greenleaf Center in 1999. Copyright © 1999 John C. Bogle and The Greenleaf Center. Reprinted with permission of the author and the publisher.

Chapter 14, "The Unique Double Servant-Leadership Role of the Board Chair," originally appeared as *Booklet 2* in the *Voices of Servant-Leadership Series,* published by The Greenleaf Center in 1999. Copyright © 1999 John Carver and The Greenleaf Center. Reprinted with permission of the author and the publisher.

Chapter 15, "Servant-Leadership in Community Colleges," is an original essay created for this collection by Ruth Mercedes Smith and Kent A. Farnsworth. Copyright © 2001 Ruth Mercedes Smith and Kent A. Farnsworth. Printed with permission of the authors.

Chapter 16, "Servant-Leadership and Philanthropic Institutions," originally appeared as *Booklet 4* in the *Voices of Servant-Leadership Series,* published by The Greenleaf Center in 2000. Copyright © 2000 John Burkhardt and Larry C. Spears, and The Greenleaf Center. Reprinted with permission of the authors and the publisher.

Chapter 17, "Foresight: The Lead That the Leader Has," is an original essay created for this collection by David S. Young. Copyright © 2001 David S. Young. Printed with permission of the author.

Chapter 18, "Servant-Leadership and Creativity," is an original essay created for this collection by Tamyra L. Freeman, Scott G. Isaksen, and K. Brian Dorval. Copyright © 2001 by Tamyra L. Freeman, Scott G. Isaksen, and K. Brian Dorval. Printed with permission of the authors.

Chapter 19, "Table for Six Billion, Please," is an original essay created for this collection by Judy Wicks. Copyright © 2001 Judy Wicks. Printed with permission of the author.

Chapter 20, "Synchronicity and Servant-Leadership," is an original essay created for this collection by Joseph Jaworski. Copyright © 2001 Joseph Jaworski. Printed with permission of the author.

Chapter 21, "Servant-Leadership: Leading in Today's Military," is an original essay created for this collection by Rubye Howard

RECOMMENDED READING

Bennis, Warren G. *On Becoming a Leader*. Cambridge: Perseus Publishing, 1994.

Blanchard, Ken, and Michael O'Connor. *Managing by Values*. San Francisco: Berrett-Koehler, 1997.

Bogle, John C. *John Bogle on Investing: The First 50 Years*. New York: McGraw-Hill, 2001.

Carver, John. *Boards That Make a Difference*. San Francisco: Jossey-Bass, 1997.

Covey, Stephen. *Leadership Is a Choice*. New York: Simon & Schuster, 2001.

DePree, Max. *Leadership Is an Art*. New York: Doubleday, 1989.

_____ . *Leadership Jazz*. New York: Dell Publishing, 1992.

_____ . *Leading Without Power*. San Francisco: Jossey-Bass, 1997.

Greenleaf, Robert K. *The Institution as Servant*. Indianapolis: The Greenleaf Center, 1976.

_____ . *Servant Leadership*. New York: Paulist Press, 1977.

_____ . *The Leadership Crisis*. Indianapolis: The Greenleaf Center, 1978.

_____ . *The Servant as Religious Leader*. Indianapolis: The Greenleaf Center, 1982.

_____ . *Seminary as Servant*. Indianapolis: The Greenleaf Center, 1983.

_____ . *My Debt to E. B. White.* Indianapolis: The Greenleaf Center, 1987.

_____ . *Old Age: The Ultimate Test of Spirit.* Indianapolis: The Greenleaf Center, 1987.

_____ . *Teacher as Servant: A Parable.* Indianapolis: The Greenleaf Center, 1987.

_____ . *Education and Maturity.* Indianapolis: The Greenleaf Center, 1988.

_____ . *Have You a Dream Deferred.* Indianapolis: The Greenleaf Center, 1988.

_____ . *Spirituality as Leadership.* Indianapolis: The Greenleaf Center, 1988.

_____ . *Trustees as Servants.* Indianapolis: The Greenleaf Center, 1990.

_____ . *Advices to Servants.* Indianapolis: The Greenleaf Center, 1991.

_____ . *The Servant as Leader.* Indianapolis: The Greenleaf Center, 1991.

_____ . *On Becoming a Servant Leader.* San Francisco: Jossey-Bass, 1996.

_____ . *Seeker and Servant.* San Francisco: Jossey-Bass, 1996.

_____ . *The Power of Servant Leadership.* San Francisco: Berrett-Koehler, 1998.

Hesse, Hermann. *The Journey to the East.* New York: The Noonday Press, 1992.

Hock, Dee. *Birth of the Chaordic Age.* San Francisco: Berrett-Koehler, 1999.

Jaworski, Joseph. *Synchronicity: The Inner Path of Leadership.* San Francisco: Berrett-Koehler, 1996.

Jones, Michael. *Creating an Imaginative Life.* Berkeley: Conari Press, 1995.

McGee-Cooper, Ann, Duane Trammell, and Barbara Lau. *You Don't Have to Go Home from Work Exhausted!* New York: Bantam Books, 1992.

McGee-Cooper, Ann, and Gary Looper. *The Essentials of Servant-Leadership: Principles in Practice.* Waltham: Pegasus Communications, 2001.

Moxley, Russ S. *Leadership and Spirit.* San Francisco: Jossey-Bass, 1999.

Renesch, John, editor. *Leadership in a New Era.* San Francisco: New Leaders Press, 1994.

Schuster, John P., Jill Carpenter, and M. Patricia Kane. *The Power of Open Book Management.* New York: Wiley, 1996.

Spears, Larry C., editor. *Reflections on Leadership: How Robert K. Greenleaf's Theory of Servant-Leadership Influenced Today's Top Management Thinkers.* New York: Wiley, 1995.

_____ . *Insights on Leadership: Service, Stewardship, Spirit, and Servant-Leadership.* New York: Wiley, 1998.

Wheatley, Margaret J. *Leadership and the New Science Revised: Discovering Order in a Chaotic World.* San Francisco: Berrett-Koehler, 1999.

Wicks, Judy et al. *White Dog Café Cookbook: Multicultural Recipes and Tales of Adventure from Philadelphia's Revolutionary Restaurant.* Philadelphia: Running Press, 1998.

Williams, Lea E. *Servants of the People: The 1960s Legacy of African American Leadership.* New York: St. Martin's Press, 1996.

Young, David S. *Servant Leadership for Church Renewal.* Scottdale: Herald Press, 1999.

Zohar, Danah. *Rewiring the Corporate Brain.* San Francisco: Berrett-Koehler, 1997.

INDEX